# Maryland's Western Shore

# The Guidebook

### Katie Moose

**Conduit Press**
**Annapolis, Maryland**

Copyright ©2001   Conduit Press

Cover *Dove* ©Historic St. Mary's City (Courtesy of Historic St. Mary's City)

Cover design by Jean Harper Baer Graphic Design, Baltimore, Maryland

Published by the Conduit Press, 111 Conduit Street, Annapolis, Maryland 21401

Library of Congress Cataloging-in-Publication Data

Printed and Bound by Victor Graphics, Inc., Baltimore, Maryland, USA

ISBN: 0-9666610-4-4

# Table of Contents

# Photographs

# Introduction

The history of Maryland begins on the Western Shore of Maryland where Native Americans, such as the Algonquin, Susquhannocks, Piscataway and Mattapani lived. In 1634 English settlers arrived at St. Clement's Island in Southern Maryland. The colonists moved up the Chesapeake Bay or inland along the many creeks and rivers. Sadly a number of rivers are now silted in due to the development of agricultural products, and more particularly tobacco. However, great and not so great cities, villages and towns survive. This book will explore these very special places, citing history, places of interest, lodging, dining and favorite traditions. The area also is noted for yachting and waterfowl. Baltimore, which has a number of good guidebooks and Annapolis (see Annapolis: The Guidebook by Katie Moose) are not included.

For several years my grandfather was stationed at Aberdeen Proving Grounds. My grandparents later retired to "Harmony Hills Farm" in Havre de Grace. Following World War II my parents lived at "Mount Pleasant" in Havre de Grace and after my birth stayed on for almost a year. The next ten years were spent in New Castle, Delaware. Many week-ends and holidays we would venture to "Harmony Hills", my grandparent's farm. There are memories of those drives and singing "London Bridges" as we went under the many bridges along some of the back roads. Sunday dinner might be at "Harmony Hills", but once in a while we would drive over to the Susquehanna and feast looking out over the Bay and river. Often my grandfather would leave early to go hunting in Havre de Grace or even the Eastern Shore. These were carefree times spent with family - fishing in the pond, sledding, swimming in the stream and avoiding black snakes.

Many years later I moved back to Maryland and settled in Annapolis. The Western Shore of Maryland became a place to explore and ponder its place in American history. So much happened here - from the early exploration of Captain John Smith, the Calverts, the Carrolls and so many other well known families, including my own Clag(g)ett family, to Annapolis as capital, and Baltimore one of the premier U.S. cities. The Western Shore is two very diverse regions - the Northern and Southern - and each sided during the Civil War, and with many families divided also during the Revolutionary War. Even today Southern Maryland is mainly agricultural and genteel; Northern Maryland more developed and industrialized. Even so, they are part of one of America's most historic states.

The book starts in the most northern part of Maryland and meanders its way to St. Mary's City and St. Clement's Island where all the history started. Enjoy!

**Drum Point Lighthouse, Calvert Marine Museum, Solomons**

# Chapter 1

## Western Shore Informative Tips

### Traveling to the Western Shore

The easiest way to travel by car to the Western Shore is by taking Rte. 95 north or south.

Welcome and information centers are located at the I-95 North and South Welcome Centers, mile marker #37, Savage; Chesapeake House Welcome Center, I-95 North/South, marker #97. Perryville; the State House Visitors Center, Maryland State Capital, Annapolis; Crain Memorial Visitor Center, Newburg; and BWI Airport Welcome Center.

The speed limit is 65 on interstate highways, 55 in many places, unless otherwise noted. All passengers are required to use safety belts. Children under 3 or weighing less than 40 pounds must be in approved child-safety seats.

The Maryland State Police monitor CB Channel 9. Motorists traveling with cell phones may report disabled vehicles or accidents by dialing #77.

There are seven tollbooths on state roads for highway, tunnel or bridge use. Fees range from $1.00 to $2.50.

The Western Shore of Maryland presently has two telephone area codes – 301 and 410. You must dial all ten digits when calling in the state.

# Calendar of Events

## January

Baltimore Woodworking Show, Maryland State Fairgrounds, Timonium
Fishing Expo and Boat Show, Maryland State Fairgrounds, Timonium
Polar Bear Plunge, Sandy Point State Park, Annapolis
Paper Americana Show, Elkton

## February

Chesapeake Bay Boat Show, Baltimore Convention Center
Maryland International Auto Show, Maryland State Fairgrounds, Timonium
Maryland Recreational Vehicle Show, Maryland State Fairgrounds, Timonium
Hunt Valley Antiques Show, Hunt Valley

## March

Maryland Home, Flower and Spring Craft Show, Maryland State Fairgrounds, Timonium
St. Patrick's Day - parades, special events
Maryland Day Celebration, Baltimore, Annapolis
Maryland Days - Historic St. Mary's City

## April

Maryland Archeology Month
Marlborough Hunt Races, Roedown Farm, Davidsonville
Maryland Orchid Society's Annual Orchid Show, Owings Mills
My Lady's Manor Steeplechase Races, Monkton
Upper Chesapeake Skipjack Invitational Races, Havre de Grace
Maryland Hunt Cup, Glyndon
Maryland House and Garden Pilgrimage

## May

Baltimore Women's Show, Maryland State Fairgrounds, Timonium
Decoy, Wildlife and Sportsmen Festival, Havre de Grace
Southern Maryland Spring Festival, Leonardtown
Ladew Plant Sale, Monkton
Burning of Havre de Grace Reenactment, War of 1812, Havre de Grace
Chesapeake Bay Bridge Annual Walk
Montpelier Spring Festival, Montpelier Mansion, Laurel
Preakness Race, Baltimore. Third Saturday

East Coast Rally, Aberdeen Proving Ground
Reservoir Hill Garden Tour, Baltimore City
Chesapeake Bay Blues Festival, Sandy Point State Park, Annapolis
Antique Vehicle Run, Chesapeake Beach
Bowie Heritage Day, Belair Mansion, Bowie
Dundalk Art Show, Dundalk
Memorial Day - parades, concerts

## June

Maryland Rose Society, Inc. Rose Show, Cylburn Arboretum, Baltimore
Secret Garden Tour, Hammond-Harwood House, Annapolis
Strawberry Festivals
Scottish Festival, Havre de Grace
Montpelier Summer Concert Series, Montpelier Mansion, Laurel
Party Music Crab Feast, Baltimore
Maritime Festival, Havre de Grace
Mid-Atlantic Chevelle Show, North East
Gospel Music Crab Feast, Baltimore
Annual Antique Show, Havre de Grace
Annual Classic Boat Show, Havre de Grace
Susquehanna Wine Festival, Havre de Grace

## July

Fourth of July - parades, concerts, fireworks
John Paul Jones Days, US Naval Academy, Annapolis
Harford County Farm Fair, Bel Air
Cecil County Fair, Fair Hill

## August

Rotary Crab Feast, Annapolis
World War II Cradle of Invasion, Calvert Marine Museum, Solomons Island
Howard County Fair, Howard County Fairgrounds, West Friendship
Susquehanna River Festival, Port Deposit
Kunta Kinte Festival, Annapolis
North Beach Bayfest, North Beach
Maryland State Fair, Maryland State Fairgrounds, Timonium
Calvert County Jousting Festival, Port Republic
Maryland Renaissance Festival, Annapolis

## September

Maryland Seafood Festival, Annapolis
Annual Duck Fair, Havre de Grace
Star-Spangled Banner Week-end, Baltimore
Fall Maryland RV Show, Maryland State Fairgrounds, Timonium
Charles County Fair, LaPlata
Defenders Day Remembered, Dundalk
Havre de Grace Corn Festival, Tydings Memorial Park, Havre de Grace
Aberdeen Heritage Day, Aberdeen
Solomons Island Biathlon, Solomons
War of 1812 Re-enactment, St. Leonard
Calvert County Fair, Barstow

## October

Mid-Atlantic Boat Show, Maryland State Fairgrounds, Timonium
United States Sailboat Show, Annapolis
United States Powerboat Show, Annapolis
Darlington Apple Festival, Darlington
Woodland Indian Culture Days, St. Mary's City
Patuxent River Appreciation Days Festival, Solomons
Chocolate Festival, Baltimore
Great Chesapeake Bay Schooner Race, Baltimore to Norfolk, VA
St. Mary's County Oyster Festival. Fairgrounds, Leonardtown. Third week. The National Oyster Cook-off is a highlight of the festival
West River Heritage Day Oyster Festival. Capt. Salem Avery House, Shady Side.
Blessing of the Fleet. St. Clement's Island. 1st full week-end

## November

Maryland Historical Society Antiques Show, Baltimore
Antique Bottles and Collectibles Show and Sale, Elkton
Harford County Day School Antique Show, Bel Air
Potter's Guild of Baltimore Holiday Show, Baltimore
Annapolis by Candlelight, Annapolis
Lights on the Bay, Annapolis

## December

Governor's Open House, Annapolis
Lighted Boat Parade, Baltimore, Annapolis, Solomons
A Plantation Christmas, Sotterley Plantation, Hollywood

Christmas Candlelight Tours, Montpelier Mansion, Laurel
Candlelight Tour of Belair Mansion, Bowie
Port Deposit "Susquehanna Festival of Lights", Port Deposit
Candlelight Tour & Carver Celebration of Historic Havre de Grace
Victorian Yuletide by Candlelight, Surratt House Mansion, Clinton
AMC Holiday House Tour, Bel Air
Holiday Mart, Ellicott City
Garden in Lights, Solomons
Christmas Madrigal Evenings, St. Mary's City
Colonial Christmas at Smallwood, Marbury
First Night Annapolis

## Important Numbers

Emergency Number                    911
U.S. Coast Guard Search and Rescue. Baltimore. 410-576-2520
U.S. Coast Guard. 1-800-418-7314
Maryland Department of Natural Resources. 410-260-8888
Maryland Poison Center. 1-800-492-2414
Maryland State Police, Annapolis. 410-268-6101
Maryland State Police, Bel Air. 410-838-4101
Maryland State Police, Essex. 410-686-3101
Maryland State Police, North East. 410-398-8101

## Airports

Baltimore-Washington International. 410-859-7111
Ronald Reagan Washington National. 703-419-8000
Washington Dulles International. 703-572-2700
Martin State Airport. Middle River. 410-682-8800
Lee Airport. Edgewater. 410-956-2114
Freeway Airport. Off Route 50. 301-390-6424
St. Mary's County (Hollywood) Airport. 301-373-2101

## Car Rentals

Alamo. 1-800-327-9633
Allstate Auto Rentals. 410-363-6500
Avis. 1-800-331-1212
Budget. 800-527-0700
Dollar. 800-800-4000

Enterprise Rent-A-Car. 800-Rent-A-Car
Hertz. 800-654-3131
National. 800-328-4567
Thrifty Car Rental. 800-367-2277

## Taxis/Limousines

American Limousine. 410-522-0400
Carey Limousine Service. 410-880-0999
Celebrity Limousine, Inc. 410-496-1303
International Limousine Service, Inc. 410-799-1400
Presidential Limousine. 410-780-8181
Davis Limousine Service. 410-526-5667
Prime Time Sedan & Limousine Services. 443-562-0067
Zbest Limousine Services, Inc. 410-768-1148
BWI Airport Shuttle. 800-258-3826
About Town Airport Express. 410-838-6449 (Harford County)

## Motorcoach Transportation

Greyhound. Baltimore. 410-752-1393. Washington. 202-289-5154
Annapolis Transit. 410-263-7964
Maryland Transit Authority (Annapolis, Baltimore, Washington). 410-539-5000
Quick Trip Tours. Churchville. 410-836-0297
Superior Tours. 410-602-1704
Bill Rohrbaugh's Charter Service, Inc. 7694 Belair Road. Baltimore. 410-882-7501

## Trains/Subways

Amtrak. 800-872-7245 Penn Station. 1501 N. Charles Street. Baltimore
Amtrak. New Carrollton. 410-539-5000
Metro. Washington area. 202-637-7000
MARC. 410-539-5000
Light Rail. 410-637-5000

## Walking Tours

North East: A Strolling Guide. 410-287-2658
Havre de Grace Welcomes You. 410-939-3303

Baltimore Architecture Foundation Walking Tours. 410-625-2585
Ellicott City Walking Tour. 8267 Main Street. 800-288-8747
Chesapeake Marine Tours. City Dock, Annapolis. 410-268-7600
Historic Annapolis Foundation Tours. 26 West Street. 410-263-5533
Naval Academy Tour Guide Service. Visitors Center. Gate 1. 410-263-8120
Three Centuries Tours. 48 Maryland Avenue, Annapolis. 410-263-5401
Discover Annapolis Tours. Departs from 26 West Street, Annapolis. 410-626-6000
Historic Annapolis African-American Heritage Walking Tour. 410-268-5576
Revolutionary Annapolis. Museum Shop. 77 Main Street. The pamphlet is $4.50. 410-267-7619
Eastport Historic Walking Tour. Annapolis Maritime Museum. 410-295-0104
Historic St. Mary's City. 301-862-0990

**Visitor Centers and Chambers of Commerce**

North East Chamber of Commerce. 410-287-2658
Cecil County Office of Tourism. 1 Seahawk Drive, North East, MD 21901. 410-996-6290
Baltimore Area Visitors Center. 300 W. Pratt Street, Baltimore. 410-837-4636
Baltimore Area Convention & Visitors Association, Legg Mason Tower, 12th Floor, 100 Light Street, Baltimore, MD 21202. 410-659-7300
Baltimore County Conference and Visitors Bureau, 111 Shawan Road, Hunt Valley Mall, Hunt Valley, MD 21030. 410-329-1001
Discover Harford County Tourism Council. 224 Washington Street. Havre de Grace. 410-575-7278
Havre de Grace Tourism Commission & Chamber of Commerce Office. 224 N. Washington Street. 410-939-3303
Essex Middle River Chamber of Commerce. 439 Eastern Blvd. 410-686-2233
Howard County Tourism Council, 8267 Main Street, Ellicott City, MD 21043. 410-313-1900
Prince George's County, MD Conference and Visitors Bureau, Inc., 9200 Basil Court, Suite 101, Largo, MD 20774. 301-925-8300
Annapolis &Anne Arundel County Conference and Visitors Bureau, 26 West Street, Annapolis, MD 21401. 410-280-0445
Calvert County Department of Economic Development and Tourism, 175 Main Street, Prince Frederick, MD 20678. 410-535-4583
Charles County Office of Tourism, PO Box B, LaPlata, MD 20646. 301-645-0558
St. Mary's County Division of Travel and Tourism, PO Box 653, Leonardtown, MD 20650. 301-475-4411
St. Mary's Chamber of Commerce. 28290 Three Notch Road. Mechanicsville. 301-884-5555

# Newspapers

Cecil Whig. 601 Bridge Street. Elkton. 410-398-3311
The Aegis. 10 S. Hays Street. Bel Air. 410-838-4400
The Capital. 2000 Capital Drive, Annapolis. 410-268-5000
Washington Post. 1150 15th Street, NW, Washington, DC. 202-334-6000
The Washington Times. 3600 New York Avenue, NE, Washington, DC. 202-269-3419
Baltimore Sun. 501 N. Calvert Street, Baltimore. 800-829-8000
Maryland Gazette. 306 Crain Highway S.W., Glen Burnie. 410-766-3700
Crofton News-Crier. PO Box 790. Bowie. 410-20715
West County News. PO Box 170. Odenton. 410-280-5922
The Publick Enterprise. Annapolis. 410-268-3527
New Bay Times. Deale. 410-867-0304
Calvert County Recorder. 310 Main Street. Prince Frederick. 301-855-1029
Calvert Independent Newspaper. Prince Frederick. 301-855-1000
Enterprise Newspaper. Lexington Park. 410-326-4039
The Southern Maryland Voice. 9020 Bay Avenue. North Beach. 301-855-0711

# Magazines

Baltimore. 1000 Lancaster Street, Baltimore. 410-974-3973
Inside Annapolis. 519 Burnside Street. 410-263-6300
Spin Sheet. 301 Fourth Street. Annapolis. 410-216-9309
Chesapeake Life. PO Box 3323. 410-280-2777
Chesapeake Bay Magazine. 1819 Bay Ridge Avenue. Annapolis. 410-263-2662
The Mariner. 500 S. Main Street. North East. 410-287-9430

# Hospitals

The Johns Hopkins Hospital. Baltimore. 410-955-5000
Sheppard Pratt Health System.6501 N. Charles Street. Baltimore. 410-938-3000
Union Hospital. Elkton. 410-398-4000
Union Memorial Hospital. 201 E. University Parkway, Baltimore. 410-554-2000
Harbor Hospital. Baltimore. 410-347-3509
Harford Memorial. 501 S. Union Avenue. Havre de Grace. 410-939-2400
University of Maryland Medical Center. Redwood & Greene Streets, Baltimore. 410-328-6722
Union Memorial Hospital. Charles Street, Baltimore
Mercy Hospital. 301 St. Paul Place, Baltimore. 410-332-9000
Sinai Hospital. 2401 W. Belvedere Avenue, Baltimore. 410-601-9000
Sheppard Pratt. 6501 N. Charles Street, Towson. 410-938-3000

Laurel Regional Hospital. 7300 Van Dusen Road. Laurel. 301-725-4300
Prince George's Hospital. Cheverly. 301-618-2000
Anne Arundel Medical Center. Jennifer Road. Annapolis. 410-267-1000
North Arundel Hospital. 301 Hospital Drive, Glen Burnie. 410-787-4000
Calvert Memorial Hospital. 100 Hospital Road. Prince Frederick. 410-535-4000
St. Mary's Hospital. 25500 Point Lookout Road. Leonardtown. 301-475-8981

## Tickets

Baltimore Tickets. 1-888-Balt-Tix

## Theaters/Theatre Groups

Cecil County Community College Cultural Center. North East. 410-287-1037
Covered Bridge Theatre Company. North East. 410-287-1023
Phoenix Festival Theater. Harford Community College. 410-836-4211
Timonium Dinner Theatre. 9603 Deereco Road. 410-560-1113
Baltimore Actors' Theatre. Hunt Valley. 410-337-8519
Maryland Arts Festival. Towson University, Towson. 410-830-2076
Dundalk Community Theatre. Baltimore. 410-285-9667
CenterStage. 700 N. Calvert, Baltimore. 410-332-0033
Everyman Theatre. 700 N. Calvert Street, Baltimore. 410-332-0033
Fell's Point Community Theatre. Baltimore. 410-276-7837
Morris Mechanic Theater. 25 Hopkins Plaza, Baltimore. 410-625-4230
Peabody Conservatory of Music. One E. Mount Vernon Place, Baltimore. 410-6598124
Thomas Hopkins. Merrick Barn, Johns Hopkins University, Baltimore. 410-516-7159
Vagabond Players. 806 S. Broadway, Baltimore. 410-563-9135
Howard County Center for the Creative Arts. 8510 High Ridge Road. Ellicott City. 410-313-2787
Annapolis Summer Garden Theater. 143 Compromise Street. 410-268-0809
Chesapeake Music Hall. 339 Busch's Frontage Road, Annapolis. 410-626-7515
Colonial Players. 108 East Street, Annapolis. 410-268-7373
Maryland Hall for the Creative Arts. 801 Chase Street, Annapolis. 410-263-5544
Pasadena Theatre Co. Chesapeake Center for Creative Arts. Brooklyn Park. 410-969-1801
Alice Ferguson Foundation: Hard Bargain Players. Accokeek. 301-292-5665
Port Tobacco Players. La Plata. 301-932-6819

11

## Music

Tydings Park, Havre de Grace. Summer Sunday evening concerts
Baltimore Symphony Orchestra. Meyerhoff Symphony Hall. 1212 Cathedral Street. 410-783-8000
Baltimore Opera Company. Lyric Opera House. 140 W. Mount Royal Avenue, 410-494-2712
Baltimore Choral Arts Society. 410-523-7070
Charlestown Chapel Concert Series. Catonsville. 410-536-4762
Annapolis Symphony. Maryland Hall for the Creative Arts. 801 Chase Street. 410-263-0907
Annapolis Chorale. Maryland Hall for the Creative Arts. 410-263-1906
Annapolis Opera. 410-267-8135
United States Naval Academy. Mitscher Hall. 410-293-2439
Chesapeake Youth Symphony Orchestra. Annapolis. 410-544-0314
Susquehanna Symphony Orchestra. Forest Hill. 410-838-6465
City Dock. Annapolis. Summer concert series. Tuesday evenings at 7:30
Rip Miller Field. US Naval Academy, Annapolis. Summer evenings at 7:30
William Paca Garden. Annapolis. Summer Sunday evenings. 410-267-7619
South County Concert Association. 410-867-1584
Campus Green. St. Mary's College of Maryland. Summer Friday evening concerts

## Yachting

See chapter on yachting.

## Golf Courses

Cecil County:
Chesapeake Bay Golf Club. 1500 Chesapeake Club Drive, North East. 410-287-0200.
Chantilly Manor Country Club. 128 Karen Drive. Rising Sun. 410-658-4343
Brantwood Golf Club. 1190 Augustine Herman Highway. Rising Sun. 410-398-8848

Harford County
Bulle Rock. 320 Blenheim Lane. Havre de Grace. 410-939-8887
Churchville Golf & Baseball. 3040 Churchville Road. Churchville. 410-838-1411
APG-Plumb Point Golf Course. Aberdeen Proving Ground. 410-278-9994
APG-Ruggles Golf Course. Aberdeen Proving Ground. 410-278-4794

Exton Golf Course. Aberdeen Proving Ground. 410-671-2213
The Wetlands Golf Club. 740 Gilbert Road. Aberdeen. 410-273-7488
Beechtree Golf Club. 811 Stepney Road. Aberdeen. 410-297-9700
Geneva Farms Golf Club. 217 Davis Road. Street. 410-836-8816
Mt. Vista Golf Course. 11101 Raphael Road. Bradshaw. 410-592-5467

Baltimore County
Mountain Branch Golf Course. 1827 Mountain Road. Joppa. 410-836-9600
Longview Golf Course. 1 Cardigan Road. Timonium. 410-628-6362
Pine Ridge Golf Course. 2101 Dulaney Valley Road. Lutherville. 410-252-1408
Rocky Point Golf Course. 1935 Back River Neck Road. Essex. 410-391-2906

Prince George's County.
Patuxent Greens Country Club. Laurel. 301-776-5533
Marlborough Country Club. Upper Marlboro. 301-952-1300

Howard County
Turf Valley Resort & Conference Center. 2700 Turf Valley Road. Ellicott City.
410-465-1500
The Timbers at Troy. 6100 Marshalee Drive. Elkridge. 410-313-GOLF

Anne Arundel County:
Crofton Country Club. 1691 Crofton Parkway. Crofton. 410-721-3111
Annapolis Golf Club. 2638 Carrollton Road. Semi-private. 410-263-6771
Bay Hills Golf Club. 545 Bay Hills Drive, Arnold. Semi-private. 410-974-0669
Dwight D. Eisenhower Golf Club. Generals Highway, Crownsville. 410-222-7922
Severna Park Golf Center.1257 Ritchie Highway, Arnold. 410-647-8618
South River Golf Links. Routes 2 and 214, Edgewater. 410-798-5865
Night Hawk Golf Center. 814 Rte. 3 South. Gambrills. 410-721-9349
Old South Country Club. 699 Marlboro Road. Lothian. 410-741-6037

Charles County
Indian Head Golf Course. Indian Head Naval Ordnance Station. 301-743-4000
Swan Point Country and Yacht Club. Issue. 301-259-4411
White Plains Golf Course. DeMarr Road and St. Charles Parkway, near Waldorf.
301-645-1300
Hawthorne Country Club. Rte. 225. LaPlata. 301-934-8422

Calvert County
Twin Shields Golf Course. 2425 Roarty Road. Dunkirk. 301-855-8228
Chesapeake Hills Golf Club. H.G. Trueman Road. Lusby. 410-326-4653
Mellomar Golf Park. 6215 Scaggs Road. 410-286-8212

St. Mary's County
Breton Bay Golf & Country Club. Society Hill Road. Leonardtown. 301-475-2300
Wicomico Shores Golf Course. 301-884-4601

## Football

Redskins          1-877-478-SEAT
Ravens            301-261-7283
US Naval Academy       410-US4-NAVY
University of Maryland   301-314-7070

## Baseball

Baltimore Orioles - Camden Yards, Baltimore. 410-481-SEAT
Baysox. Route 301, south of Rte. 50. 301-805-6000
Naval Academy. 410-268-6060
Aberdeen Arsenal. 410-272-2332

## Basketball

University of Maryland   301-314-7070
US Naval Academy.       1-800-US4-NAVY

## Bicycle Rentals and Sales

Broadway Bicycle. 415-7 S. Broadway, Baltimore. 410-276-0266
Bike Doctor. 150 Jennifer Road, Annapolis. 410-266-7383
Sea Dive & Cycle. S&W Shopping Center, Solomons. 410-326-4386
Starrk Moon Kayaks. Kayak and bike rentals. Havre de Grace. 410-939-9500
Jody's Jalopies. 843 Otsego Street. Havre de Grace. 410-939-2453. 4-wheel bikes!
Blue Wind. 9001 Three Notch Road. California. 301-737-2713
Bike Doctor. 2957 Festival Way. Waldorf. 301-932-9980
Loveville Bike Shop. Rte. 5, Loveville.
Mike's Bikes. 447C Great Mills Road, Lexington Park. 301-863-7887
Mike's Bikes. 3262 Leonardtown Road, Waldorf. 301-870-600
Penn Auto. 5 Church Street, Frederick. 410-535-2222

14

Sea Dive & Bicycle. Rte 2 Solomons Island. 410-326-4386
The Bike Shop of Waldorf. 3265 Leonardtown Road. 301-645-8666
Sign and Cycles Bike Shop. Old Three Notch Road. Hollywood. 301-373-3789

## Hot Air Balloon Rides/ Ultralights

Ultraflight-Ultrafun. Havre de Grace. 1-877-FOR-A-FLY

## Riding

Happy Trails Riding Stable. North East. 410-287-2157
Tailwinds Farm. 41 Tailwinds Lane. North East. 410-658-8187
McValley Riding Stable. Port Deposit. 410-378-4166
Harford County Equestrian Center. N. Tollgate Road. Bel Air. 410-638-3528
Equilibrium Horse Center. 1685 Underwood Road. Gambrills. 410-721-0885
Loftmar Stables. 17620 Central Avenue. Bowie. 301-249-7893
Relax & Ride. 1837 Underwood Road. Gambrills. 410-721-0100
Piscataway Riding Stables & Horse Farm. Clinton. 301-297-9808
PG Equestrian Center/Show Place Arena. 14900 Pennsylvania Avenue. Upper
Marlboro. 301-952-7999. Equestrian sports and events.
Battlecreek Horse Farm. Port Republic. 410-586-2477
Maiden Point Farm. Newburg. 301-259-2442
Mary's Go Round. 15320 Noah's Place, Waldorf. 301-888-1426

## Race Tracks

Pimlico Race Course. Hayward and Winner Avenue. 410-542-9400
Laurel Park. Rte. 198 and Race Track Road. Laurel. 301-725-0400
Rosecroft Raceway. 6336 Rosecroft Drive. Fort Washington. 301-567-4000

## Fishing

There is good fishing on the Chesapeake Bay, rivers, lakes and creeks. Bass,
stripers (otherwise known as rockfish), oysters, crab, and other fish are available
locally. Some need licenses.

# Swimming

North East Beach. Rte. 272. 410-287-5333
Sandy Point State Park. Rte. 50, Annapolis
Breezy Point Beach & Campground. Breezy Point Road. Chesapeake Beach. 410-535-0259
Point Lookout State Park. Scotland. 301-872-5688
Elm's Beach. Dameron. 301-475-4572
Greenwell State Park. Hollywood. 301-872-5688
Chesapeake Beach Water Park. 4079 Gordon Stinnett Avenue. Chesapeake Beach. 410-257-1404
Bay Front Park. Chesapeake Beach. 410-257-2230
Calvert Cliffs State Park. Rte. 765. Lusby. 301-872-5688
Flag Ponds Nature Park. Flag Ponds Parkway. Lusby. 410-586-1477
North Beach Public Beach. North Beach. 410-257-9618

# Ice Rinks

Herbert Wells Ice Rink. 5211 Paint Branch Road, College Park. 301-277-0654
Benfield Pines Ice Rink. I-97 and Benfield Road. 410-987-5100
Dahlgren Hall Ice Rink. US Naval Academy. 410-293-2350
Northwest Ice Rink. 5731 Cottonworth Avenue. Baltimore. 410-732-4614

# Raceways

Cecil County Dragway. Theodore Road. Near North East. 410-287-5486

# Parks/Wildlife Refuges

Cecil County:
Fair Natural Resource Management Area. Fair Hill
Elk Neck State Park, Rte. 272, near North East. 410-287-5333
Elk Neck Demonstration Forest. Irishtown Road. 410-287-5675

Harford County:
Susquehanna State Park, 3318 Rocks Chrome Hill Road, Jarrettsville. 410-557-7994. 2,639 acre park
Gunpowder Falls State Park. Hereford. 410-592-2897. 13,020 acre park
Rocks State Park. Rte. 24. 410-557-7994

Chesapeake Bay National Estuarine Research Reserve. Otter Point Creek, Edgewood

Baltimore County:
Soldiers Delight NEA. Off Rte. 26. 410-461-5005
Hart-Miller Island. 410-477-0757
North Point State Park. Off Old North Point Road. Edgemere. 410-477-0757

Howard County:
Patapsco State Park. 8020 Baltimore National Pike. Ellicott City. 32 miles along the Patapsco River with 12,699 acres

Anne Arundel County:
Baltimore Annapolis Trail Park. Glen Burnie to Annapolis
Bell Branch Athletic Complex. 2400 Davidsonville Road. Gambrills
Bodkin Park. Bodkin Avenue. Pasadena
Broadneck Park. Broadneck Road. Pasadena
Crofton Park. Davidsonville Road. Crofton
Cypress Creek Park. Cypress Creek Road. Severna Park
Deale/ Tracy's Park. Tracy's Landing. Deale
Downs Park. 8311 John Downs Loop. Pasadena. 230 acre park on Chesapeake.
Jug Bay Wetlands Sanctuary. 1361 Wrighton Road. Lothian. 620 acre natural preserve.
Lake Waterford Park. Pasadena Road and B&A Blvd. Pasadena. Lake, picnic area.
Sandy Point State Park. Rte. 50. Annapolis
Smithsonian Environmental Research Center. Rte. 468. This 2600 acre center has trails, docks, and information on the Chesapeake Bay.

Prince George's County:
Greenbelt Park. Greenbelt. 1,176 acre park
Lake Artemesia Park. College Park
Oxon Hill Farm. Oxon Hill
Patuxent River Park. The 6,500 acre park has canoeing, hiking, nature studies
Merkle Wildlife Refuge. Croom Road. 301-888-1410
Rosaryville State Park. Rte. 301. This 990 acre park also has the ancestral home, Mount Airy, of the Calvert family.
Cedarville State Forest. Cedarville Road. 301-888-1410. There are over 3,000 acres of woods and swampland. The Zekiah Swamp is located on the winter camp of the Piscataway Indians. Hiking,
The Accokeek Foundation at Piscataway Park. 3400 Bryan Point Road. Accokeek. 301-283-2113. The National Colonial Farm, trails, and Robert Ware Strauss Ecosystem Farm are located on the banks of the Potomac across from Mount Vernon

Fort Washington National Park. 13551 Fort Washington Road. Fort Washington. 301-763-4600. The historic park and fort overlooks Washington and the Potomac River.

Calvert County:
Calvert Cliffs State Park. Rte.765. The 1,600 acre park offers cycling, hiking, a beach, fossil hunting and various other activities.
Flag Pounds Nature Park. This is a 327 acre nature preserve on the Bay. Until 1955 a pound-net fishery operated here.
Breezy Point Beach & Campground. Breezy Point Road. Chesapeake Beach
Kings Landing Park. Kings Landing Road. Huntingtown

Charles County:
Mattawoman Natural Environment Area. Rte. 224
Chicamuxen Watchable Wildlife Center. Rte. 224. Indian Head. 301-743-4705
Doncaster State Forest. Rte. 6. 301934-2282. More than 1500 acres.
Chapel Point State Park. Chapel Point Road. Port Tobacco
Zekiah Swamp N.E.A. 301-645-0540
General Smallwood State Park. Rte. 224. 629 acre park
Gilbert Run Park. Rte 6. Near La Plata. Good for fishing
Southern Park. Rte. 257. Issue
Friendship Landing. Friendship Landing Road off Rte. 425, Nanjemoy. Boat ramp
White Plains Recreational Park. DeMarr Road and St. Charles Parkway. Golf course, picnicking
Laurel Springs Regional Park. Radio Station Road. LaPlata
Myrtle Grove Wildlife Management Area. Rte. 225. LaPlata. 301-743-5161
Ruth B. Swann Memorial Park. Bryans Road off Rte. 210
Robert D. Stethem Memorial Sports Complex.
Oak Ridge Park. Oaks Road, Hughesville
Purse State Park.Rte. 224. Indian Head. 301-743-7613

St. Mary's County:
Greenwell State Park. Rte.245. Located on Patuxent River. Hiking, horseback riding, fishing, hunting, canoeing/kayaking, swimming, beach
Point Lookout State Park. Rte. 5. 301-872-5688
St. Mary's River State Park. Camp Cosoma Road. 301-872-5688
St. Clement's Island State Park. 301-872-5688
Patuxent River Natural Resource Management Area. Golden Beach

## Zoos

Baltimore Zoo. Druid Hill Park. 410-366-5466
Zoo at Plumpton Park. 1416 Telegraph Road. Rising Sun. 410-658-6850

## Colleges and Universities

Harford Community College. 401 Thomas Run Road. Bel Air. 410-836-4000
Johns Hopkins University. 3400 N. Charles Street, Baltimore. 410-516-8000
Community College of Baltimore. 410-869-1212
University of Baltimore. 1420 N. Charles Street. 410-837-4200
Morgan State University. 1700 E. Cold Spring Lane. Baltimore. 410-885-3333
Loyola College. 4501 N. Charles Street. 410-617-2000
Peabody Conservatory of Music. One E. Mt. Vernon Place, Baltimore. 410-659-8124
Coppin State College. 2500 W. North Avenue, Baltimore. 410-383-5926
Towson University. 8000 York Road. Towson. 410-830-2000
Goucher College. Towson. 410-337-6000
College of Notre Dame. 4701 N. Charles Street. 410-435-0100
United States Naval Academy. Annapolis. 410-293-1000
St. John's College. 60 College Avenue, Annapolis. 410-263-2371
University of Maryland. College Park. 301-405-1000
St. Mary's College. Rte. 5, St. Mary's City. 301-862-0200. Rated one of the top small colleges in the United States
Anne Arundel Community College. Arnold. 410-647-7100
Bowie State University. 1400 Jericho Park Road. Bowie. 301-464-3000
Charles County Community College. 8730 Mitchell Road, La Plata. 301-870-3008
College of Southern Maryland. 22950 Hollywood Road. Leonardtown. 301-475-8700

## Schools

Cecil County Schools. 201 Booth Street. Elkton. 4100-996-5400
Harford County Schools. 410-838-7300
Baltimore County Public Schools. 6901 N. Charles Street. Towson. 410-887-4020
Prince George's County Schools. 14201 School Lane. Upper Marlboro. 301-952-6001
Howard County Schools. 10910 Rte. 108. Ellicott City. 410-313-6600
Anne Arundel County Public Schools. Riva Road. 410-222-5303

Calvert County Schools. 1305 Dares Beach Road. Prince Frederick. 410-535-1700

Charles County Schools. 301-932-6610

St. Mary's County Schools. 23160 Moakley Street. Leonardtown. 301-475-4230

Bryn Mawr. 109 W. Melrose Avenue. Baltimore. 410-323-8800

Notre Dame Preparatory School. Towson. 410-825-0590

Gilman School. Roland Avenue, Baltimore. 410-532-2300

Roland Park Country Day School. 5204 Roland Avenue. 410-323-5500

St. Timothy's. Stevenson. 410-486-7400. Girls 9-12th grades

Friends School. 5144 N. Charles Street. Baltimore. 410-435-2800

Garrison Forest. Owings Mills. 410-363-1501

St. Paul's. Brooklandville. 410-825-4400

Shrine of the Sacred Heart. Baltimore. 410-542-7406. Grades Pre-K-8th grades

Oldfields. Glencoe. 410-472-4800

McDonough School. Owings Mills. 40-998-3519

Glenelg Country School. 12793 Folly Quarter Road, Glenelg. 410-531-7348 Grades Pre-K-12th.

Archbishop Spalding High School. 8080 New Cut Road, Severn. 410-969-9105

Annapolis Area Christian School. Bestgate Road. Grades 1-12. 410-266-8251

St. Anne's Day School. 3112 Arundel on the Bay Road. 410-263-8650

The Key School. 534 Hillsmere Drive. 1-12. Nursery- grade 12. 410-263-9231

Severn School. Severna Park. 410-647-7701

Indian Creek School. Evergreen Road. Crownsville. 410-987-0342

St. Margaret's Day School. 1601 Pleasant Plains Road. Annapolis. 410-757-2333

St. Martin's Lutheran School. 1120 Spa Road. Annapolis. 410-269-1955

St. Andrew's School. 4 Wallace Manor Road, Edgewater. 410-266-0952

St. Mary's School. Duke of Gloucester Street. Annapolis. 410-263-3294

Chesapeake Academy. 1185 Baltimore Annapolis Blvd. 410-647-9612

Saint Michael's Catholic School. Lexington 301-872-5454

Belair Christian Academy. 2801 Belair Drive. Bowie. 301-262-0587

Elvaton Christian Academy. 8422 Elvaton Road. Millersville. 410-647-3224. 2 years to 5th grade

Temple Solel Religious School. 2901 Mitchellville Road. Bowie. 410-249-2424

Queen Anne School. Upper Marlboro. 301-249-5000. 6-12th grades.

Summit School. 410-798-0005. Grades 1-8th.

The Calverton School. Huntingtown. 410-535-0216. K-12th grades

Our Lady Star of the Sea. Solomons. 410-326-3171. K-8th grades

Tidewater School. Huntingtown. 410-257-0533. Pre-K-4th grades

The Cardinal Hickey Academy. Owings. 410-286-0404. Pre-K-7th grades

## Special Libraries

Maryland Archives. 350 Rowe Boulevard. Annapolis. 410-974-3914
Enoch Pratt Library. 400 Cathedral Street. Baltimore. 410-396-5430
Maryland Historical Society. 201 W. Monument Street, Baltimore. 410-685-3750

## How to Make it on the Western Shore

### Dressing the part

Dress is very important on the Western Shore. It is basically a casual region. However appropriate dress is advised. Ladies should not be seen in short shorts, low cut dresses or bathing suits.
Men should not wear tank tops, tee shirts, short shorts, or go bare-chested. No bathing suits except at the beach.

### Men

Daytime:
Khaki pants or shorts
Polo shirts

Topsiders
No socks
Foul weather gear

Evening Wear: Some restaurants and yacht clubs require coat and tie. For yacht christenings and special events navy blue blazer, tan or white pants, club or regimental tie.

### Ladies

Daytime:
Khaki, linen or silk pants
Shorts

Polo shirt
Blazers or wool sweaters
Topsiders

Evening Wear: Nice dress - silk or cotton. Silk pants and blouse.

## The Best of the Western Shore

Dining in a Historic Place

Elkridge Furnace Inn, Elkridge; Milton Inn, Sparks; Manor Inn, Monkton; Old Field Inn, Prince Frederick; Brome-Howard Inn, St. Mary's City; The Union Hotel, Port Deposit;

21

| | Howard House Restaurant, Elkton; Vandiver Inn, Havre de Grace |
|---|---|
| Tea (by reservation) | Montpelier Mansion; Riversdale Mansion; Evergreen House |
| Drinks | Overlooking Baltimore Harbor, Bay, or one of the many rivers |
| Best Dinner | Gabler's, Aberdeen; Tersiquel's, Ellicott City; Café Troia, Towson; India Palace, Cockeysville; Liberatore's Ristorante, Timonium; Hunter's Lodge, Ellicott City; Goong Jeon, Café Alberto, Glen Burnie; Windows on the Bay, Pasadena; Patrick's of Cockeysville; Oregon Grill, Hunt Valley; Brome-Howard Inn, St. Mary's City; Old Field Inn, Prince Frederick; Milton Inn, Sparks; Dry Dock, Solomons |
| Best Seafood on the Water | Portside Grille, Port Deposit; Stoney's Seafood House, Broome; Mike's Crab House, Riva; Bayside Inn, Fergie's, Surfside 7, Edgewater; Woody's Crab House, North East; Zahniser's, Bowen's, Solomons Pier, Lighthouse, Solomons; Cheshire Crab, Pasadena; Pirate's Cove, Topside, Galesvile; Herrington Harbour; Skipper's Pier, Deale; Snug Harbor, Shady Side; Deep Creek, Magothy Seafood, Arnold; Riverdale, Pasadena; McGregor's, Tidewater Grill, Havre de Grace; Gabler's, Aberdeen; Rod "N Reel, Chesapeake Beach; Vera's White Sands, Lusby; Evans Seafood, Piney Point |
| Music | Baltimore Symphony or Opera; Annapolis Symphony or Opera; summer concerts at Ladew Gardens, Montpelier Mansion, William Paca House; Chesapeake Beach Railway Museum; summer concerts on the lawn in the various towns |
| Chocolates | Kirchmayr Chocolates. 9630 Deereco Road. 410-561-7705 |

| | |
|---|---|
| Lectures | Maryland Historical Society; Historic Annapolis Foundation; Shady Side Historical Society; Montpelier Mansion; Calvert Marine Museum; Mount Clare Mansion: Riversdale Mansion; Darnall's Chance; Bel Air Mansion |
| Sightseeing | Anywhere |
| Scenic Drive | Rtes. 2,3, 4, 5 |
| Sailing | Anywhere on Bay, rivers or creeks |

## Things to do on a Great Day

Go sailing, canoeing, or kayaking
Learn to sail
Watch the sailboats
Girl watch on the harbors
Sit at one of the outdoor cafes and people watch
Take a walking tour of any of the historic towns
Take a picnic to the Bay or along one of the rivers
Walk in a park or around some of the towns' historic squares or one of the nature preserves
Take a bicycle ride
Take a balloon ride
Charter a fishing boat
Eat an ice cream cone
Go crabbing
Buy a boat
Play golf

## Things to Do on a Rainy Day

Find the best crab cakes
Go to the movies
Sit in a bar, meet new friends and be patient. Just don't get drunk as Maryland has strict DWI laws.
Go antique shopping
Go to a museum – the Decoy Museum in Havre de Grace; Museum of Industry, Maryland Historical Society, Walters Art Gallery, Baltimore Museum of Art, Baltimore; Calvert Marine Museum, Solomons; St. Mary's City.

# Places to Visit for Free

Conowingo Dam
Aberdeen Proving Grounds
Inner Harbor, Baltimore
Enoch Pratt Library, Baltimore
Lexington and Cross Street Markets, Baltimore
State Capital, US Naval Academy, Naval Academy Museum, Annapolis
Farmers Markets, throughout state
Calvert Cliffs
The Patuxent River Naval Air Museum, Lexington
Visit historic churches
Ride your bike along the many trails (Bike map of Maryland available)
Walk on the beach
Take a walking tour of the many historic Maryland towns
Walk along the Promenade in Havre de Grace
Visit a state park

# Things to do for free on a Summer Evening

Evening concerts at the local bandstand
Wednesday night sail boat races
Watch the sunset every evening
Watch the sunset every evening from your own boat
Pack a picnic and wander along the Bay

# Things to do for Free on a Winter Evening

Curl up in front of a fire with a good book
Hang out at one of the local pubs (you will have to purchase a drink or two, but you'll get some lively conversation)
Listen to some good music
Go to a lecture
Go to a book signing at a local store or library
Attend a free concert at the US Naval Academy on Friday night
Watch an old movie

# Favorite Pets

Black, yellow and chocolate Labradors and Chesapeakes (Chessies) are favorite pets, and are also used for hunting.

# Chapter 2

## History

**State House of 1676, St. Mary's City**
(Courtesy of Historic St. Mary's City – Katie Moose Photo)

The Bay was formed about 15,000 years ago by glaciers in the Susquehanna Valley. Most of the food - fish, especially rockfish, shad, crabs, and oysters came from the Chesapeake Bay and the fertile land which produced an abundance of crops.

The earliest inhabitants of the Chesapeake area were wanderers that began to settle c1,000 BC. The creation of the bow and arrow c500 AD and the cultivation of crops c 800 AD led to permanent villages. The Algonquin were the predominant group with the Susquehannocks just to the north.

The Spanish explorer Victor Hernandez is believed to have explored the Upper Chesapeake Bay in 1588. The earliest English explorer of the Chesapeake Bay was Captain John Smith who set out in 1608 from Jamestown. He mapped a great deal of the bay and reached the Upper Bay around Havre de Grace where he described the Susquehannock tribe as "a most noble and heroic nation of Indians".

George Calvert, the first Lord Baltimore, was given a grant in 1632 from King Charles I for all the land between the 40$^{th}$ parallel and the low water mark of the Potomac River to its source. He had hoped to found a colony in America, but only got as far as Newfoundland and found the area too cold and abandoned his project.

A second grant (probably 10-12 million acres) was given to his son Cecil Calvert, a Catholic, who left Virginia, which was an Anglican settlement. His wife, Anne Arundel, was the daughter of Lord Wardour. His brothers Leonard and George founded Maryland after sailing aboard the "Ark" and "Dove" with 140 passengers and landing at St. Clement's Island in the Potomac. St. Clement's Island was named for the fourth pope. In 1634 the Mattapany Indians inhabited the island and mainland. The settlers arrived on March 25, 1634. Leonard Calvert met with the Piscataway Indians, and bought a village, later St. Mary's City, and became the first Colonial Governor. He declared religious toleration for all. That day Fr. William White said the first Mass in the new colony. A wooden cross was erected and the Litany of the Cross was recited. The settlers traveled several days later to their new settlement at St. Mary's City. St. Mary's County was established in 1637.

The first governor was Leonard Calvert, brother of Lord Baltimore. Lord Baltimore, could raise an army, incorporate towns, impose duties, establish courts, appoint government officials and vest titles. In return he gave the king 2 Indian arrows every Easter, and 1/5 of the precious metals mined in the colony. St. Mary's City early on had a fort and tobacco was raised.

In 1631 William Claiborne established a trading post on Kent Island, just across from present day Annapolis. Because he claimed trading rights for the entire region and was also a Protestant, Governor Calvert sent out forces to claim the area for Maryland. In 1645 Richard Ingle arrived aboard a ship and plundered St. Mary's City. The government of Gov. Calvert was overthrown and Mr. Claiborne seized and destroyed the records of colonial Maryland. Leonard Calvert fled to Virginia. With stronger forces Gov. Calvert was able to return to power in 1646. Richard Ingle left the colony within a year. However Leonard died suddenly in 1647.

In 1648 Lord Baltimore appointed William Stone, a Protestant, governor. He purchased Leonard Calvert's House in St. Mary's City. In 1649 more than 300 Puritan settlers were expelled from Virginia for refusing to worship in the Anglican, or Established, Church. Governor Stone invited them to come to Maryland providing they took an oath of allegiance to Lord Baltimore. They settled on Greenbury's Point (now owned by the Navy) across from Annapolis and claimed land on the south side also. Edward Lloyd served as commander of the Puritans, and named the town Providence. Later it was named Anne Arundel Town in honor of the wife of Lord Baltimore.

The 1649 Toleration Act by Lord Baltimore provided freedom of worship for both Catholics and Protestants. Both Protestant and Catholic male landowners were allowed to vote in the Assembly. Lord Baltimore granted the Anne Arundel County and Calvert County charters in 1650. The Puritans overthrew the Catholic regime and moved the government to Calvert County from St. Mary's City. Also in 1650 the legislative body of Maryland was divided into two branches. The upper house consisted of the governor and members of his council appointed by the proprietor. The lower house, or general assembly, was comprised of burgesses elected by the people. Law defined the rights of Lord Baltimore.

In 1652 Robert Brooke established the first Calvert County seat in Battle Town (Calvert Town). Mr. Brooke had been asked by Lord Baltimore to come to Maryland in 1650. He was made "commander" of the county that was then called Charles County, now Calvert County. In 1652 when the parliamentary commission took over the government of Maryland, Mr. Brooke was named to the new council.

The early settlers often had problems with the Indians. Governor Stone sent a commission of five men to sign the Treaty of 1652 beneath the tulip tree "Liberty Tree" on what is now the grounds of St. John's College, Annapolis with the Susquehannock Indians.

As early as the 1640's Annapolis became a commercial port for tobacco and was made a Port of Entry in 1683. The South River was used for shipping prior to the Revolution, and LondonTowne rivaled Annapolis in trade. It was one of three sites in Anne Arundel County designated to promote trade by the 1683 General Assembly. However, the water was too shallow and Annapolis took over as the port.

The Puritans were also to settle in Calvert County under the leadership of Richard Preston who built plantation houses on the lower Patuxent River, some of which are still standing. "Charlesgift" was the site of the first assembly held in Maryland. The 1654 Protestant assembly was convened in Patuxent, which

27

acknowledged the supremacy of Oliver Cromwell and to disenfranchise the Catholics and deprive them the protection of the laws. From 1654-57 the home of Richard Preston, located near Lusby, was the provincial seat of government. In 1655 an armed band of Governor Stone's men from St. Mary's took the Puritans by surprise and seized the papers and documents that had been taken from St. Mary's by the Puritans. The Great Seal of Maryland was lost during this melee, though it is thought to be buried in the garden or walls of "Charlesgift".

From 1653-58 Oliver Cornwell, Lord Protector and a Puritan, forced Maryland to recognize him as head of the state. Governor William Stone attacked Providence (Annapolis) at the Battle of the Severn in 1655 and was defeated.. In 1656 Lord Baltimore regained control, made a treaty with the Puritans and appointed another Protestant governor, Josias Fendall. However Fendall too conspired against Lord Baltimore. When Charles II was restored to the throne in 1660 Cecil Calvert replaced Gov. Fendall with his brother Philip Calvert, and later his son Charles Calvert. Also in 1656 a jury of women met at Richard Preston's house to try Judith Catchpole for infanticide for which they found her not guilty.

The Governor's Proclamation of 1668 established 11 Ports of Entry. One of the first patents for a tract of land in Baltimore was given to John Howard in 1668. Also in that year Thomas Cole held five hundred acres known as Cole's Harbor. Later this was the area to be bounded by Paca, Mulberry, High and Lombard Streets in Baltimore. James Todd was to receive a patent for this in 1698.

The colonists in Southern Maryland cleared the oak forests and planted tobacco. The tobacco cash crop was used to support the clergy and churches and 40 pounds of tobacco was levied per taxable inhabitant. Many slaves and indentured servants came to work for the tobacco planters. Tobacco was exported, mainly to the European countries and was the prime cash crop from 1690 to 1776. Over a period of time the tobacco caused erosion. Many of the rivers and creeks began to silt up.

In 1689 King James was deposed. The throne went to William and Mary, who were Anglicans. Until 1692 the Lords Baltimore appointed the Governors. In that year Charles Calvert, the Third Lord Baltimore, and Proprietor of Maryland, lost this right. He did retain legal right to Maryland and certain benefits and profits from the Province. Now the English Crown appointed the Royal Governor, and in 1692 Nehemiah Blackiston became governor and Francis Nicholson lieutenant governor. Also in that year the royal governor, Sir Lionel Copley, convened a representative assembly in St. Mary's which voted for "the Establishment of the Protestant Religion within this Province." Quakers lost their right to sit in the provincial assembly, but could maintain separate places of worship if the 40 pound tobacco tax was paid to the established church. Roman

Catholics were not permitted to hold any office or celebrate mass except in private chapels.

Francis Nicholson, an Anglican, called his first meeting of the Maryland Assembly in September 1694, and the first order of business was the establishment of a new seat of government. Two ports of entry were established, one in Oxford on the Eastern Shore and the other at Arundellton. He ordered the transfer of the capital from St. Mary's in 1694. He had been Lt. Governor of Virginia and with Rev. James Blair founded the College of William and Mary in 1693. He later was to return to Virginia as governor twice, rector of the College of William and Mary and chair of its governing board. He also laid out the city of Williamsburg and later became governor of South Carolina.

Charles Carroll emigrated from Ireland in 1688 and was later Lord Baltimore's agent. He was to become the wealthiest person in the colonies, followed by his son who built the Charles Carroll home and was an ardent Roman Catholic, and later a grandson. He owned between 70-80,000 acres of land in Maryland, Pennsylvania and New York, raising tobacco and later wheat. The third Carroll bequeathed his estate to his four daughters who gave it to the Redemptorists (a Catholic group founded in Italy in 1732 who came to America in 1832). Charles Carroll (1737-1832) was the last of the signers of the Declaration of Independence to die. From 1704 to the Revolutionary War Catholics were not permitted to conduct services except in private homes.

The first meeting of the Assembly was held in 1695 at the home of Major Edward Dorsey on Prince George Street, Annapolis. St. John's College was founded in 1696 as King William's School, with the Rev. Edward Butler first master, and later the fourth rector at St. Anne's Church. The first State House was completed in 1697. The State House, which was also the Court House, burned in 1704, when many official records were lost, including Gov. Nicholson's plans. The State House was rebuilt in 1772 with the first Legislature meeting here in 1779 and is the oldest in America in continuous use.

The earliest trades of Maryland were furs, tobacco, and iron ore. Whetstone Point, Baltimore was made a point of entry in 1706. Iron ore was discovered at Whetstone Point in 1723 and became the Principio Furnace Company. In 1719 the government offered 100 acres to anyone who would set up a furnace and forge iron. Wheat after 1750 became the major export crop. During the 1720's and '30's many tobacco plantation owners suffered from a depression, and began raising grains. All vestiges of the early settlement of St. Mary's City were to vanish.

In 1729 Baltimore was laid out on 60 acres owned by the Carroll family. From 1731-42 and 1746-52 Samuel Ogle was governor of the state. He introduced horse racing as a gentleman's sport, importing Arabian horses with Benjamin Tasker. The Baltimore Company was formed in the 1730's for wealthy planters to mine iron ore in the Patapsco region. The group was made up of Daniel Dulany, members of the Carroll family and Benjamin Tasker.

The Tobacco Inspection Act of 1747 stipulated that tobacco had to be of a certain grade before shipping, and the tobacco due the clergy was reduced from forty to thirty pounds per taxable head.

Governor Horatio Sharp (1753-69) spoke out against the Stamp Act of 1763. General Daniel Dulany wrote about its unconstitutionality in 1765 "Consideration on the Propriety of Imposing Taxes on the British Colonies, For the Purpose of Raising a Revenue", i.e. the British were taking money without the consent of the people. In that year Zachariah Hood accepted the position of Stamp Collector and a mob tore down his house in Annapolis. He fled to the royal troops garrisoned in New York. The winter of 1765 was a particularly cold one and the Bay froze, allowing carriages to cross to Kent Island. Samuel Chase and William Paca, to defy Parliament by forcing the courts to act without stamps and to repeal the Stamp Act, formed the Sons of Liberty in 1766. Kunte Kinte, made famous in Alex Haley's "Roots" arrived at City Dock, Annapolis in 1767.

The 1767 the Townshend Act of the British government taxed glass, lead, paint, and tea. Anti-importation groups formed, and the ship "Good Intent" was sent back to England. The Stamp Act of 1774 also had an impact on Annapolis. Annapolis had its own "Tea Party" when local patriots forced Anthony Stewart to destroy his vessel, the Peggy Stewart, with a cargo of 2,000 pounds of English tea and other goods by running her aground in Spa Creek and setting fire to her. Some families did remain loyal to the Crown, such as the Dulanys, Ridouts and Ogles, with several leaving for England during the Revolution.

Lafayette and Comte de Rochambeau and the French fleet several times passed through Annapolis beginning in 1781, making it a base. The French troops encamped on Dorsey Creek, now College Creek, and Lafayette on Spa Creek in Eastport. The two Frenchmen were to return to Annapolis after Cornwallis' surrender. In 1782 William Paca became Governor of Maryland.

1783 was a very important year. Maryland Law forbade the importation of slaves. Capt. Joshua Barney, who had distinguished himself in many naval battles, and a native of Baltimore, arrived from Paris with a provisional Treaty of Paris. Annapolis was offered to Congress as a permanent home in October by Mayor Jeremiah Townley Chase, which turned out to be only temporary until 1784. Willam Paca began his second term as Governor. On December 23, 1783 the Commander-in-chief of the Continental Army, General George Washington resigned his commission as Commander at the State House. For the first time a flag with thirteen stars was designed by the noted Annapolis cabinetmaker John Shaw. Unlike the later flag with the stars in a circle this had 4,5,4 in rows. (A copy hangs in the State House). The Treaty of Paris was ratified in the same room on January 14, 1784 officially ending the Revolutionary War. In 1787 the Annapolis Convention was convened for meetings on the Articles of Confederation.

After the Revolutionary War and until the opening of the Naval Academy, Annapolis and other cities lay dormant. Baltimore took over as Maryland's port in the 1790's, and there was even word that the capital might be moved there. In 1798 the General Assembly of Maryland passed a law establishing election districts to replace the "hundreds".

The Bay was cut-off in 1813 when a squadron of British Royal Naval vessels began the blockade of the Chesapeake and Delaware Bays during the War of 1812. This war, declared by President James Madison came all too quickly after the Revolution to a country unprepared and financially getting on its feet. The war grew out of Britain and France's assaults against each other and the fact each wanted to subvert America's trade. Sailors were impressed after random checks could be made of neutral ships. In 1808 the H.M.S. Leopard attacked the *U.S.S. Chesapeake*. The Chesapeake's captain refused the random check and a British vessel shot her at broadside and three men were killed. The *Chesapeake* was unable to defend herself, so the captain ended up striking her colors and four men were impressed.

British Rear Admiral George Cockburn arrived in the Chesapeake region on March 3, 1813. A month earlier, Admiral Warren had begun the blockade of the Bay. Admiral Cockburn began terrorizing small towns along the Bay and on April 16th threatened to attack Baltimore. Instead he began to raid towns on the Upper Bay. The British burned Frenchtown and then moved up the Elk River but were repulsed by the militia at Fort Defiance, which saved Elkton. On May 3 they turned toward Havre de Grace. Grapeshot and rockets were hurled at the battery. The British took the town and destroyed many of the houses. A detachment then was sent to Bell's Ferry where they burned a warehouse and five vessels. Adm. Cockburn then proceeded by boat to Principio Creek and destroyed 46 cannons at Samuel Hughes Principio cannon factory.

During this time Commodore Joshua Barney came out of retirement and formed the "Chesapeake Flotilla", after lobbying the Maryland legislature to build a fleet of small boats to harass the British. The legislature refused, but Commodore Barney was able to get money from Congress. For about four months he was able to keep the British from closing in on Washington. At one time the British trapped him inside St. Leonard's Creek, but his men escaped to the Patuxent and burned the barges near where the Jefferson Patterson Park & Museum is located.

In August 1814 a British force of 4,000 soldiers arrived in Benedict in Charles County and then marched north through Upper Marlboro and on to Bladensburg. Commodore Barney and his men scuttled the "Chesapeake Flotilla" and joined the ground defense. They were routed near what is now the Fort Lincoln Cemetery.

In September the British moved to Baltimore. They were held off by the troops at Fort McHenry. Francis Scott Key, a graduate of St. John's College, Annapolis wrote "The Star Spangled Banner", on the night of September 14th, as he watched the bombardment over Baltimore. The British then turned to Washington and burned White House.

Following the War, tobacco growing declined, but shipbuilding became an important industry. The first steamboats began service in 1813 with the *Chesapeake* sailing from Baltimore. The Baltimore Steam Packet Company, or popularly known as the Old Bay Line was founded in 1839 and lasted until the 1960s linking cities and towns along the Chesapeake Bay.

Besides agriculture, harvesting the Chesapeake Bay took a prominent role. Oysters were shipped to Baltimore and Philadelphia. The opening of the Chesapeake and Delaware Canal in 1829 allowed produce and seafood to be transported north more quickly. In 1831 the Baltimore & Ohio's first 13 miles connected Baltimore with Ellicott Mills. The first railroad terminal in the nation was built in Ellicott Mills in 1832. The first curved stone-arch bridge in the country carried the B&O rail line over the Patapsco River near Elkridge. The Thomas Viaduct was built in 1835 and is 700 feet long.

In 1840 the Annapolis and Elkridge Railroad opened allowing transportation between Washington and Annapolis. Annapolis was linked to the main line of the Baltimore and Ohio Railroads on Christmas Day 1840. The Baltimore and Potomac opened in 1872 and the Annapolis Shortline in 1887. With these railroad lines Baltimore, Washington and Annapolis, plus outlying areas became easily accessible. The Washington, Baltimore, and Annapolis mainline opened this up even more in 1908, not only for transportation of passengers, but freight as well. South of Annapolis transportation still relied on sailing vessels and steamers that plied the Bay, rivers and creeks.

By 1860 Prince George and Charles Counties were to have over 22,000 slaves. During the Civil War, like the Revolution, people had divided loyalties, some to the Confederacy, others to the Union. Slavery had played an important role in growing tobacco, but with its decline slaves were freed, many living in Annapolis or settling on the Eastern Shore as watermen. Maryland was a slave-holding state under its Constitution, but remained loyal to the Union under Gov. Thomas Hicks.

The upper Chesapeake region was part of the Underground Railroad. Many Quakers and Methodists who opposed slavery lived here. Their farms provided a refuge for those slaves heading to Pennsylvania. Forests along the Bay and Susquehanna River provided cover for the runaways.

Further south in Howard County, there were both plantations and large mills. The railroad and bridges were targets for the Confederate Army and Union soldiers guarded the Thomas Viaduct.

In 1861 the Naval Academy students in Annapolis were moved to Newport, RI and St. John's College became the College Green Hospital in 1863, Hospital #2, and the Naval Academy Hospital #1. During the War Northern troops were located at Horn Point (in Eastport) and later camped at the Naval Academy.

With the Emancipation Proclamation in 1864 only slaves in states "in rebellion against the United States" were freed. Maryland had to write a new Constitution to free them. The schools were segregated until the 1950's, the libraries until the 1940's.

Oystering began in earnest during the Civil War, and was to reach its peak in the 1870's with more than 11 million bushels accounted for. During this time the oystermen of Maryland and Virginia staked out claims on the Bay, which was not settled till 1877 when boundaries were set.

In the late 19th century towns along the Western Shore became resorts, linked either by railroad or steamboat. Among these were Bay Ridge, Chesapeake Beach and Piney Point. African Americans also developed their own resorts at Arundel on the Bay, Sparrows Beach, Highland Beach and Carr's Beach which had big name entertainers such as Duke Ellington perform there.

In 1868 an act of the Maryland Legislature granted the Southern Maryland Railroad Company a franchise to begin plans for a railroad from Washington, DC to St. Mary's County. In 1872 the Washington City & Point Lookout Railroad, a rival company, was founded. Also that year the railroad bed was graded from Mechanicsville to Point Lookout and in 1881 service to Charlotte Hall and Mechanicsville from Prince George's County was started. However, in 1889 railroad service was suspended until 1891 when the Washington City & Point Lookout Railroad resumed service.

The Washington & Potomac Railroad was incorporated in 1894 and the Washington, Potomac & Chesapeake Railroad in 1901. In 1918 the tracks were sold for junk to Joseph Josephs Brothers & Company for $92,000. In 1918 the Washington, Brandywine & Point Lookout Railroad was incorporated. By 1942 the line was extended to the Naval Air Station Patuxent River. The line was sold to the Penn Central Railroad in 1954 and the railroad was finally abandoned in the 1970s.

In 1915 the Maryland legislature adopted a law requiring "that public schools for white youth remain in session 180 days each year, public schools for colored youths, at least 140 days". The Maryland General Assembly also decreed a mandated one pay scale for white teachers and a lower one for black teachers even though they had the same certification. In 1939 the Maryland legislature set a 180-day school year for all students.

By the 1930s steamboats disappeared and cars, plus a few short distance rail lines such as the Brandywine and Point Lookout took over as the means of transportation. The golden age of railroads 1908-1935 brought visitors to various places in the state and also facilitated transportation of crops. It also led to growth in population in much of farmland Maryland. The Baltimore, Annapolis and Washington Railroad converted from steam to electric power on its track from Annapolis to Annapolis Junction. The Annapolis and Elk Ridge Railroad Track was combined with a new double track from Baltimore to Washington, DC. Villages sprang up along the railroad lines.

During Prohibition the Western Shore of Maryland had a number of sites that became notorious for drop-offs, but also in some areas, because of their isolation, particularly in Southern Maryland, bootlegging became a prosperous business. In 1921 federal agents confiscated six stills and more than 100 gallons of moonshine in Severn, including some in the back yard of Deputy Sheriff William Crouse. Children also sold pint and half-pint bottles to bootleggers for extra spending money!!!

The highway system was developed in the 20$^{th}$ c. The main routes connecting Maryland's Western Shore are 95, Crain Highway, Ritchie Highway, Baltimore Washington Parkway, Rtes. 2 and 4 going north and south, Rtes. 32, 50, 100 and Defense Highway east and west.

In 1941 with the railroad extending to the Naval Air Station Patuxent River, the Bureau of Aeronautics decided that Cedar Point would meet the requirements for a test center site and became the home of the United States Naval Test Pilot School.

Ferry service across the Bay was discontinued in 1952 with the opening of the first span of the Bay Bridge (the William Preston Lane Bridge, named for the governor 1947-51). The single span bridge begun in 1949 cost $112 million and is 4.2 miles long. Beginning in 1997 painting the bridge will cost $79 million.

The United States has maintained a number of military facilities on the Western Shore besides the U.S. Naval Academy. These include the Old Bainbridge facility, Aberdeen, Naval Air Station at Cedar Point (1942), Naval Surface Warfare at Indian Head, Patuxent Naval Air Station, Andrews Air Force Base, and others.

Maryland, even though it had divided loyalties during the Civil War, was very slow to desegregate its schools. The Baltimore Public Schools were desegregated beginning in 1954. However parochial and some private schools remained segregated until 1962, or later.

The Baltimore-Washington Parkway opened in 1954. Up until that time Rte. 1 and Rte. 40 were the main north-south roads. Interstate 95 now handles most of the traffic.

The Baltimore Harbor Tunnel is 6,300 feet long, the longest open-trench tunnel.

Some of the Western Shore counties still grow tobacco, though many farmers have switched to soy beans, sorghum, corn, and hay. A recent proposal in the Maryland Legislature was proposed to pay off the farmers growing tobacco to produce grapes for wine instead!!!! Tobacco auctions are held in the spring in Hughesville.

**Did You Know?**

Cecil County was founded in 1674 and named for Cecil Calvert, the second Lord Baltimore.

Governors from Cecil County include Thomas W. Veazey (1774-1842), James Black Groome (1838-93), Austin L. Crothers (1860-1912)

Harford County was formed in 1773 and named for Henry Harford, the son of Frederick Calvert, the sixth and last Lord Baltimore, proprietor during the Revolutionary War. Harford Town was the county seat of Harford County from 1774-81. Harford Village at the head of the Bush River was a post office in 1789. Harford Furnace was an iron works. The county has many lovely farms raising dairy cattle, horses, grains, and other vegetables and fruit trees. The county was part of Baltimore County until 1774.

Famous people from Harford County include the Rodgers, Hopkins and Tydings families:

Commodore John Rodgers was Commodore of the United States Navy squadron posted in the Atlantic against the British forces during the War of 1812. Rodgers brother, George Washington Rodgers also served in the war. His brother-in-law, William Pinkney, a Harford county lawyer, ratified the Constitution, was a member of the House of Delegates, served as a major in the Baltimore militia and was wounded at the Battle of Bladensburg. Jared Sparks, a tutor and eyewitness of the British attack, later became President of Harvard University and wrote one of the first biographies of George Washington.

Dr. John Archer who obtained the first medical degree from the Philadelphia Medical College in 1768 was a signer of the Bush Declaration and later raised a militia during the Revolutionary War. Dr. Archer and his son, Dr. Thomas Archer founded the Medical and Chirurgical Faculty of Maryland in 199. Dr. John Archer served for two terms in Congress and then founded a medical school in his home. Another son, Stevenson Archer, also served in Congress, was chief judge of the Circuit Court, and chief judge of the Court of Appeals.

Governors from Harford County include William Paca (1740-90) and Augustus W. Bradford (1806-81).

Gunpowder River flows from the Chesapeake Bay between Harford and Baltimore Counties. It is also called Gunpowder Falls. There are several stories surrounding its name. One states that the Indians thought the gunpowder could be grown.

Baltimore County was named for Cecil Calvert, the second Lord Baltimore and proprietor of Maryland. Baltimore County was formed in 1659. The first county seats were Old Baltimore on the Bush River and Joppa, both now in Harford County. Baltimore County and Baltimore City were separated in 1854. In 1715 the population of Baltimore County was 3,000, 1890 72,909 and in 1990 692,134. The seal of the county depicts the Calvert and Crossland coats of arms and seven stars, and was designed by Adelaide M. Haspert. The county seat is Towson.

Governors from Baltimore County include Charles Ridgely of Hampton (1760-1829).

Baltimore City was named for the first Lord Baltimore, George Calvert, and for the port of Baltimore in County Cork, Ireland. The author visited Baltimore, County Cork in July 2000. The town was established in 1727. Baltimore was incorporated in 1797 and the city seal adopted in 1827.

Locust Point in Baltimore was once known as Whetstone Point after it was established as a Port of Entry in 1706. It was named after the section of London called Whetstone by Charles Carroll. In 1720 the Maryland Legislature ordered a survey to be made of Baltimore town, beginning at a locust post on what is now the grounds of Ft. McHenry.

Governors from Baltimore City include John Eager Howard (1752-1827), William Pinkney White (1824-1908), John Lee Carroll (1830-1911), Herbert R. O'Conor (1896-1960), Theodore R. McKeldin (1900-74), Spiro T. Agnew (1967-69 resigned), Marvin Mandel (1969-79), and William Donald Schaefer (1987-94). (See Howard County where several of the governors also lived).

Prince George's County was founded in 1696 and is named for Prince George of Denmark who married Queen Anne, queen of England from 1702-14. The county had originally been part of Calvert County. Charles Beckwith from Patuxent designed the county seal in 1696. The seal represents Queen Anne and the countries of France, England, Scotland and Ireland.

The first county seat of Prince George's County was Charles Town in 1683. In 1718 the seat was moved to Marlborough, now Upper Marlboro. The court met for the first time in 1721.

Famous people from Prince George's County are:

The Claggett (Clagett) family settled in Maryland with a land grant in Prince George's County in the 1670s. The ancestral home, Weston was built near Upper Marlboro. Bishop Thomas John Claggett was born in 1743 in Nottingham and became the first Episcopal Bishop of Maryland.

Today the Clagett family includes Hal Clagett of Davidsonville who grew up at Weston and won the Distinguished Flying Cross as a World War II pilot, practiced law in Maryland, and served as president of the State Bar Association. He was the author of a bill in the early 1960s that created the Maryland Racing Fund, which established bonuses for Maryland-bred horses. His farm Roedown breeds horses. His son, Hal Clagett III, now owns Weston.

In 1784 Peter Carnes of Bladensburg was the first man in the country to send up a hot air balloon. The first balloon was unmanned, but later he sent up Edward Warren, aged 13, of Baltimore in the first manned flight.

Dr. Richard Brooke developed a vaccination for smallpox and did research on wind and weather.

The Bowie family produced several governors of Maryland. Robert Bowie served three terms beginning in 1803. Oden Bowie was governor 1869-72. He was one of the founders of the Pimlico Race Course.

37

Bladensburg was named for Thomas Bladen, a colonial governor, and is the oldest incorporated town in the area, established in 1742.

Benjamin Stoddert served in the continental Army during the Revolutionary War and went on to become the first Secretary of the Navy.

Governors from Prince George's County include Thomas Sim Lee (1745-1819), Robert Bowie (1750-1818), and Samuel Sprigg (1783-1855).

In 1659 Howard County became part of Baltimore County and remained until 1726 when it became part of Anne Arundel County. Howard County was established in 1851. The county is named for Col. John Edgar Howard, Governor of Maryland 1788-91. Edward Stabler designed the county seal in 1840. The tobacco and wheat represent the important crops of that period.

Famous citizens of Howard County include:

Andrew Ellicott and Benjamin Banneker, a free Black man and neighbor who had worked with the city designer L'Enfant, were commissioned to survey the boundaries for the new capital, Washington, DC in 1791. Mr. Banneker later was to build the first clock made in America and to publish Almanacs from 1792-97.

Four men from Howard County have served as Governors of Maryland – George Howard (1831-33), Thomas Watkins Ligon (1854-58), John Lee Carroll (1876-1880), and Edwin Warfield (1904-08).

Anne Arundel County is the third oldest county in Maryland, following St. Mary's and Kent Counties. The county was named for Anne Arundel, wife of Cecil Calvert, second Lord Baltimore. The county seal is red and gold, gold from the coat of arms of the Calverts and red from the coat of arms of the Crosslands, George Calvert's mother's family. George Calvert was the first Lord Baltimore.

Among the famous citizens from Anne Arundel County are:

Charles Carroll "The Settler" was a lawyer in England and came to Maryland as Attorney General in 1688. However he lost his position almost immediately since he was a Roman Catholic and King William, a Protestant had become king. He settled in Annapolis in 1701 after living on the Eastern Shore. He received an appointment as a judge under Charles Calvert, third Lord Baltimore. He purchased property along Spa Creek and by 1716 owned ¼ of Annapolis. When he died in 1720 he owned 47,000 acres of land, the largest landowner in Maryland.

Dr. Charles Carroll was raised as a Roman Catholic, eventually becoming a Protestant. He moved to Annapolis from England c 1715. He began importing English goods and acquiring land. In 1718 he bought 2400 acres from Charles Carroll "The Settler", a cousin and eventually acquired 31,259 acres.

Charles Carroll was born in 1702 and educated in England. He built the first brick house on Spa Creek in Annapolis and later Doughoreagan Manor in Howard County on 10,000 acres. He did not marry his wife, Elizabeth Brook, until his son Charles was twenty years of age, and needed permission from the Catholic Church to be married.

Charles Carroll of Carrollton was born on September 19, 1737 and was sent to Belgium and France to be educated with his second cousin, John Carroll, the first Roman Catholic Bishop of the United States. He later studied law in France and England and returned to Annapolis in 1765 to assist in his father's business. He married Mary Darnall in 1768. They were to add onto and change the family house on Duke of Gloucester Street to a more Georgian home and built a seawall along Spa Creek. He also had extensive property on the Monocacy River in Frederick County.

Mr. Carroll was elected to the first Maryland Senate, while also having a seat in the Continental Congress, commuting to Philadelphia 1777-1779. He was a member of the Maryland Convention (1775), the Commission to Canada (1776). He was later to serve as a U.S. Senator in the first Congress (1789-92). He lived to 1832, aged 95, the last of the Signers of the Declaration of Independence, and the only Roman Catholic Signer.

Charles Carroll of Carrollton's son married Harriet Chew, daughter of the Chief Justice of Pennsylvania. The wedding present from his father was land in Baltimore where he built Homewood in Baltimore in 1801. Mr. Carroll owned slaves for his numerous properties, which meant he had to reconcile his belief in slavery with his Catholic belief in equality of men before God.

Daniel Dulany (1685-1753) came to Port Tobacco as an indentured servant in 1703. Under George Plater he began an apprenticeship as a lawyer. He began acquiring land and by 1720 owned 27,200 acres, much of it in western Maryland. In 1720 he moved to Annapolis, and here worked on the issue of rights for Maryland citizens and in 1728 wrote "The Rights of the Inhabitants of Maryland". He founded Frederick Town and along with Benjamin Tasker and Charles Carroll of Carrollton owned the Baltimore Iron works. His home in Annapolis was off Church Circle, now the site of the County Court House.

Thomas Bladen was the only colonial governor born in the colonies.

Samuel Chase was a Signer of the Declaration of Independence, served in the Continental Congress, the Maryland House of Delegates 1777, and on the Supreme Court 1796.

William Paca was elected to the Maryland Senate in 1776 and 1778. In 1782 he was elected Governor of Maryland. In 1783 Mr. Paca welcomed George Washington to Annapolis for his resignation from the Continental Army and hosted a dinner at Mann's Tavern followed by a ball at the State House. In 1786 he was elected to the lower house of the Maryland Assembly and in 1789 Judge of the US District Court for the District of Maryland.

Bowie is named for Oden Bowie, Governor of Maryland 1869-72.

Johns Hopkins was born near Millersville at Whitehall in 1795. The house was probably built in the 1760s by his grandfather. His family were Quakers, and in 1778 after the Baltimore Yearly Meeting condemned slavery, the family's slaves were freed. Mr. Hopkins left the farm in 1812 to work in his uncle's wholesale grocery business in Baltimore. In 1819 he started his own wholesale grocery business. With his fortune he founded Johns Hopkins University and Hospital.

The singer, Toni Braxton, was born in Severn, where her father is a minister. She won two Grammy awards in 1997.

Calvert County was founded on July 3, 1654, the fourth oldest county in Maryland. The county originally contained parts of what are now Charles, Prince George's, Montgomery and Frederick Counties. The earliest settlements in Calvert County were settled soon after the colonists arrived in St. Mary's. The first records appear in the General Assembly in 1642. In 1696 when Prince George's County was established Calvert County assumed almost its present area. Lord Baltimore, a Catholic, established the county. However, the first governor, a friend of Lord Baltimore's and a Protestant, was Robert Brooke, who arrived with his wife, ten children and 28 servants in June 1650.

Famous Citizens from Calvert County include:

Thomas Parran who was Surgeon General of the Armies during the Revolutionary War.

Louisa Catherine Johnson became the wife of President John Quincy Adams and Margaret Mackall Smith the wife of President Zachary Taylor.

Roger Brooke Taney, Attorney General under President Andrew Jackson, served as Secretary of the Treasury and Chief Justice of the Supreme Court where he wrote an opinion in the Dred Scott Case.

Governors from Calvert County include Thomas Johnson (1732-1819) and Joseph Kent (1779-1837)

Leonard Calvert bought property from King Yocomico that was first named Augusta Carolina, later becoming St. Mary's County, and patron saint of the settlers aboard the *Ark* and *Dove*. The settlers arrived on the Feast of the annunciation, March 25, 1634. St. Mary's County was founded in 1637 and is the oldest in the state. St. Mary's County still produces the largest amount of tobacco in Maryland. In April 2000 the Maryland Treasurer, William Donald Schaeffer announced that he would like to turn the area into a first class wine-growing region.

St. Mary's County has a large Amish population that came from Pennsylvania in the 1940 and 1950s. They farm the land and at Charlotte Hall hold an open-air farmers' market twice a week.

Famous citizens of St. Mary's County include:

Margaret Brent lived at "Sisters' Freehold". At his death in 1647 Governor Calvert made her his executrix. She settled not only his affairs, but also for the province. In 1648 she appeared before the Assembly and demanded two votes, one as landowner in her own right and one as attorney for Lord Baltimore. This was the first time in the colonies that a woman had sought equal rights with a man.

In 1659 Edward Prescott, owner of the ship *Sarah Artch*, was brought to trial at Fenwick's Free at the complaint of Colonel John Washington, great-grandfather of George Washington. He was accused of being an accessory to the death of Elizabeth Richardson who had been hanged at the yardarm as a witch on the voyage to the colony, on which Mr. Washington was a passenger. He was acquitted.

There are a number of legends about the some of the original colonists, including witches. Moll Dyer's rock is located in front of the old jail in Leonardtown. Her story dates back more than 300 years when she lived in a small cabin along a creek. The winter of 1697 was one of the worst on record and townspeople were convinced she was a witch, cursing the town. They burned her cabin and forced Moll and her dog out into the cold, where she froze to death clinging to a rock. When she was pried loose, her handprint was left in the rock, which remains today. People have even seen her walking with her white hair, white dress and white dog!!!

The Rev. William Wilkinson arrived in Maryland in 1650 and was the first Anglican rector. He served the congregations of St. Clement's Manor, St. George's Episcopal Church, and other churches in the area.

William and Diana Nuthead of St. Mary's City operated the first printing press in the southern colonies beginning in 1685.

Mathias de Sousa was the first man of African descent to serve in a legislature in the colonies (1642).

Jerome White laid out St. Mary's City in 1666, inspired by the Italian Baroque style.

Governors from St. Mary's County include George Plater (1735-92) and James Thomas (1785-1845).

Charles County was established in 1658. There were several Charles for whom the county could have been named, but is probably named for the eldest son of Lord Baltimore. The county first included all of Maryland lying north and west of St. Mary's and lands in Western Maryland. Prince George's took this over in 1659.

During the Civil War Charles County remained loyal to the South. Following the emancipation of the slaves, most slaves moved elsewhere. Many of the plantations were abandoned.

The Charles County seat is La Plata. The flower is the wild carrot, also called Queen Anne's Lace; the county tree, the dogwoo;, and the county bird, the Great Blue Heron.

Among the famous citizens of Charles County are:

General William Smallwood (1732-92) who lived at Smallwood's Retreat and led the Maryland regiment against the British at the Battle of Long Island. He was also Governor of Maryland.

Daniel of St. Thomas Jenifer was President of Maryland's Council of Safety during the Revolutionary War, and later a member of the Continental Congress. His home, "Charleston" overlooks the Port Tobacco River.

John Hanson was born near Port Tobacco in 1720. He was a member of the Lower House of the Assembly and active during the Revolutionary War. In 1774, under his leadership, the delegates to the Maryland Convention from Prince Frederick County advocated independence. Mr. Hanson served as the eighth president of the Continental Congress in 1781 and died in 1783. He lived at Mulberry Grove and was related to the Jenifers.

Thomas Stone, a Signer of the Declaration of Independence, lived at Habre de Venture, now the Thomas Stone National Park near Port Tobacco. He also maintained a home in Annapolis.

Dr. Gustavus Brown, who attended George Washington during his last illness, lived at "Rose Hill" overlooking the Potomac and Port Tobacco Rivers.

Dr. James Craik was also a physician to George Washington and lived at "La Grange", near La Plata.

Governors from Charles County include John Hoskins Stone (1750-1804).

The Patapsco River flows into the Chesapeake at Baltimore. Its name most likely comes from an Algonquin word meaning, "jutting ledge of rocks".

The Patuxent River was named for the Patuxent Indians. The name means "at the little rapid".

Maryland Route 235 follows a trail laid out in 1672 from Mattapany on the Patuxent River north. The road is known as Three Notch Road. In 1702 a law required that roads be marked as to their destinations – three equidistant notches on a tree marked a road to a ferry; two notches with another higher marked a road to a courthouse; and two notches towards the ground with slit marked the road to a church.

The Potomac River was called Patawmoke by Captain John Smith in 1608. The name means, "landing place for goods".

The Wicomico River is one of two rivers by the same name; the other located on the Eastern Shore. This river was named for an Indian village called "Wighcocomoco" which means "pleasant village of dwelling sites".

Mattowoman Creek was named for an Indian village "Mataughquamend" which means, "where one goes pleasantly".

Najemoy Creek is named for the Indian Village "Nushemoick" which means "one goes on downward".

The Susquehanna River is the longest non-navigable river in the United States. The river begins in Cooperstown, NY and only 20 miles of the 448 miles are in

Maryland. The Susquehanna provides half of the fresh water in the Chesapeake Bay.

Pomonkey Creek is a tributary off the Potomac River. It was known for its fresh spring waters, and is named for an Indian village "Pamunkeya" or "twisting in the lands".

Zekiah Swamp has been spelled several ways – Zakayo, Zakeia, and Zachio. The name comes from the Algonquin-Fox dialect "Sacaya" which means "a dense thicket".

The Thomas J. Hatem Memorial Bridge crosses the Susquehanna River between Perryville and Havre de Grace. The bridge was opened August 28, 1940 and cost $4.5 million. Prior to that a ferry had crossed the river for over two hundred years. A vehicle bridge was opened in 1910, and a railroad bridge in 1873. In May 1986 the bridge was dedicated to Mr. Hatem, a resident of Harford County who devoted his life to public and civic service.

The Governor Harry W. Nice Bridge crosses the Potomac River between Maryland and Virginia carrying Rte. 301. The bridge was originally called the Potomac Bridge and was renamed in 1968 to honor the governor during whose term the bridge was built. Until 1940 no bridges south of Washington, DC crossed the Potomac. In 1937 Governor Nice approved crossings for the Potomac, Susquehanna and Patapsco Rivers and the Chesapeake Bay.

Rte. 2, Governor Ritchie Highway between Baltimore and Annapolis is named for Governor Albert Cabell Ritchie, governor of Maryland for four terms.

York Road was opened in 1743 as the Susquehanna Road and became a turnpike in 1807.

Wades Bay is named for Zachariah Wade. During the Civil War soldiers grew hemp. Dr. Grace G. Purse willed 148 acres near the Bay to the state in the 1960s.

In 1772 the first umbrella to be introduced in the colonies came to Baltimore from India.

Maryland produced many fine craftsmen. Among these are:

*Furniture:*

William and Matthew Atkinson were clockmakers in the later 18th c in Baltimore.

Jacob Mohler (1744-1773) was born in Lancaster County, PA and learned the clock making trade. He came to Baltimore in the mid 1760s. He made and repaired clocks, watches and jewelry on South Street, Baltimore.

Peter Mohler, son of Jacob, began his apprenticeship with Matthew Atkinson. He made clocks and operated the Mohler brass foundry on Harrison Street in Baltimore.

John Shaw arrived in Annapolis in 1763 from Glasgow and worked for John Brice. He started business as a cabinetmaker and in 1770 formed a partnership with Archibold Chisholm. Much of their work was for Edward Lloyd and later furnishings for the State House. John Shaw completed work on the Capital dome with the acorn on the pinnacle as a symbol of wisdom. He was named State Armorer in 1777.

John and Hugh Finlay of Baltimore were noted for their painted furniture, which included chairs for the White House during President Madison's administration that were designed by the architect Benjamin Henry Latrobe. A number of their fine pieces are also displayed at Hampton National Historic Site.

William Camp introduced "Grecian" style furniture to Baltimore c1812-14, having worked for a short period in Philadelphia before settling here.

John Needles worked in Baltimore from 1810-52 and designed many elegant tables, sideboards, desks, chairs and other pieces.

Anthony H. Jenkins took over his family's cabinetmaking business in Baltimore after his father's death in 1832.

Other Baltimore cabinetmakers include David Bodensick and Edward Yearly. Baltimore clockworks were also designed by Samuel Steele.

Pianos and piano fortes were produced by Knabe and Joseph Hiskey of Baltimore. James Stewart designed classical pianos in Baltimore.

## Painters

The painter, Charles Willson Peale (1741-1827), was born in St. Anne's County, and later was apprenticed to a saddler in Annapolis. He painted signs for which he received recognition. In 1767 he was sent to London to study under Benjamin West by his patron William Paca. He painted the portraits of George Washington and William Pitt that hang in the State House. Other notable paintings were of William Buckland, William Paca, the Edward Lloyd Family, plus many others.

Mr. Peale moved to Philadelphia in 1776, and became of America's most noted painters.

James Peale, brother of Charles, also was a noted painter and lived in Annapolis, before joining his brother in Philadelphia. He painted many miniatures until his eyesight failed him in 1818.

Rembrandt Peale was a son of Charles Willson Peale who studied in Europe and later opened a museum in Baltimore with his brother Raphaelle. He painted many famous Baltimoreans.

Raphaelle Peale was the eldest son of Charles Willson Peale and painted still lifes and portraits.

The earliest painter in Annapolis was Justus Englehardt Kuhn, a German immigrant whose first records appear about 1708. He painted many of the area's well-to-do families such as the Carrolls. His painting of Henry Darnall III which hangs at the Maryland Historical Society in Baltimore, is thought to be the first representation of a slave in American portraiture.

Gustavus Hesselius, born in Sweden, arrived in Philadelphia with a letter of introduction from William Penn. He moved to Prince George's County sometime before 1826. He painted Thomas Bordley, Mrs. Charles Carroll and the Darnall family. He too moved to Philadelphia.

His son, John, was also to paint in Maryland, Delaware and Virginia. In 1763 he married Mary Young Woodward, the widow of Henry Woodward of Primrose Hill, an estate near Annapolis. He painted such people as the Calverts, Samuel Chew, Col. Edward Fell and Anna Bond Fell – for whom Fell's Point in Baltimore is named, and Mrs. Richard Galloway.

The other prominent Annapolis painter was John Wollaston who arrived about 1752 from London. He too painted many famous Maryland families.

Bouche was a French portrait painter and drawing teacher who came to Maryland from Santo Domingo in 1794. He opened a drawing school in Baltimore in 1795.

Alfred Jacob Miller painted the famous panorama of the bombardment of Ft. McHenry in 1829. The painting is on display at the Maryland Historical Society in Baltimore, with a copy on display at Ft. McHenry. He later made his name as a painter of Indian life in the American West.

Nicolino Vicomte de Calyo was born in Naples, Italy and appeared in Baltimore c1834. He painted scenes of Baltimore that include the *Balloon Ascension at Fairmount Park* and *View of the Port of Baltimore.*

Cornelius de Beet came from Amsterdam to Baltimore c1810. He painted chairs for the Finlay brothers and still lifes.

Anson Dickinson, a Connecticut miniaturist, painted in Baltimore between 1824-33.

Oliver Tarbell Eddy, a portrait painter, painted in Baltimore from 1842-51.

Thomas Sully, an Englishman, spent much time in America and painted a number of prominent Marylanders, including Charlotte Augustus Norris Calvert, Mary Mackall Bowie Johnson and Governor Charles Ridgely of Hampton.

Richard Caton Woodville was born in Baltimore in 1825, studied in Germany and painted portraits and copies.

Charles Volkmar (1809-1880) painted in Baltimore and is known to have done landscapes that were purchased by the Ridgely family for Hampton.

*Silversmiths:*

Among the noted craftsmen were the silversmith William Faris, Sr. and his sons. He was born in London and came to Philadelphia in 1729, moving to Annapolis in 1757. His shop on West Street produced elegant silver pieces, many of which are now displayed at Winterthur, The Metropolitan Museum of Art, and the Baltimore Museum of Art.

Charles C. Stieff founded The Baltimore Sterling Silver Company in 1892. in 1904 the name was changed to The Stieff Company. In 1979 Stieff purchased Samuel Kirk and Son, Inc. becoming Kirk-Stieff, Inc.

Samuel Kirk was born in 1792 in Pennsylvania and came from a long line of silversmiths. He came to Baltimore in 1815 and went into partnership with John Smith, but basically worked on his own becoming Baltimore's most prominent silversmith. His works can be seen in many museums and at places such as Hampton National Historic Site.

William Ball was considered one of Baltimore's finest silversmiths in the neo-classical style. He was born in England in 1763 and worked in Baltimore until his death in 1815.

Andrew Ellicott Warner began working as a silversmith in Baltimore in 1805. His brother Thomas, and father Cuthbert were also silversmiths. He was the most prominent silversmith in Baltimore between 1819-23, and a major competitor to Samuel Kirk.

Standish Barry was born in Baltimore in 1763. He became a silversmith, but because of possible financial problems advertised as a merchant in 1810. He was elected sheriff of Baltimore in 1824. He served in both the Revolutionary War and War of 1812.

Charles Louis Boehme came to Baltimore in 1799 and served several apprenticeships, but like several silversmiths, entered other businesses, becoming successful in real estate.

Ira and William Buckingham Canfield came to Baltimore from Connecticut and worked at 227 West Baltimore Street. They exhibited at the Maryland Institute Exhibitions in the 1850s.

Philip Syng, Sr. (1676-1739) moved to Annapolis from Philadelphia in about 1730 to open a silver and watch shop.

John Inch worked from 1741-1763 as a silversmith. He may have served an apprenticeship with Philip Syng before opening his own shop.

George Aiken was born in Philadelphia in 1765 and advertised his business in Baltimore in 1787. His wife was the daughter of Peter Leret, also a silversmith.

Andrew Ellicott Warner made silver repousse items in the second quarter of the 19th century.

*Jewelers:*

Christopher Hughes immigrated to Baltimore from Dublin, Ireland in 1771? He became a noted goldsmith and jeweler.

For more information on the history of each city, town or village, please refer to the chapter on these places.

# Chapter 3

## Cities, Towns and Villages of the Western Shore

This chapter starts from the most northern part of Maryland and wends its way to Point Lookout and the southern region. Scenic roads are routes 2, 4, 5, 40 and 301.

## Fair Hill

**Rock Presbyterian Church**

Fair Hill was once called Fairhill Cross Roads, and later the post office Fayette.

**Attractions**

Rock Presbyterian Church. Rte. 273 and 841. The church dates c1761, but has been remodeled several times.

Fair Hill Natural Resource Area. Rtes. 273 and 213. The Cecil County Fair, Scottish Games are held here.

Fair Hill Races. Fair Hill Natural Resource Area. 410-398-6565. The estate was originally owned by William DuPont, Jr. and is located on 5,600 acres. The race meet is held on Memorial Day.

Big Elk Creek Covered Bridge. Fair Hill Natural Resource Area. 410-398-1246. The bridge dates to c1860.

## Dining

Fair Hill Inn. 3370 Singerly Road. 410-398-4187. The inn dates to c1714. The fireplace in the dining room bears the date 1764. Lafayette may have visited the inn and sent the cherry trees to the proprietor.
Wesley's. 3700 Telegraph Road. 410-398-3696
Hilltop Inn. 825 Hilltop Road. 410-398-1512

# Rising Sun

Rising Sun was originally located in Pennsylvania as part of the Nottingham Lots. When the Mason-Dixon Line was established in 1765 Rising Sun became part of Cecil County, Maryland. By 1730 the town was known as Summer Hill. The tavern was located at the center of town where five wagon trails met and was called "The Rising Sun". The town was located at the crossroads between Baltimore and Philadelphia during the Revolutionary War. In 1815 the name was changed to Rising Sun, and incorporated in 1860. The town was a trading center for grain and dairy products.

## Attractions

West Nottingham Academy. Rte. 276. The Nottingham Presbyterian Church and Academy dates c1741. The school was one of the oldest private academies in the country. The Honorable Richard Stockton and Dr. Benjamin Rush, both Signers of the Declaration of Independence, were students at the academy.

Brick Meeting House (East Nottingham Friends Meeting House). Old Rte. 273. The building was constructed in 1724 and enlarged in 1752. During the Revolutionary War the building served as a hospital for the wounded men of General Smallwood's Continental Army. Those who died here were buried near the south door.

Plumpton Park Zoo. 1416 Telegraph Road. 410-658-6850. Zoo, picnic area and nature trails.

# Childs

Traveling north or south on I-95 one cannot help but notice the Shrine of our Lady of the Highways. This is located on the property of the Oblates of St. Francis de Sales, a Roman Catholic order of priests and brothers. The shrine was built in 1972 in memory of three people who died in an automobile accident nearby in 1968. May it be an inspiration to all who travel.

Childs was Childs Station on the Baltimore & Ohio Railroad, named for George W. Childs, editor of the Philadelphia *Ledger*. He owned the nearby Marley Paper Mill.

# Elkton

Elkton is located at the head of the Elk River, and could be considered part of the Eastern or Western Shores of Maryland. The land was patented in 1681 as "Friendship", though the river was mentioned as early as 1652. The town was once called Head of Elk, and was a port for shipping wheat and later flour. The creeks supplied water for paper mills and textile factories. Later the river was to silt in and Elkton lost its importance as a port. Elkton has been the county seat for Cecil County since 1786, and was incorporated in 1787.

During the Revolutionary War the British troops passed through the town on their way to Philadelphia in 1777. Count Rochambeau and General Washington left here in 1781 for Yorktown, and eventually the final surrender of the British.

During the War of 1812 some of British Adm. George Cockburn's fleet attacked the town but were driven back

Until recently Elkton was known as the Wedding Capital when Pennsylvania and New Jersey relaxed their requirements for marrying. Elkton received national recognition when the town offered nuptials without a blood test or waiting period. Since the railroad came through here couples could leave the trains, hop into waiting taxi cabs, and get married immediately. In 1938 a 48 hour wait was mandated, but even so couples continued to descend on the town. Among those married here were Joan Fontaine in 1964, Willie Mays in 1956, and former U.S. Attorney General John Mitchell and his wife Martha in 1957.

**Attractions:**

Mitchell House. 131 Main Street. Private. This house was built in 1769 by Dr. Abraham Mitchell, a physician, and became a hospital during the Revolutionary War. The house was passed on to his son, Dr. George Mitchell of Fair Hill who was a member of the Pike expedition to Canada in 1813 and a member of Congress. Dr. Mitchell introduced the resolution for Lafayette to tour the United States in 1824.

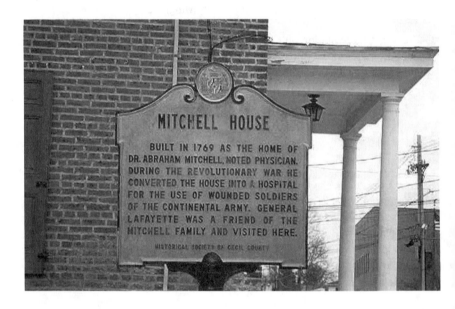

The Hermitage. 323 Hermitage Drive. Private. Part of the mansion was built in 1735, possibly by Robert Alexander, Delegate to the 1775 Continental Congress. He left his wife, family and 2000 acres and sailed to England with General Howe in 1777. The estate was confiscated and sold in August 1782.

Partridge Hill. 129 West Main Street. Private. Col. Henry Hollingsworth built the house in 1768 on property that once extended all the way to the head of the Elk River. Col. Hollingsworth supplied munitions, food and transportation to the Continental Army.

Gilpin Manor. Rte. 316. Private. The house was built c1760 for Joseph Gilpin.

The Historical Society of Cecil County. 135 East Main Street. 410-398-1790. The society was incorporated by an act of the General Assembly of Maryland in 1931. The building was constructed in 1830 as a bank. By the mid 1800s John Groome was practicing law and Dr. Joseph Wallace operated a drug store. In 1865 the Farmers' and Merchants' Bank of Elkton opened its doors, to be followed by the National Bank of Elkton in 1922. Levi Cameron, an architect, renovated the building in 1890s. It was last owned privately by Henry H. Mitchell, a mayor of Elkton. In 1955 the Cecil County Library obtained the building. The Historical Society occupied the building in 1988. The society also maintains the Research Library, the museum, a country store, the Reverend William Duke's log house, and the Sheriff John F. Dewitt Military Museum with memorabilia from the War of 1812.

The Courthouse. Main Street. The building was constructed in 1938 on the site of the Fountain Inn.

Elk Landing. 410-260-6400. The site is situated at the confluence of the Little Elk and Big Elk Creeks. The site is important for the number of events that have taken place here. The earliest settlers were Swedes and Finns who established a trading post known as Transtown. Zebulon Hollingsworth then acquired two parcels and named it Elk Landing. 18,000 British troops passed through here in August 1777 on their way north to capture Philadelphia. The British returned in 1813, but Elkton was saved by defense from Forts Hollingsworth and Defiance. During the 19th c Elk Landing was a port, and in 1887 Henry Diebert began constructing a canal. The town of Elkton was offered the property by Hollingsworth descendants and in 1999 acquired 42 acres. Today the property is a private foundation seeking funding to become a living history museum.

## Dining

Howard House Restaurant. North and Main Streets. 410-398-4646. The building dates to c1846.
Lyon's Pharmacy. 107 E. Main Street. 410-3982820. The pharmacy has been around since 1875, and still serves breakfast and lunch.
Baker's Restaurant. 1075 Augustine Herman Highway. 410-398-2435
Main Street Café. Main Street
Bentley's Restaurant. 902 E. Pulaski Highway. 410-398-3252
Iron Skillet Restaurant. Petro Shopping Center. 410-392-3052
San Lin East Chinese Restaurant. 953 Pulaski Highway. 410-620-5009
Smokin' Joe's Café. 128 West Main Street. 410-620-4130

# Elk Mills

The Baldwin Manufacturing Company once produced damask. Nearby is the Baldwin House which is thought to have been built before the Revolutionary War.

## Attractions

Elk Forge. Rte. 277. The stone building was constructed in 1761 by a group of Philadelphia businessmen to manufacture bar iron from pig iron produced in Lancaster County, PA. The British attacked the forge on their way to Philadelphia, and the property was confiscated during the Revolutionary War, as one of the owners was John Roberts of Philadelphia, a Loyalist. A gristmill stood near the creek. When the British asked the miller for flour he mixed glass in the flour, but was hanged for his treachery.

# North East

North East is located at the head of the North East River. John Smith explored the area in 1608. The river was mentioned by Cyprian Thorowgood c1634. George Talbot, a cousin of Charles Calvert, the third Lord Baltimore, petitioned for the river to be named the Shannon River in 1684.

Mills have played an important role in the town. In 1711 a mill was built where the Big and Little North East Creeks meet and in 1716 a mill was constructed at the falls of North East.

At one time herring fishing was an important industry and the town was nicknamed Herringtown.

## Attractions

The town has a number of antique shops, boat yards and craft shops.

St. Mary Anne's Church. Main Street. The General Assembly established the North Elk Parish in 1706. Fire destroyed the original structure. This church was built 1742-43. Some of the items that came from Queen Anne's funds were a silver chalice and paten made in London in 1716-17, the Bible printed in Oxford, England in 1716, and a Book of Common Prayer. Richard Brookings, founder of the Brookings Institute in Washington, DC is buried here. His family donated the bell tower in the south wall in 1904. The fieldstone grave markers in the churchyard are said to mark Native American graves.

**St. Mary Anne's Church**

Old Town Lockup. Rte. 7. This was built c1885 and once served as the town hall.

North East United Methodist Church. Main Street. The church dates from 1781. The first Methodist Parsonage in the United States was on the property.

Upper Bay Museum. End of Walnut Street. 410-287-2675 The structure was built in 1880 and was used as a fish house. Today it has items related to the Bay, particularly hunting and fishing.

West Log Home. Main Street. The 18th c house was used as an inn and stage stop. The First National Bank of North East now owns the building.

England's Colony on the Bay Decoy & Gift Shop. Main Street. Roney and Wells was a hardware store until it closed in the early 1990s.

Elk Neck Forest. Irishtown Road. 410-287-5675. The 3500 acre forest has hiking trails, camping, shooting and archery ranges.

Elk Neck State Park. Rte. 272 South. 410-287-5333. The 2200 acre park is on the water, and has trails, beaches, conference center, miniature golf and boat rentals.

Turkey Point Lighthouse is located in the park and is one of the Bay's oldest continuously operating lighthouses, built c1833. The lighthouse was established to route sailors into the C&D Canal. The lighthouse appeared in the Clint Eastwood movie *Absolute Power*.

Gilpin's Falls Covered Bridge. Rte. 272. The bridge dates from c1860.

Day Basket Factory. 714 S. Main Street. 410-287-6100. Tours available

Cecil County Dragway. Theodore Road. 410-287-5486. Races are held March to December.

## *Lodging:*

The Mill House B&B. 102 Mill Lane. 410-287-3532. This charming home built in 1710 was built as two buildings - one for the miller and the other for the kitchen and servant quarters. Francis DuPont for Winterthur purchased the parlor paneling for the Cecil bedroom.
North Bay B&B. 9 Sunset Drive. 410-287-5948. Located at the head of the Bay on the water.
Chesapeake Lodge at Sandy Cove. 410-287-5433. Christian conference center and resort.
Crystal Inn. Rte. 272. 410-287-7100
Sandy Hill Retreat & Conference Center. 3380 Turkey Point Road. 410-287-5554
Bayside Jacuzzi Suite. 111 S. Main Street. 410-287-8320
North Bay B&B. 9 Sunset Drive. 410-287-5948. Offers sailboat charters

## *Dining:*

Pier 1. 1 North Main Street. 410-287-6599
The Blue Heron Restaurant, Bar & Grill. 410-287-0200
The Cookery. One Center Drive. 410-287-7108
Aft Deck. 200 Cherry Street. 410-287-6200. Serves brunch
Windows on Main & Tavern on the Main. 101 S. Main Street. 410-287-3512
Moore's Tavern. 107 South Main Street. 410-287-3512
Woody's Crab House. 29 South Main Street. 410-287-3541
Golden Wall Chinese Restaurant. North East Station. 410-287-2955

China Gardens. 238 North East Plaza. 410-287-3785
Jean Marie's Restaurant. 508 South Main Street. 410-287-6111
Nino's Pizza. North East Station. 410-287-3737
Pat's Pizzeria. 2305 Pulaski Highway. 410-287-5050
North East Seafood. 19 South Main Street. 410-287-8380. Ships oysters and crabs.
Pear Tree Café and Bakery. 32 S. Main Street. 410-287-0959
The Lantern Queen. 40 Harry's Lane. 410-287-7217. The *Lantern Queen* is a replica of a Mississippi riverboat that serves meals.
Schroeder's Deli and Liquors. Rte. 272 & I-95. 410-287-6465
Billie's Chuck Wagon Restaurant. Rte. 40
The Galley Snack Bar. Jackson Marine. Hances Point. 410-287-9400
Crystal Inn. Rte. 272. 410-287-7100

# Charlestown

Charlestown, located on the banks of the North East River, was established by an act of the Maryland Assembly in 1742 and incorporated in 1786. The town is named for Charles Calvert, Lord Baltimore. From 1782-87 Charlestown was the county seat for Cecil County. It was a port at the head of the Chesapeake Bay with some shipbuilding. During the Revolutionary War Charlestown was a supply depot for the Continental Army. The town was once considered as the location for the nation's capital and as the county seat. Fishing was an important industry and salted herring were exported along the East Coast and further west. In 1974 the town received approval for the Historic District which is on the original 150 acres and contains about 175 structures.

## Attractions

Indian Queen. Market Street. Private. The frame house has a central fireplace which was unusual for an 18[th]c Maryland house. The house may have been a tavern. George Washington is thought to have stopped here in 1795.

The Tory House. Market and Cecil Streets. 410-287-8793. The house is also known as the 107 House and may have been run as a tavern by Tories during the revolution. The house was built in the "Dutch" style and was restored by Colonial Charlestown, Inc.

Town Hall.241 Market Street. 410-287-6173. The School Commissioners of Cecil County deeded a lot for a schoolhouse in 1877. A two-room schoolhouse was built in 1878 for grades 1-6. In 1961 the Board of Education deeded the property back to the town, and it now houses the Post Office and Town Hall.

*Dining*

Wellwood River Shack. Historic Charlestown. 410-287-6666
Beachcomber Restaurant. 410-287-5629
Market Street Café. 315 Market Street. 410-287-6374
Wellwood Yacht Club Restaurant. 410-287-6666

# Principio Furnace

Principio Furnace is located on the Old Post Road between Baltimore and Philadelphia. Joseph Farmer chose the site and while building the furnace was joined in partnership with Stephen Onion and Thomas Russell, Sr. who in 1722 bought 22,000 acres to supply the iron ore and timber for the furnace. John England arrived in 1723, finished the furnace and located the iron ore deposits on the Patapsco River. From 1735-80 the furnace produced pig iron. George Washington's father, Augustine Washington, and brother maintained an interest in the furnace.

The furnace was confiscated from the British in 1780 and operated by Thomas Russell and his son. It was then leased to James and George Whitaker in 1829. The Whitakers built a third furnace in 1837, the second having been built after the British destroyed the furnace in 1813. In 1847 Jethro McCullough, Delaphine McDaniel and Edward Harvey purchased the furnace. The McCullough and Iron Company was formed in 1861 and produced the first galvanized sheet iron in the United States. Pig iron was produced here until 1889.

# Conowingo

The Conowingo is a tributary of the Susquehanna River. The Conowingo Dam, meaning "at the rapids" in Susquehannock language, was opened in 1928. The dam is located three miles upriver from Havre de Grace.

Just north of Conowingo was a place called Bald Friar. The crossing was on the main route to Philadelphia. Lafayette and Comte de Rochembeau's crossed here in 1781 to head to Yorktown. Mile's Island, which has since been covered with water from the lake, was a Native American site. Relics from here are on display at the Maryland Academy of Science in Baltimore.

# Attractions

Conowingo Dam. U.S. Rte.1. 410-457-5011. Even as a child I thrilled crossing over this dam. Over the years we have seen the 14 mile lake rise and fall, but even so it has long been a good fishing hole. The dam is one of the largest hydroelectric projects in the U.S. Tours are given of the plant. The annual "fish-lift" is held in the spring.

The Philadelphia Electric Company built the dam 1926-28. Over 4,000 workers came from nearby counties to complete the project. The adjoining power plant was completed and put into operation in 1928.

Stark Valley Farm. 724 Conowingo Road. 410-378-3280

## Dining

The Susquehanna Inn. 177 Conowingo Road. 410-378-3789
Conowingo Diner. Rtes. 1 and 222. 410-378-3073
Conowingo Crab Shack. Rtes. 1 and 222. 410378-3480
Dave's Family Restaurant. 390 Conowingo Road. 410-378-5112

# Port Deposit

Port Deposit is a sleepy town along the banks of the Susquehanna River, with many stone buildings constructed of Port Deposit granite. The town was settled c1720. Thomas Cresap was known to have operated a ferry here in 1729. An early name for the town was Creswell's Ferry operated by the Creswell family that owned the Anchor and Hope Farm just above Port Deposit. The Susquehanna Canal was built c1783 and some of the canal beds can still be seen. In 1812 Philip Thomas laid out the town and the legislature named it Port Deposit in 1813. Agricultural and other products were floated down the river and canal to Port Deposit and then loaded on larger ships. Herring and shad fishing began in earnest, followed by quarrying. In 1849 an iron factory was opened and later was to produce the Armstrong stove in the 1870s.

The canal was closed in the 1890s when rail transportation was found to be more economical. In 1910 a dam was built just north of Port Deposit which was to adversely effect the fishing industry.

A ferry landing for crossing the Susquehanna was located in front of the Union Hotel. A sawmill was also located near the hotel. Most of the buildings are three stories high, due to the river flooding that often took place. In 1972 Hurricane Agnes ravaged the town.

In 2000 several projects were announced to bring some life back along the waterfront. A new marina, Tome's Landing, condominiums and a park have been constructed.

## Attractions

The Donaldson Brown Center. 410-378-2555. The Georgian mansion overlooks the Susquehanna River. Small meetings are permitted on the property.

The Gerry House. Main Street. The building was constructed c1813 in the Greek Revival style probably by David Megrady. Cornelius Smith of Philadelphia willed the house to his step-grandson Lucius A.C. Gerry. Mr. Gerry served under Capt. Alonzo Snow's Battery B in the Civil War.

Paw Paw Building. N. Main Street. The building supposedly was named for the two trees that were near the front door. It was constructed in 1821 as a Methodist Church, built of Port Deposit granite. Since then it has been used as an academy and Masonic Lodge, and now a museum.

Town Hall. 64 S. Main Street. 410-378-2121. Adams Hall was built in 1904 with designs from Boring and Tilton. The original building once had a swimming pool and basketball court. The structure was renovated in 1983 as the Town Hall, and the library added in 1986.

Washington Hall. Main Street. The brownstone building was built in 1894 for the Tome Institute. Mr. Jacob tome made his fortune in lumber and gave very generously to Port Deposit, including $1.5 million to the Tome Institute, and the town schools. The Tome School opened in 1902 on the bluff behind Port Deposit, but closed in 1941.

88 Main Street. A brick and stone staircase has been built into the side of the bluff that climbs to the Tome School. A waterfall cascades down beside the steps, and is just an awesome sight.

Port Deposit Quarries. Rte. 222. Quarrying began here in 1816-17 to build a bridge across the Susquehanna River.

Smith's Falls. Captain John Smith who ventured up the Susquehanna River in the early 1600s named them "Smith's Fales".

Bainbridge Naval Training Center. Lowe Enterprises Community Development

Corp. of Los Angeles has received exclusive rights to negotiate with the Bainbridge Development Corp. to develop the 1,200 acre former Naval Training Center. The former Navy boot camp has been vacant since 1960. Included in the project will be a conference center, an industrial park and other facilities.

Bainbridge was located on property once owned by Jacob Tome who built the Jacob Tome Institute, a college preparatory school. Later the property was the site of a WAVE-recruit training command base and then the training center.

Physick House. Rte 222. Private. The 2½ story house was built c1830 with a hipped roof.

**Rock Run Mill**

Rock Run Mill. Rte. 269. Open on week-ends Memorial Day to Labor Day. The stone mill was built c1725 by John Steel and operated until 1731.

**Dining**

Portside Grille. 600 Rowland Drive. 410-378-4600. Innovative cuisine overlooking the river

The Union Hotel. 1282 Susquehanna Road. 410-378-3503. The hotel was built c1783 and was an important location along the canal.

Winchester Hotel Pub & Restaurant. 15 S. Main Street. 410-378-3701. The building dates to c1869.

Donna's Shoppe. 14 S. Main Street. 410-378-5505.

CM Tugs Food & Spirits. 10 S. Main Street. 410-378-8338

Crother's Market & Seafood Restaurant. Rte. 222N. 410-378-0045

Rick's Crabs. 1205 Tome Highway. 410-378-3710

# Perryville

Captain John Smith explored the area in 1608. In 1722 Edward Palmer was granted a patent for a settlement on Garrett Island and Perryville had its first settlement. During the 17th c Lord Baltimore granted George Talbot 31,000 acres which included Perryville. Perry Point was known to have been surveyed in 1658. In 1710 Captain Richard Perry of London bought the property.

Perryville was a staging area during the Revolutionary War. Colonel John Rodgers who operated the inn and ferry raised the 5th Company of the Maryland Militia. His son, John Rodgers, was to become Commodore of the American Navy and helped rid the Tripoli pirates from the Mediterranean. Commodore Rodgers served in the War of 1812 and is known as the "Father of the American Navy".

Perryville has been called Chesapeake, Lower Ferry and Susquehanna. The town lies on the Old Post Road, and is on the north side of the Susquehanna River across from Havre de Grace. Ferries crossed between the two towns. In 1835 when the railroad was built, ferries carried the railroad cars across the river. The post office was known as Perryville in 1837. The first bridge was built in 1866 by the Pennsylvania Railroad.

*Attractions:*

Rodgers Tavern. Old Post Road. The tavern was believed to have been a tavern in 1745 operated by William Stephenson. In 1771 Col. John Rodgers, the father of Commodore John Rodgers, a naval hero during the War of 1812, bought the building. The tavern was visited many times by Martha and George Washington who crossed the river by ferry here.

**Rodgers Tavern**

Perry Point Hospital. The facility is a veteran's hospital for the mentally ill. The superintendent formerly owned Perry Point Mansion (now private). The property was patented in 1658 by John Bateman and named Perry Point. Richard Perry and his sons owned the land from 1710-29. The Thomas family purchased the property in 1729 and built a mill and the house. John Stump bought about 1800 acres in 1800. The farm was turned over to the Union Army during the Civil War and much damage was done to the house. The U.S. government bought 516 acres in 1918 from the Stump family. The VA hospital was built in 1930.

Perryville Train Station. The station dates to c1904.

Prime Outlets at Perryville. Heather Lane. Outlet shopping

*Lodging:*

Comfort Inn. 61 Heather Lane. 410-642-2866

*Dining:*

Rendezvous Bar and Restaurant. 362 Front Street. 410-642-0045
Buddy's Seafood Restaurant & Lounge. Rte. 40. 410-642-6456
Island Inn Restaurant. 648 Broad Street. 410-642-3448

# Garrett Island

The island lies just inside the mouth of the Susquehanna River between Perryville and Havre de Grace. In 1608 John Smith found the Susquehannocks on the island. Later William Claiborne fortified the island for the Virginia Company. Then Edward Palmer received it as a King's Grant and named it for himself.

During the mid 19th century the B&O Railroad bought the island as a base for the bridge across the river and named it for John W. Garrett, the chairman of the B&O. Another bridge was built for Route 40 by the state. Interestingly enough the railroad also allowed fishermen to haul seine nets for shad, and process them there during the 19th and 20th c.

In 1997 the CSX, the successor to the B&O sold Garrett Island to a developer, who then put it up for sale again. The board of the Cecil Land Trust has formed a limited liability corporation to possibly purchase the property.

# Havre de Grace

Havre de Grace was laid out in 1658 for Godfrey Harmer, and called "Harmer's Town". In 1659 Mr. Harmer assigned the town to Thomas Stockett. It then became known as "Stockett's Town". In 1695 the "Lower Ferry" crossed here and after 1700 the town was known as Susquehanna Lower Ferry.

In 1781 Rochembeau's troops camped here on their way to Yorktown, mapping the area. In 1782 on their return, they again drew a map, but placed the camp on the eastern side of the river. One soldier noted that a city was to be built, called Havre de Grace. By 1783 there were seven houses, and by 1798 forty. In 1789 Havre de Grace almost became the capital of the United States. The House of Representatives met to vote on the location with a tie resulting between Havre de Grace and Washington. The Speaker cast the deciding vote for Washington.

The town was incorporated in 1795 as Havre de Grace or "Harbour of Grace". General Lafayette and other Frenchmen thought the town resembled Le Havre in France. The Old Post Road between Baltimore and Philadelphia brought stages, and the port continued to grow as a ferry operated between Perryville and Havre de Grace.

Just south of Havre de Grace is Spesutia Island. Robert Smith, Secretary of the Navy 1801-1809, was a resident of the island and prepared the Navy for the War of 1812. He changed the sailor's "rum ration" to "rye whiskey".

On May 3, 1813 during the War of 1812, the British fleet under the leadership of Admiral George Cockburn attacked with fifteen barges and burned about 60% of the homes in Havre de Grace. One of those belonged to Commodore John Rodgers who was Commodore of the United States Navy squadron posted in the Atlantic against the British forces. Rodgers' brother, George Washington Rodgers also served in the war. His brother-in-law, William Pinkney, a Harford County lawyer, ratified the Constitution, was a member of the House of Delegates, served as a major in the Baltimore militia and was wounded at the Battle of Bladensburg.

In May 1813 British vessels shelled the town, and the only officer present, John O'Neill was taken captive aboard the *Maidstone*. John O'Neill, a member of the local militia tried to defend Havre de Grace with cannon and musket fire, manning three guns at the "Potato Battery". He was wounded by the recoils of one of his guns, captured by Admiral Cockburn, and was sentenced to be hanged. Matilda, his daughter, rowed out to the *Maidstone* and pleaded with the admiral to save her father's life. He granted her request and then burned the town. For his bravery Commodore O'Neill was given the position of lighthouse keeper for the Concord Point Lighthouse. The lighthouse position passed down through the O'Neill family until the lighthouse became powered by electricity in 1920.

Jared Sparks, a tutor and eyewitness of the British attack, later became President of Harvard University and wrote one of the first biographies of George Washington.

The town was slow to recover after the War of 1812. However, a steamship line, a railroad and the building of the canal brought prosperity to the area. The Susquehanna and Tidewater Canal was started in 1836 and completed in 1840 to increase commerce and carry crops between Baltimore and Pennsylvania. Lancaster, Pennsylvania was connected through the Conestoga Canal. 29 locks linked Havre de Grace with Wrightsville, Pennsylvania, a distance of 45 miles. The mule drawn canal boats were raised a total of 233 feet, thus making the trip several days. As railroad travel became faster and cheaper the canals were shut down. The most profitable year for the Susquehanna and Tidewater Canal was c1870, closing down 1890-1900.

The railroad passed through here in 1835 with railroad cars being ferried from Perryville. The first car bridge was built in 1906. The Route 40 bridge was built in 1939 and the Millard Tydings Bridge in 1963, named after Millard Tydings, U.S. Senator elected from here in 1926. Mr. Tydings authored the bill giving the Philippines their independence.

65

During the cold winter of 1852 railroad tracks were laid across the ice on the Susquehanna from January 15$^{th}$ to February 29$^{th}$. The construction of the first railroad bridge across the river was completed in 1866 and used until 1939.

Fishing, boat building, exportation of grain and lumber from Pennsylvania, coal and canning brought economic growth to Havre de Grace.

Over a period of time Havre de Grace became noted for duck hunting, fishing, and the carving of decoys. The Havre de Grace Decoy Museum preserves these traditions. From 1919-52 a thoroughbred racetrack brought horse lovers to town. On September 29, 1920 *Man O' War*, one of racing's most famous horses, won the Potomac Handicap. The Maryland National Guard now owns the property.

The author, although she was born in Baltimore, spent her first year in Havre de Grace at "Mount Pleasant", with her maternal grandparents living nearby at "Harmony Hills", now "Bonita Farm".

**Attractions**

The town has a number of antique stores, an old bookstore and Bombay's homemade Candy (322 Market Street). Much of the area comprises the National Register Historic District.

Concord Point Lighthouse. Foot of Lafayette Street. 410-939-2165. Open week-ends April to October. The property was the site of a battery where the Susquehanna River meets the Chesapeake Bay. The lighthouse was built in 1827 by John Dunahoo and was the oldest lighthouse in continuous use in Maryland. The lighthouse was decommissioned in 1975.

Havre de Grace Decoy Museum. 215 Giles Street. 410-939-3739. The museum is built on the site where Jim Currier carved his duck decoys, many of which are now displayed in the museum. In fact the museum has over 2,000 decoys on display that were carved locally or around the Bay. During the year there are carving demonstrations, a Decoy Festival and annual Duck Fair. (See Waterfowl chapter)

Bayou Hotel. Overlooking the Flats. The building was constructed beginning in 1917, but delayed by World War I. It was opened as a luxury hotel in 1920. During the Great Depression the hotel closed and became a residence for the Franciscan Sisters. In 1953 the building was converted to apartments, and in 1984 luxury apartments.

The Susquehanna Museum of Havre de Grace. Conesteo Street. 410-939-0253. Open Friday, Saturday, and Sunday, May to October. The museum preserves the history of the Havre de Grace and the canal The property was given to the City of Havre de Grace by the Philadelphia Electric Company. The Locktender's House was constructed c1840 to serve as both the Canal office and locktender's family house. The house was restored in 1982. Inside are memorabilia and history of the canal, and a gift shop. A pivot bridge was reconstructed which allowed passage of traffic over the canal to the river and tow path.

**Locktender's House and Canal**

Steppingstone Farm Museum. 461 Quaker Bottom Road. 410-939-2299. Week-ends, May to October. Located in the Susquehanna State Park the museum offers insights into the rural arts and crafts of the 1880-1920 period. This working farm has a large collection of hand tools donated by J. Edmund Bull and others.

Havre de Grace Maritime Museum. Lafayette Street. 410-939-4800. Week-ends May to September. The museum offers educational programs and preserves Havre de Grace's maritime heritage.

Skipjack *Mary W. Somers*. William T. Young built the skipjack on Youngs Creek in Parksley, VA. The boat is a wooden 55 foot 7 ton sloop rigged skipjack.

Pensell Propeller. Lafayette Street. The propeller was built in 1895 and installed on the 135 foot tug *Sea King*. In 1917 the tug reported for war at Havre de Grace to replace a steam boiler, but with the end of the war she was no longer needed. She was abandoned and sunk. In 1953 while moving her to build the Tidewater Marina, George Pensell salvaged the shaft and propeller.

Thomas Hopkins House. 229 N. Union Street. The house was built in 1839 for Dr. Thomas C. Hopkins, a member of the Maryland Legislature, 1842-43 and 1865-66.

Skipjack *Martha Lewis*. Foot of Congress Avenue. 800-406-0766

Skipjack *Applegarth*. Tydings Park Marina. 410-879-6941.Captain Paul Thomas purchased the *Applegarth* from Paramount Pictures in 1995 after filming of the movie "I.Q.". The boat is a mini skipjack which was used for crabbing, fishing and oystering, and is now used for Bay cruises

North Park Trail. Three trail systems lie along the Susquehanna River.

The Promenade. The boardwalk is adjacent to Tydings Park and the Decoy Museum. It is a perfect place to look out on the Bay and Susquehanna River.

Tydings Park. The park was named for U.S. Senator Millard E. Tydings, who was raised in Havre de Grace and went on to author the Philippine Independence Bill. During the summer the Concert in the Park series is held beginning in June and continuing through August.

O'Neill House. Washington Street. The house was owned by John O'Neill, who defended Havre de Grace during the War of 1812. Most of the house dates from 1865.

Rodgers House. 226 N. Washington Street. The Georgian brick house is the oldest structure in Havre de Grace, built in 1787.

Aveilhe-Goldsborough House. Union and Green Streets. The house was built in 1801 for Baptiste Aveilhe, a Frenchman.

Seneca Mansion. Union and Pennington Streets. William Plack designed the large Victorian house which was built in 1885 for Stephen J. Seneca, an entrepreneur who donated the Methodist Church and was mayor of Havre de Grace 1893-94.

City Hall. 121 N. Union Street. The building was erected in 1870 as a school and town hall. It was later an opera house and town hall. A fire caused extensive damage in 1920's. A new building elsewhere is used as the city hall.

St. John's Episcopal Church. Union and Congress Streets. The church was built in 1809 and is the oldest in Havre de Grace. The financing for the building came through a lottery in 1802, though the church was not built until 1809. The church was damaged by the British in 1814 and gutted by fire in 1832. The building was renovated c1863 and the belfry was added c1884. The church has Flemish bond brick walls and round arched windows. The author was christened here.

Methodist Church. 101 S. Union Street. The structure was donated by Stephen J. Seneca in 1901 and is built of Port Deposit granite with Indiana limestone trim.

Old Ordinary. Congress Avenue. The building dates to c1800. The lot was first leased by Gabriel Peterson Vanhorn, a partner in the overland stage line from Baltimore to the Lower Ferry, from Robert Young Stokes, the founder of Havre de Grace in 1782.

Abraham Jarrett Thomas House. The house was built in 1834 and owned by Mr. Thomas, a banker. Prior to his ownership the property had belonged to the Havre de Grace Ferry Company, who had bought the property from William B. Stokes, who operated a stage line between Baltimore and Philadelphia and the ferry across the Susquehanna River. From c1856 to the 1940s the building was hotel and in its final years the Lafayette Hotel. Today it is the Joseph L. Davis Post American Legion Home.

Sion Hill. Rte. 155. Private. The property is named for the estate of the Dukes of Northumberland on the Thames River, England. Rev. John Ireland, rector of St. George's Parish, owned the land from 1789-95. He opened Sion Hill Seminary, a boy's school, which went broke. In 1795 Gabriel Dennison of Philadelphia bought the farm. His daughter married Capt. John Rodgers, a naval hero during the War of 1812, and commander of the naval forces at the Battle of Baltimore.

Swan Harbor Farm. 401 Oakington Road. 410-939-6767. The 463 acre farm overlooks the Chesapeake Bay. The property has facilities for meetings and special events.

Susquehanna State Park. 410-557-7994. Located three miles northwest of Havre de Grace the park has horseback riding, trails, mountain biking, boating, bird watching and other outdoor activities. On the property is the Rock Run Grist Mill built in 1794, a New Jersey tool house and the Archer Museum. The area is noted for the breeding grounds of the bald eagle.

Oakington. Oakington Road. Private. Just outside Havre de Grace is the 555 acre estate of Senator Millard D. Tydings and now owned by his son, Joseph Tydings, also a former Senator. John Stump of Stafford built the house in 1810. Two wings were added in 1900. Some of the property has now been sold, and "Ashley", a rehabilitation center, is located there.

## Lodging:

Spencer-Silver Mansion. 200 S. Union Avenue. 410-939-1485. The house was built in 1896 for John Spencer, a merchant, and was later bought by Charles Silver, a canner. The carriage house also accommodates guests.
Vandiver Inn. 301 S. Union Avenue. 1-800-245-1655. This historic home was built by the mayor of Havre de Grace, Murray Vandiver in 1886.
La Cle D'or. 226 North Union Avenue. 410-939-6562. The home was built in 1868 and was home to the Johns Hopkins family.
Currier House B&B. 800 South Market Street. 410-939-7886. The Currier family came to Maryland in 1648. Matthew Currier moved to Havre de Grace in 1861 after his livestock and farm products were appropriated to the Union Army. He lived in a portion of the present house. In 1882 the house was sold to the Thomas family, and enlarged. Ollie Currier, a grandson of Matthew purchased the home in 1937. In 1995 Jane Currier Belbot, a great-granddaughter of Matthew and John Currier, Matthew's great-grandson renovated the house and has filled it with family heirlooms.
Super 8. 929 Pulaski Highway. 410-939-1880

## Dining:

Tidewater Grill. 300 Franklin Street. 410-939-3313.
Price's Seafood. 654 Water Street. 410-939-2782.
Bayou. Pulaski Highway. 410-939-3565 A local favorite for good crabcakes and crab soup.
MacGregors Restaurant &Tavern. 331 Saint John Street. 410-939-3003. On the water
Heritage Tea Room. 421 St. John Street. 410-942-0290. Lunch and tea
Stone Creek Crossing. 320 Blenheim Lane. 410-939-8887
Vandiver Inn. 301 South Union Avenue. 410-939-5200
The Crazy Swede Restaurant & Bar. 400 N. Union Avenue. 410-939-5440
Ice Creams. 209 N. Washington Street. 410-939-1525. Sandwiches, ice cream
Java by the Bay. 118 N. Washington Street. 410-939-0227. Coffee, tea, muffins and bagels
Bobby Griffin's Fishermen's Café. Tydings Park
Le Café de Galleria. 113 S. Washington Street. 410-939-4230. Southwestern food in the Abbe Art Gallery
Deli-Mart. Restaurant & Carry-out. 1123A Revolution Street. 410-939-0090

Bay City Market. 200 Congress Avenue. 410-939-3116
Fortunato Brothers Pizza. 103 N. Washington Street. 410-939-1401
Vancherie's. 419 Union Avenue. 410-939-1151
Coakley's Pub. 406 St. John Street. 410-939-8888
Goll's Bakery. 234 N. Washington Street. 410-939-4321
The Havre de Grace Ritz. 100 N. Washington Street. 410-939-5858. Desserts
and ice cream
The Lighthouse Diner & Restaurant. 913 Pulaski Highway. 410-942-0302

# Darlington

Col. Nathan Rigbie once owned a 2,000 acre estate called "Philip's Purchase".
From 1728-31 portions of the property were sold to Thomas Jones, Gerard
Hopkins, and Henry Coale.

Quakers were to settle in the area and the Deer Creek Friends' Meeting House
was organized in 1737 and rebuilt in 1784. On April 13, 1781 Lafayette's army
camped here. The post office was known as Darlington in 1819, but changed to
Woodlawn in 1821 and Battle Swamp in 1853. Later the name was changed
back to Darlington. The Darlington Academy opened in 1836 to provide public
school instruction.

**Attractions**

Nathan Rigbie House. Castleton Road. Private. The house is believed to have
been built before 1732. On April 13, 1781 Lafayette visited with Col. James
Rigbie, captain of the militia and sheriff of Harford County. While here
Lafayette's troop tried to mutiny. Lafayette tried Walter Pigot for treason for
selling flour to the British. He was found guilty and hanged. The house is a
National Register landmark and sits on 320 of the original 2,000 acres.

Deer Creek Friends Meeting. Rte. 161. The meeting house was built in 1784 and
had two sections that separate the men and women's sides. In the cemetery is the
grave of Sarah Rumsey Rigbie, wife of Col. Nathan Rigbie.

Prospect School. Greenspring Road. The school is listed on the National
Register and was built c1830 by Joshua Stevens, a stone mason.

Bonita Farm. 3745 Harmony Church Road. Private. The 400 acre farm was once
known as "Harmony Hills" and owned by the author's grandparents. The farm

was bought following World War II by Col. and Mrs. Grafton Sherwood Kennedy.

The north wing of the house was built in 1810 by Zephaniah Bayless, the founder of the Deer Creek Harmony Presbyterian Church, which still stands on the corner of the property. A formal addition was added to the house in 1844, and a boxwood garden planted. Anna Merven Carrere, the daughter of the New York architect, John Carrere, owned the house in the 1930s and 1940s adding the east wing and formal gardens.

**Bonita Farm**

The property now has extensive stables, a racetrack and a large stone barn. The owner breeds and trains racehorses, which include *Disputed Testimony* and *Parfaitment*.

## *Lodging*

Darlington Manor B&B. 1114 Main Street. 410-457-9021

# Hickory

The town was known as Hickory Tavern in 1831.

**Attractions**

Walter's Mill. Rte. 543. The mill on Deer Creek began operating in 1803. The present mill dates to c1890 built on the foundation of the original mill.


# Churchville

Churchville was once known as Lower Crossroads. The first graduate of the Philadelphia School of Medicine, Dr. Archer, was born here in 1741 and graduated in 1768. By 1828 Churchville was known as Herberts Cross Roads.

**Attractions**

Holy Trinity Episcopal Church. Rte. 155. Dr. David Harlan of Churchville, Medical Director of the U.S. Navy and the Rev. Edward A. Colburn, rector of Deer Creek Parish, founded the church in 1866. Dr. Harlan donated the land and the first church building which burned in 1877. He also donated the present church which was built in 1878 and designed by George Archer. The church is built in 13th c English Gothic style of stone that was quarried near Churchville, trimmed with Port Deposit granite and roofed with slate quarried in Cardiff, Harford County.

Churchville Presbyterian Church. Rte. 136 and 155. The congregation was founded in 1739. The church was built in 1820 and remodeled in 1870.

Calvary United Methodist Church. Calvary Road, just south of Churchville. The church was founded in 1821 and is the oldest, continuously operating Methodist church in the Baltimore area. Calvary is part of the Abington Charge with Cokesbury United Methodist Church.

Greenwood. Old Level Road. Private. The house was built in 1841 by the Rev. William Finney and is listed on the National Register of Historic Places.

Big M Drive-in. This is one of two drive-in movie theaters left in Maryland.

# Aberdeen

The settlement was founded in 1669. In 1683 Aberdeen was designated the colony's official port-of-entry, and served as a marine hub between New England and Virginia. Aberdeen was formerly known as Halls Cross Roads and Mechanicsville. In 1892 the town was incorporated and the Pennsylvania, Wilmington and Baltimore Railroad passed through here. The station was named Aberdeen, after Aberdeen, Scotland, the home of Mr. Winston, the postmaster.

**Attractions:**

Ripken Museum. 3 West Bel Air Drive. 410-273-2525. Baltimore's Baseball hero has a museum dedicated to the Ripken family, the history of baseball, and memorabilia from Cal, Jr. and Bill.

Aberdeen Rooms Archives and Museum. 58 North Parke Street. 410-273-6325. Open Tuesday, Thursday and first Saturday of month. The museum has memorabilia from the city of Aberdeen.

Old Spesutie Church. Perryman Road. The first church was raised in 1760. The present church was built in 1851 with the plans of John Rudolph Niernsee and J. Crawford Neilson. The church serves St. George's Parish, one of the original Anglican churches in Maryland. The Vestry House was built in 1766, and used as a school. Buried on the grounds is Col. Thomas White, father of the first bishop of the Protestant Episcopal Church in the United States, William White.

Aberdeen Proving Ground. Rte. 715. Aberdeen Proving Ground opened in 1917, occupying 17,000 acres, now over 80,000 acres. The Proving Ground is on the site of Baltimore County's first seat of government and the county's first human settlement. The nonprofit Old Baltimore Foundation plans to collect artifacts from the site and build a "virtual reality" village or reconstruct the settlement at Swan Harbor Farm, a county owned property near Havre de Grace.

The author's godfather, Maj. General Alfred Bixby Quinton was once Commanding General of Aberdeen Proving Ground and her grandfather Colonel Grafton Sherwood Kennedy also served here.

The facility was established to develop and test ordnance. On the grounds are many displays of U.S. and foreign tanks and other artillery, plus quarters for staff and training grounds.

U.S. Ordnance Museum. Maryland and Aberdeen Boulevards. 410-278-3602. The museum has an extensive collection of combat vehicles, artillery, arms, a

German V-2 rocket, and General Pershing's Locomobile. Outside is the "Tank Park".

Spesutie Island. The island is now part of Aberdeen Proving Ground. Col. Nathaniel Utie settled on the island in the 1600s when he was commander of the northern frontier. The name means "Utie's Hope".

**Aberdeen Proving Grounds- Commanding General's Quarters**

## *Lodging*

Four Points Hotel by Sheraton Aberdeen. I-95 and Rte. 22. 410-273-6300
Holiday Inn Chesapeake House. 1007 Beards Hill Road. 410-272-8100
Budget Inn of Aberdeen. 1112 S. Philadelphia Blvd. 410-272-2401
Holly Hill Motel. Rte. 40. 410-272-0900
Red Roof Inns. I-95 at S.R. 22. 410-273-7800
Quality Inn & Suites. 793 W. Bel Air Avenue. 410-272-6000
Knights Inn. 744 S. Philadelphia Blvd. 410-272-3600
Super 8 Motel. 1008 Beards Hill Road. 1-800-800-8000
Days Inn. 783 W. Bel Air Avenue. 410-272-2525
Econo Lodge. 820 W. Bel Air Road. 410-272-5500
Ken's Motel. 636 S. Philadelphia Boulevard. 410-272-6650

*Dining*

Gabler's. 2200 Perryman Road. 410-272-0626
Japan House. 984 Beards Road. 410-272-7878
Durango's Colorado Steak & Pub. 980 Hospitality Way. 410-273-6300
Olive Tree Restaurant. 1005 Beards Hill Road. 410-575-7773

# Bush

Bush was the first county seat of Harford County (1744-82). The town was once called Harford Town, named for Henry Harford, the last lord proprietor. In 1775 thirty-four members of the Committee of Observation for Harford County signed the Bush Declaration to support the Continental Congress. The Bush River is a tributary of the Chesapeake Bay.

# Fountain Green

**Attractions**

Tudor Hall. 410-838-0466. Private. Junius Brutus Booth purchased "Tudor Hall" in 1821.His sons, Edwin and John Wilkes Booth were born in an earlier house built on the property. Edwin Booth was a Shakespearean actor. John Wilkes Booth, also an actor, murdered Abraham Lincoln on April 14, 1865 at Ford's Theater in Washington, DC. Small meetings are permitted on the property.

# Fulford

**Attractions**

Medical Hall. Greer Road. Private. Dr. John Archer who obtained the first medical degree from the Philadelphia Medical College in 1768 built the house. He was a signer of the Bush Declaration and later raised a militia during the Revolutionary War. Dr. Archer and his son, Dr. Thomas Archer founded the Medical and Chirurgical Faculty of Maryland in 199. Dr. John Archer served for two terms in Congress and then founded a medical school in his home. Another son, Stevenson Archer, also served in Congress, was chief judge of the Circuit Court, and chief judge of the Court of Appeals.

# Bel Air

In 1782 Harford County voted to move the county seat and land was purchased for a courthouse in Scott's Old Field. The town consisted of 40 lots, with 15 of those owned by Thomas A. Hays. The courthouse burned down and a new one was erected in 1858-59. In 1794 it was known as Bellair from the French meaning "fine air". Bel Air is the Harford County seat.

## Attractions

Hay's House. 324 Kenmore Avenue. The house was built prior to 1711 on another site and moved here and restored in the 1960's. In 1784 Lafayette spent the night here.

The Historical Society of Harford County 143 N. Main Street. 410-838-7691. The society was organized in 1885 and has a wealth of records on the county and the War of 1812.

Liriodendron. 502 W. Gordon Street. 410-879-4424. The house was built in 1898 by a Johns Hopkins' physician. On the grounds are a Palladian style house and elegant boxwood gardens. The house is open for special events.

Rockfield Manor. 501 Churchville Road. 410-638-4536. The 1921 prairie style house demonstrates the crafts of the 1880-1920s. The property is located on part of one of the original Thomas Hays lots, which was sold in 1920 to Charles and Adele McComas, who built the house. In 195 John and Jenovefa Hoza purchased the property. They had moved here from Czechoslavakia. He was part of the management team for the Bata Shoe company. In 1991 Harford County purchased 46 of the 55 acres and in 1993 the County deeded the land to Bel Air for use as a community park. In 1996 the town purchased the five remaining acres and house and outbuildings creating the Rockfield Foundation. The house is open for social events and meetings.

## *Dining*

Bill Bateman's Raw Bar & Grille. 1226 Bel Air Road. 410-879-7748
Du Claw Brewing Co. 16-A Bel Air S. Parkway. 410-515-3222

Scotto's. Festival at Bel Air. 410-515-2233
Red Ox Café & Grill. 5 Belair South Parkway. 410-569-3700

# Belcamp

Belcamp is located at the head of the Bush River. The name means "good camp" or "good field". Prior to World War II the Bata Shoe Company was founded here by Czechoslovakian refuges, and was once the largest industrial plant in Harford County.

# Abingdon

Abingdon was founded in 1779 by John Paca, father of William Paca, a Signer of the Declaration of Independence and Governor of Maryland. Mr. Paca was born at "Chilberry Hill" in 1740. The town was once home to the first silk hat factory in America.

In 1785 the cornerstone for Cokesbury College, named for Bishops Asbury and Coke, and the first Methodist College in America, was laid here. The building was destroyed by fire in 1795. The bricks were used in other Methodist churches and the bell is now at Goucher College.

**Attractions**

Anita C. Leight Estuary Center. 700 Otter Point Road. 410-612-1688. Open Saturday and Sundays. The 600 acre center has special programs, canoeing, nature trails, children's and educational activities.

Cokebury College Site National UM Landmark. MD 7. 410-638-0744.

William Paca Historical Marker. Rte.7. The marker commemorates the birthplace of William Paca.

# Edgewood

Edgewood Arsenal. Rte 24. The U.S. facility is located on Gunpowder Point. The facility was the U.S. Army chemical warfare station and was merged with Aberdeen Proving Ground in 1971.

*Lodging*

Best Western Invitation Inn. 1709 Edgewood Road. 410-679-9700
Comfort Inn Edgewood Conference Center. 1700 Van Bibber Road. 410-679-
0770
Sleep Inn. 1807 Edgewood Road. 410-679-4700
Days Inn of Edgewood. 2116 Emmorton Park Road. 410-671-9990

*Dining*

Giovanni's Restaurant. 2101 Pulaski Highway. 410-679-9797

# Magnolia

The town was a post office in 1866. It is probably named for the magnolia tree.

# Joppa

Joppa or Joppatowne is located near the Gunpowder River and is named for
Jaffa in Israel. In 1712 the Baltimore County seat was moved here from
Baltimore Town. The seat was held here until 1768. Industry in the area included
tobacco farming and exporting, and the Joppa Iron Works. A shipyard is also
thought to have been located here. Benjamin Rumsey, a Signer of the Bush
Declaration, bought the courthouse and prison in 1773.

In April 1781 John Paul, Walter Pigot and two other men were arrested for
supplying flour to the British. Mr. Paul escaped, but Mr. Pigot was court-
martialed and hanged.

**Attractions:**

Rumsey House. 600 Church Road. James Maxwell, a justice of the county, built
the house. It was enlarged about 1771 and sold to Benjamin Rumsey, a member
of the Continental Congress who died here in 1808. The building is now the
office of the Harford County Executive.

Mariner Point Park. Off Joppa Road. 410-612-1608. 38 acre waterfront park

Site of Joppa Town. Bridge Drive.

*Lodging*

Super 8 Motel. 1015 Pulaski Highway. 410-676-2700

*Dining*

The Grille & Pub at Mountain Branch. 1827 Mountain Road. 410-836-9600

# Jarrettsville

Jarrettsville was originally called Carmens, and the name changed to Jarretsville in 1838 for the Jarrett family. Jesse Jarrett became the real estate assessor for Harford County in 1798.

**Attractions**

Rocks State Park. 3318 Rocks Chrome Hill Road. 410-557-7994. 850 acre park on Deer Creek. The park has interesting rock formations.

# Fallston

Fallston was once known as "White House" and in 1849 the name was changed to Fallston. During the Civil War Fallston was a stop on the Underground Railroad.

**Attractions**

Little Falls Meeting House. Old Fallston Road. The meeting was established in 1758 as a branch of the Gunpowder Meeting, and in 1815 established its own meeting. The meeting house was built in 1843 with separate entrances and a partition for men and women.

Bon Air. Laurel Brook Road. Private. The house is the only 18th c French house in North America, outside of French Canada. The house was built in 1794 by Claudius Francis Frederick de la Porte, a merchant and ship owner who had fled from his home in San Domingo during slave revolts. He brought with him carpenters to build the house. Black walnut grown on the property was used in the interior. Mr. de la Porte may have been a colonel in Rochembeau's army, which was led by Lafayette and marched through Harford County en route to Yorktown and the defeat of Cornwallis.

Gunpowder Falls State Park. The park has over 10,000 acres and lies along the Gunpowder River and Big and Little Gunpowder Falls.

Marker for a copper works. In 1815 Levi Hollingsworth established a $100,000 copper-rolling mill, one of the earliest in the United States.

## Dining

Josef's Country Inn. 2410 Pleasantville Road. 410-877-7800
Mo's Seafood Restaurant. 2403 Bel Air Road. 410-877-3336
Weber's Landing. 2607 Bel Air Road. 410-893-2035
Fusion Grille. 2402 Pleasantville Road. 410-877-1550


# Pleasant Hills

### Attractions

Olney Farm. Old Joppa Road. Private. The original tract was called Prospect and was taken up in the 1700s by John Saurin Norris, a Quaker, who built the house in 1810. Olney was named for the house of the English poet, William Cowper.


# Baldwin

During the 1800s the Baldwin family settled in this area. Thomas Baldwin sold general merchandise, and A.S. Baldwin and Charles A. Baldwin were physicians.


# Kingsville/ Jerusalem

Even though George King was postmaster here in 1834, the town is probably named for Abraham King who came to Maryland from Pennsylvania.

The village was built around a mill that David Lee, a Quaker, built on Little Gunpowder Falls in 1772. The tract of land was patented "Jerusalem" in 1687.

## Attractions

Jerusalem Mill. Gunpowder Falls State Park. 410-877-3560. The mill is located on the banks of the Little Gunpowder Falls River. In 1769 millwright Isaiah Linton and miller David Lee entered into a partnership to build the mill. In 1772 David Lee began milling flour under the "White Silk" label for Baltimore and the surrounding area. Until the 1870's the mill was known as Lee's Merchant Mill. The mill was converted to electricity after a dam broke in 1940. The mill continues to operate. Also on the property is a restored Blacksmith Shop, the Jerusalem Gun Factory, and the Jericho Covered Bridge. The Friends of Jerusalem Mill was founded in 1985 to restore the buildings and preserve the area.

**Jerusalem Gun Factory**

Kingsville Inn. Jerusalem Road. The house was built before 1740. The Rev. Hugh Dean of St. John's Parish added an addition. His son-in-law, John Paul, was a Quaker and British sympathizer. Mr. Paul was arrested in April 1781 for supplying flour to the British, but was able to escape.

Site of Ismael Day's House. On July 28, 1864 Mr. Day shot and killed a Confederate sergeant, William Fields of Baltimore who was trying to take Mr. Day's Union flag. Mr. Fields was part of a cavalry detachment led by Harry Gilmor which burned the railroad bridge over the Gunpowder River as part of the Confederate plan to capture Washington.

# Perry Hall

Perry Hall was once called Germantown. In 1774 Harry Dorsey Gough purchased the land and built a home named for an English ancestral castle.

## Attractions

Perry Hall Mansion. Perry Hall Road. Private. The house was built c1773 and sold to Harry Dorsey Gough in 1774. Additions were made to the house after the Revolutionary War. In 1787 Mr. Gough's daughter married James Carroll of "Mount Clare' in Baltimore. Mr. Gough was very involved in the Methodist Church and often entertained preachers such as Francis Asbury and Thomas Coke. In 1784 after a meeting at Perry Hall the Methodist Church in America was organized in Baltimore. In 1786 Mr. Gough was elected first president of the Society for Improvement of Agriculture in Maryland. A fire destroyed part of the mansion in 1824.

# Monkton

My Lady's Manor was a 10,000 tract that was bestowed on the wife of the third Lord Baltimore. The town was originally called Charleotte Town, then Monkton after Monkton Priory in Wales.

## Attractions

Ladew Topiary Gardens. 3535 Jarrettsville Pike. 410-557-9466. The gardens were planted between 1929-76 by the late Harvey S. Ladew. There are fifteen gardens on twenty-two acres.

Mr. Ladew purchased the farmhouse and land in 1929 for fox hunting. During his many visits to England he became aware of topiary gardens, and returned to establish his own. The gardens rang from whimsical to gorgeous rose gardens, each completely different. Our favorite is the topiary Hunt Scene.

The house was built in the late 1700s and early 1800s. Mr. Ladew added the porticos, raised the roof and made other additions. The oval library has been cited as one of the most beautiful rooms in America.

Mr. Ladew died in 1976 and bequeathed the house and gardens to the public establishing a foundation to run them. The house and gardens are on the National Register of Historic Places. During the summer there are concerts in the Great Bowl, lecture series, and many other special events, including My Lady's Manor Steeplechase Races that benefit Ladew Gardens. Also on the site are a Café, Gift Shop, Carriage Museum and Nature Walk.

**Ladew Gardens Manor House**

My Lady's Manor Course. Pocock Road and Rte. 146. A point-to-point horse race and other races are held on this course.

St. James's Church. Monkton Road. The church was built about 1750, and was part of St. John's Parish of Joppa Town.

*Dining*

Manor Tavern. 15819 Old York Road. 410-771-8155. The historic building was known to have existed as a stable in the mid 18$^{th}$ c.

# Hunt Valley

*Lodging*

Courtyard by Marriott. 221 International Circle. 410-584-7070
Chase Suites by Woodfin. 10710 Beaver Dam Road. 410-584-7370
Embassy Suites. 213 International Circle. 410-584-1400
Marriott's Hunt Valley Inn. 245 Shawan Road. 410-785-7000

*Dining*

Oregon Grille. 1201 Shawan Road. 410-771-0505

# Cockeysville

The town was named for John Cockey who purchased land in 1728. Cockeysville Marble, which was used to build the Washington Monument in Washington, DC and St. Patrick's Cathedral in New York, was quarried here for many years.

**Attractions**

Baltimore County Historical Society. 9811 Van Buren Lane. 410-666-1876

Oregon Ridge Nature Center. 13555 Beaver Dam Road. 410-887-1815. Wildlife, quarries, iron ore pits and nature center.

Sherwood Episcopal Church. York and Sherwood Roads. The church was erected in 1830 and named for the English home of the Cockey family. In 1876 the building was enlarged and the belfry added.

*Lodging*

Cockeysville EconoLodge. 10100 York Road. 1-800-553-2666

*Dining*

Patrick's Restaurant and Pub. Cranbrook Shopping Center. 410-683-0604
India Palace. 35 Cranbrook Road. 410-628-6800
Bamboo House. 26 Yorktowne Plaza. 410-666-9550
Beijing Empire Restaurant. 11222 York Road. 410-527-1999
The Corner Stable. 9942 York Road. 410-666-8722
Fazzini's Italian Kitchen. 578 Cranbrook Road. 410-667-6104
Pacific Rim. 9726 York Road. 410-666-2336
Vito's Café. 10249 York Road. 410-666-3100
York Inn. 10010 York Road. 410-666-0006
The Treehouse Bar & Grille. 9926 York Road. 410-628-2190

# Sparks

## Attractions

Loveton Mansion. York Road. Private. Dr. Thomas Love built this Federal/Italianate home in 1804. The house was enlarged and completed by his son, Capt. Thomas Love in 1848. He established a dairy farm which was to produce milk for Baltimore City and County customers until 1909. Love's granddaughter, Bessie Motague Merryman, was born in the house. She was Wallis Warfield Simpson's (later the Duchess of Windsor) aunt and confidante. The house was the 2000 Baltimore Symphony Associates Decorator Showhouse.

McCormick & Company. McCormick is the world's largest spice and flavorings company. The company was founded in 1889 in Baltimore by Willoughby M. McCormick and a staff of three. They produced root beer, flavoring extracts, fruit syrups and juices, "Iron Glue", "Uncle Sam's Nerve and Bone Liniment". In 1896 the company bought F. G. Emmett Spice Co. of Philadelphia, which moved its operations to Baltimore. In 1900 the company opened an export office in New York, and in 1902 established its "Banquet Brand" for spices and mustard. The Great Baltimore Fire of 1904 wiped out the company and its records. Within ten weeks the company had built a new five story building.

In 1905 the company introduced the "Bee Brand Tea" which was sold in pouches, and tea bags were introduced in 1910. The House of McCormick on the Baltimore Harbor was built in 1921. The headquarters included a Tea House and replica of a 16$^{th}$ c English village. In 1972 the company acquired 435 acres in Hunt Valley and moved to Sparks in 1991.

86

*Dining*

Milton Inn. 14833 York Road. 410-771-4366. The historic inn was once a coachmen's inn c1740. In 1847 the inn became a boy's school. One of the students to study here was John Wilkes Booth, who assassinated President Lincoln.

## Timonium

The town was named for Mrs. Archibald Buchanan's home "Timonium Mansion" after the tower near Alexandria, Egypt. She suffered extensive grief after she lost a friend at sea. The tower in Alexandria was where Mark Anthony withdrew after his friends deserted him.

**Attractions**

Maryland State Fairgrounds. The annual Maryland State Fair is held here.

*Lodging*

Holiday Inn Select. 2004 Greenspring Drive. 410-252-7373
Days Inn. 9615 Deereco Road. 410-560-1000
Red Roof Inn. 111 W. Timonium Road. 410-666-0380

*Dining*

Au Poitin Stil. 2323 York Road. 410-560-7900
Liberatore's Restaurant. 9515 Deereco Road. 410-561-3300
Edo Sushi. 53 E. Padonia Road. 410-667-9200
Damon's. 2306 York Road. 410-453-9555
The Charred Rib. 12 W. Ridgley Road. 410-561-0060
Michael's Café Raw Bar & Grill. 2219 York Road. 410-252-2022
Gibby's. 22 W. Padonia Road. 410-560-0703
JJ's Everyday Café. 2141 York Road. 410-308-2700
Padonia Station Bar Grille & Games. 63 E. Padonia Road. 410-252-8181
Rothwell's Grille. 106 W. Padonia Road. 410-252-0600

# Lutherville

John G. Morris, the owner of "Oak Grove", named the town for Martin Luther. The Lutherville Female Seminary, chartered in 1853, later became the Maryland College for Young Ladies. The college closed in 1952.

**Attractions**:

Fire Museum of Maryland. 1301 York Road. 410-321-7500. The museum has more than 40 fire trucks dating from 1806-1957.

*Dining*

Joey Chiu's Greenspring Inn. 10801 Falls Road. 410-823-1125
Harvey's Restaurant. 2360 W. Joppa Road. 410-296-9526
Nichi Bei Kai. 1524 York Road. 410-321-7090
Ocean Pride Seafood. 1534 York Road. 410-321-7744
Peppermill Restaurant & Lounge. 1301 York Road. 410-583-1107

# Cross Keys

An inn and village were once located on this site. The Rouse Company developed the present town.

*Lodging*

Radisson at Cross Keys. 5100 Falls Road. 410-532-6900

*Dining*

Crossroads. Cross Keys Inn. 410-532-6900
Bun Penny. 410-464-1802
Crepe du Jour. Cross Keys
Donna's Coffee Bar. 410-532-8818

# Dickeyville

Dickeyville is part of Baltimore, but was once a village located near a mill operated by water from Gwynns Falls and owned by the Tschudy family. The town dates back to 1719 with the establishment of Gwynns Falls Mill, a grain mill. William J. Dickey purchased the mill in 1871. During the Civil War the mill was confiscated to make Confederate uniforms. For a short time in 1911 the name was changed to Hillsdale.

Much of Dickeyville – 81 homes, three mills, and a mansion –was sold for $42,000 to a developer. The village was named to the National Register of Historic Places in 1968.

Today Dickeyville is little changed with rows of mill houses, a few newer homes, and Hillsdale, Gwynns Falls and Leakin Parks that offer open space for hiking and other outdoor pleasures. Only one mill remains and is used for offices. The village has a web page, but no stores or offices.

**Attractions**

Hillsdale United Methodist Church. The church was built in 1849.

Dickey Memorial Presbyterian Church. The church was organized in 1877.

# Stevenson

*Lodging*

Gramarcy Mansion B&B. 1400 Greenspring Valley Road. 410-486-2405

# Brooklandville

Charles Carroll of Carrollton once owned "Brooklandwood". The property was later purchased by Isaac Emerson, the inventor of Bromo Seltzer. Today it is St. Paul's School.

*Attractions*

Villa Julie College. Greenspring Valley Road. Private women's college.

Villa Pace. Greenspring Valley Road. Private. This was once the home of Rosa Ponselle, the opera singer who performed with the Metropolitan Opera in New

York. The Rosa Ponselle Foundation in Stevenson sponsors symposiums and vocal competitions.

Sater's Church. Falls Road. The oldest Baptist church in Maryland was founded in 1742, and reorganized in 1865.

## Dining

Valley Inn. 10501 Falls Road. 410-828-8080. Lovely old inn.

# Hampton

**Attractions**

Loch Raven Reservoir. Rte. 146. The reservoir was built as a dam in 1881 on the Gunpowder River to channel water to Lake Montebello and Lake Clifton. The city of Baltimore created the reservoir in 1914, submerging the village of Warren.

# Towson

Towson was named for a family that kept a tavern. Earliest records mention the name in 1771. Ezekial Towson petitioned for the York Road to pass in front of his tavern. It was formerly known as Towsontown. Towson is the county seat of Baltimore County.

**Attractions:**

Hampton National Historic Site. Hampton Lane. 410-823-1309. Henry Darnall, a cousin of Lord Baltimore, was granted the Northampton property in 1695. Colonel Charles Ridgely acquired a 1,500-acre tract of land in 1745 from Mr. Darnall's daughter, Ann Hill. In 1762 Charles Ridgely established an ironworks on the land. He owned a fleet of merchant vessels to transport the iron and cash crops to Europe, mills, quarries, orchards, and a general merchandise business in Baltimore. He owned more than 300 slaves, making this one of the largest slave plantations in Maryland.

The Georgian mansion was built between 1783 and 1790 as a county seat for Captain Charles Ridgely "The Builder". At that time the house was the largest in America. Later his nephew and heir Charles Carnan Ridgely "The Governor" lived here followed by his son John Ridgely and his wife Elizabeth. The Sixth Master of Hampton, John Ridgely, Jr. sold the property to a Mellon family trust which donated Hampton to the federal government. The National Park Service assumed full responsibilities for the site in 1979. Of the original 24,000 acres only 60 acres remain.

The Great Hall of the house measured 51 feet by 21 feet and could comfortably seat 50 guests. Much elaborate entertaining was done at the house, and guests included Charles Carroll. The furnishings include many Baltimore pieces by John Needles, William Camp, and John and Hugh Finlay, plus some magnificent Samuel Kirk silver.

**Hampton**

On the property is an ice house built at the same time as the mansion. The Orangery has replaced a Greek Revival structure that was built in 1825 and destroyed by fire in 1929. The Great Terrace was a bowling green and has wonderful views of the gardens. The stables were built in 1803 and 1857. Hampton was famous for breeding and racing horses beginning in the late 1700s. The Ridgely family cemetery is on the property.

Towson University. 8000 York Road. The university was founded in 1866 to prepare teachers for the public schools. Towson was originally located in Baltimore and was moved here in 1915.

Asian Arts Center-Roberts Gallery. Towson University. 410-830-2807

Goucher College. Rte. 146. The college is located on 300 acres that were purchased in 1935. The college originally opened as the Women's College of Baltimore, a Methodist college, in 1888 at St. Paul and 23$^{rd}$ Streets in Baltimore. In 1914 the college became nonsectarian and the name was changed to Goucher College in honor of the former president of the college, John F. Goucher.

*Lodging:*

Burkshire Guest Suites & Conference Center. 10 W. Burke Avenue. 410-324-8100
Days Inn. 8801 Loch Raven Boulevard. 410-882-0900
Holiday Inn Cornwell Bridge. 1100 Cornwell Bridge Road. 410-823-4410
Ramada Inn. 8712 Loch Raven Boulevard. 410-823-8750
Sheraton. 903 Dulaney Valley Road. 410-321-7400

*Dining:*

Café Troia. 28 W. Allegheny Avenue. 410-337-0133
Orchard Market & Café. 8815 Orchard Tree Lane. 410-339-7700
Casa Mia. 40 York Road. 410-321-8707
Mahi Mahi Japanese Restaurant. 22 W. Allegheny Avenue. 410-825-2181
StraPazza. 12 W. Allegheny Avenue. 410-296-5577
Souris' Saloon. 537 York Road. 410-296-1997
F. Scott Black's Dinner Theatre. 100 E. Chesapeake Avenue. 410-321-6595
Wolford's European Bakery & Deli. 31 W. Chesapeake Avenue. 410-828-4760
Cedar Deli. 246 Burke Avenue. 410-823-3326. Good Middle Eastern food
Kabob Hut. 13 Allegheny Avenue. 410-821-8005
Bill Bateman's Bistro. 7800 York Road. 410-296-2737
Crackpot Seafood Restaurant. 8102 Loch Raven Blvd. 410-828-1095
Fisherman's Wharf. 826 Dulaney Valley Road. 410-337-2909
Rigatoni's. 204 E. Joppa Road. 410-821-8888
Frisco Burritos. 3 W. Chesapeake Avenue. 410-296-4004
Hampton's of Towson. 204 E. Joppa Road. 410-821-8888
The Melting Pot. 418-420 York Road. 410-8216358
Orient. 319 York Road. 410-296-9000
Golden Gate Noodle House. 6-8 Allegheny Avenue. 410-337-2557
Purim Oak. 321 York Road. 410-583-7770
Sander's Corner. 2260 Cromwell Bridge Road. 410-825-5187

That's Amore. 720 Kenilworth Drive. 410-825-5255
Rainforest Café. Towson Town Center. 410-321-0300

# Ruxton

Ruxton was first noted in 1694 in the Maryland Archives when Thomas Hooker
was granted a patent between what is now known as the area around Charles
Street and Falls Road. In the 1700s this became a very popular area to build
summer homes, outside the city of Baltimore. Lake Roland is in the center of the
area.

In the late 18th c Nicholas Ruxton Moore, a Revolutionary War officer and later
Maryland Congressman owned the farm just east of the Ruxton railroad bridge.

**Attractions**

St. John's Church. Bellona Avenue. The original log house was built in 1835 and
was destroyed by fire c1876. The present church was erected in 1886 in the
Gothic Revival style. The church was for African-Americans who lived on
nearby plantations or owned houses along Falls Road. The church is listed on the
National Register of Historic Places.

Tyrconnell. Woodbrook Lane. Private. The house was built in 1826 for John
O'Connell, son of Capt. O'Connell whose family was in the China trade business
and established Canton in Baltimore.

# Parkville

Parkville was originally called Lavender Hill.

*Dining*

Valley View Inn. 8712 Satyr Hill Road. 410-668-0255
Perring Place. Perring Parkway at McLean Blvd. 410-661-0630
El Salto. 8816 Waltham Woods Road. 410-668-3980

# Carney

*Dining*

The Barn Restaurant & Crab House. 9527 Harford Road. 410-882-6182

# White Marsh

White Marsh was originally named Cowenton when it was a station for the B&O Railroad. Several large quarries were mined for sand and gravel.

*Lodging*

Hilton Garden Inn White Marsh. 5015 Campbell Blvd. 410-427-0600
Hampton Inn. 8225 Town Center Drive. 410-931-2200

*Dining*

Red Brick Station Restaurant & Brew Pub. 8149 Honeygo Boulevard. 410-931-7827
Bayou Blues. 8133-A Honeygo Boulevard. 410-931-BLUE
Della Rose's Avenue Tavern. 8153-A Honeygo Boulevard. 410-933-8861
Williamsburg Inn. 11131 Pulaski Highway. 410-335.3172

# Chase

Chase was named for Charles Chase who came from New England to collect a debt and received land instead. Mr. Chase was related to Samuel Chase, a Signer of the Declaration of Independence.

*Dining*

The Corner Stable. 3321 Eastern Avenue. 410-238-7204

# Middle River

Glenn Martin bought a 1200 acre farm on the Middle River in 1928 to be used as a sportsmen's club. Though born in Iowa in 1886, he had taught himself how to fly. He built his first airplane factory in California in 1917 and then one in Cleveland. However he wanted to be on the East Coast. After purchasing the farm he built an airplane company and within a year had employed over 1,000 people. The plant expanded in the 1930s and began producing bombers for France and England, and by 1942 was the largest airplane manufacturer in the United States. Mr. Martin is still remembered today with the Lockheed Martin plant on the Middle River, the Glenn L. Martin State Airport, and the Glenmar Sailing Association.

This area was also the site of the first Bethlehem Steel mill which was built on the Back River in 1886. The mill expanded to Sparrows Point on the Patapsco River in the early 1900s and was the largest steel mill in the United States.

**Attractions**

Glenn Martin Aviation Museum. 701 Wilson Point Road. 410-682-6122

*Dining*

Crab Quarters. 2909 Eastern Boulevard. 410-686-2222

# Essex

Essex began to grow as a community after 1914 when the Glenn Martin plant opened.

**Attractions**

Ballestone Manor House. 1935 Back River Neck Road. 410-887-0218. The house dates from 1780-1880.

Heritage Society of Essex & Middle River. 516 Eastern Boulevard. 410-574-6934

*Lodging*

Bauernschmidt Manor B&B. 2316 Bauernschmidt Drive. 410-687-2223

*Dining*

A-1 Crab Haven. 1600 Old Eastern Avenue. 410-687-6000
Al's Seafood. 1551 Eastern Boulevard. 410-687-3264
River Watch Restaurant and Marina. 207 Nanticoke Road. 410-687-1422
Cactus Willie's. 7940 Eastern Avenue. 410-282-8268.
Crew's Quarters. 534 Riverside Drive. 410-780-3938
Schultz's 1732 Old Eastern Avenue. 410-687-1020
Carolina Gardens. 1625 Holly Tree Road. 410-335-7775
Decoys. 1110 Beech Drive. 410-391-5798

# Bowley's Quarters

Bowley's Quarters was named for Captain Daniel Bowley, born in Gloucestershire, England in 1715, who had planned on settling in Jamaica, but when his ship collided with another ship, was brought to America.

*Dining*

Wild Duck Café. Maryland Marina. 410-335-2121

# Dundalk

In 1886 the Pennsylvania Steel Company established a foundry. In 1895 William McShane established a bell factory and named the town for Dundalk, Ireland. Later in 1916 Bethlehem Steel purchased 1,000 acres to house their workers at Sparrows Point. Today there are not only steel mills, but also the Dundalk Marine Terminal.

**Attractions**

Battle Acre Monument. 3219 Old North Point Road. 410-583-7313. The monument is dedicated to the 5th Regiment's defense against the British in 1814.

*Dining*

Captain Harvey's Submarines. 3435 Dundalk Avenue. 410-284-7772
Costa's Inn. 4100 North Point Boulevard. 410-477-1975

Mariners Landing. 601 Wise Avenue. 410-477-1261
Ever Spring Chinese Restaurant. 1786 Merritt Boulevard. 410-284-5176

# Baltimore

Baltimore has its own guidebooks and history, but there are several special places to be visited that are pertinent to the history of the Western Shore of Maryland. These are highlighted in this section.

Baltimore was laid out by the Legislature in 1729 on land owned by Charles Carroll. Early on it was a local inspection port. In 1745 Jones-Town, which was laid out in 1732, became part of Baltimore. Beginning in the 1750s wheat was exported to England and the West Indies. This brought about the development of the city, and by 1801 Baltimore was the third largest city in the nation.

The name comes from the Calvert family who became the Lord Baltimores. George Calvert became Lord Baltimore of the Barony of Baltimore in Ireland in 1625.

The first Protestant Episcopal Parish Church was built in 1739 at what is now St. Paul's Church, Charles and Saratoga Streets. In 1761 a market house and town hall were built at Gay and Baltimore Streets. Charles Carroll built the first of the grand Baltimore homes. "Mount Clare" was not in an "ideal" section of Baltimore and the family soon lived elsewhere. In 1752 Baltimore had 25 wooden houses, and reached a population of 30,000 in 1800. In 1768 Baltimore was made the county seat. A courthouse was erected at the site of the present Battle Monument.

Much of the downtown area of Baltimore was destroyed by fire in 1904. Today the downtown is thriving, thanks mainly to the Rouse family and their development of the harbor front, and a wonderful inner city that has elegant structures and private homes.

## Attractions

Carroll Mansion (Baltimore City Life Museums). 800 East Lombard Street. 410-396-3523. This home was built by Charles Carroll of Carrollton, the last surviving signer of the Declaration of Independence, who wintered in the Federal-era mansion from 1820 until his death in 1832. His granddaughter, Mary Caton, was considered one of the most beautiful women in Baltimore. She married Robert Patterson whose sister at the time was married to Jerome, brother of Napoleon Bonaparte. Their grandson Charles J. Bonaparte served as U.S

Secretary of the Navy and Attorney General in Theodore Roosevelt's cabinet. After Mr. Patterson's death she moved to England and married the Marquess Wellesley, the Duke of Wellington's brother.

Baltimore Maritime Museum. Inner Harbor. 410-396-3854. The museum has three historic ships, including the lightship *Chesapeake* and the Coast Guard cutter *Taney*, named for Roger Brooke Taney, Chief Justice of the United States, whose statue is at the State House in Annapolis. The *Taney* is the only warship still afloat that saw action December 7, 1941 at Pearl Harbor.

Fort McHenry National Monument. E. Fort Avenue. 410-962-4290. The fort was named for James McHenry who served as President George Washington's first Secretary of War. At the time of the War of 1812 Major George Armistead ordered a large flag that would not be missed by the British. Mary Pickersgill made the 42 by 30 foot flag that flew over the fort when the British attacked.

**Fort McHenry**

In September 1814, Francis Scott Key, a graduate of St. John's College, Annapolis, wrote the "Star Spangled Banner". At the time he was a lawyer and had set out from Washington with Col. John S. Skinner, U.S. Commissioner General of Prisoners, to seek the release of Dr. William Beanes, arrested for allegedly violating a pledge of good conduct after the Battle of Bladensburg. They had sailed from Washington on September 5 and reached the British fleet on the 7th. After spending several days in negotiations, the release of Dr. Beanes was arranged. However, because they had learned the British had planned to attack Baltimore they were detained until after the assault. Francis Scott Key, Col. Skinner and Dr. Beane witnessed the bombardment of Baltimore from the deck of a U.S. truce ship. Mr. Key jotted down the poem and finished it on September 16th. It was first titled "Defence of Fort McHenry", and published the next day. The poem was then sung to the tune of "To Anacreon in Heaven". The song became the National Anthem in 1931. The original manuscript is owned by the Baltimore Historical Society. The original flag hangs in the Smithsonian Institution in Washington, DC.

During the Civil War Union soldiers used the fort as a prison camp for the detention of Confederate soldiers, Southern sympathizers, and political prisoners. From 1917 to 1923 U.S. Army General Hospital No. 2 was located here to serve World War I troops. During World War II part of the 43 acre park was used by the U.S. Coast Guard. The National Park Service began administration of the park in 1933.

Over the years granite slabs could be spotted off Fort McHenry. Recently divers using a forklift were able to retrieve six of these slabs that Northern troops used to support their artillery during the Civil War. Each is four to six feet long and weighs about 500 pounds. They were stationed on an overlook and formed a semicircular stage so that the soldiers could maneuver oversized weapons that they aimed at Baltimore. The stones were installed in 1842, used during the Civil War and then discarded during renovations in 1939. The project was undertaken by the Maryland Underwater Services, a private organization for divers.

Baltimore Civil War Museum. 601 President Street. 410-385-5188. The museum is in part of a former train station that was a stop on the Underground Railroad.

The Star-Spangled Banner Flag House. 844 East Pratt Street. Home of Mary Pickersgill who made the 30 X 42 foot flag that flew over Ft. McHenry on September 13, 1814 when Francis Scott Key wrote the "Star Spangled Banner".

"Pride of Baltimore II". Baltimore Harbor. The Pride is a replica of 1812 Baltimore sailing clipper.

Constellation. The Constellation was built in Baltimore in 1797 and was the first ship in the U.S. Navy. She served in the War of 1812. She was recently renovated and brought back to Baltimore.

SS John W. Brown. Highlandtown Station. 410-661-1550. Tours are given on this World War II Liberty Ship, one of only two still left.

The National Aquarium. 501 Pratt Street. 410-576-3800. The former Director was Nicholas Brown, a graduate of the U.S. Naval Academy in Annapolis. The author is also a descendant of the Brown family of Rhode Island.

Maryland Historical Society. Monument Street. 410-625-3750. The society maintains an excellent collection on Maryland memorabilia and the original manuscript of "The Star Spangled Banner".

Peale Museum. 225 Holliday Street. The structure was built by Rembrandt Peale in 1813 in memory of his father Charles Willson Peale. In 1816 the first use of gas lighting was demonstrated here.

**Mount Clare Mansion**

Mount Clare Museum House. 1500 Washington Boulevard. 410-837-3262. The house was built beginning in 1756 and finished in 1760 for Charles Carroll the Barrister, author of the Maryland Declaration of Independence and member of the Continental Congress. He had studied in England and most of the materials used in building the house were sent from there. He also maintained a home in

Annapolis, now demolished but said to resemble the Jonas Greene House. He married Margaret Tilghman, his cousin.

In 1766 Charles Carroll contributed to a purse to enable Charles Willson Peale, a saddle maker in Annapolis, to study painting in England. Mr. Peale was to paint oils of the home in 1775, and later portraits of Mr. and Mrs. Carroll that are presently in the Mount Clare collection.

The house was dramatically changed to a grand Palladium home in 1766-67, influenced by the Upton Scott and Ridout homes in Annapolis. When Annapolis was laid out in 1683-84, it was divided into 100 one-acre lots. At the time of the Barrister's death he owned seven of these.

On July 4, 1828 Charles Carroll of Carrollton, aged 90, laid the cornerstone of the Baltimore and Ohio Railroad at Mount Clare. In 1829, also at Mount Clare, the New York inventor, Peter Cooper began to build his experimental locomotive, the *Tom Thumb*.

The furnishings of the house are presently maintained by the National Society of Colonial Dames of America in the State of Maryland.

Shot Tower. The building was built in 1829.

Baltimore Museum of Art. Art Museum Drive at North Charles and 31st Streets. 410-396-7100. The museum has an excellent art collection and fine Baltimore pieces.

Baltimore Museum of Industry. 1415 Key Highway. 410-727-4808. The museum is located in an 1865 oyster cannery. Exhibits include food canning, the Bunting Pharmacy where Noxema was invented, and learn about the city that developed the world's first disposable bottle cap, the first umbrella factory, world's first typesetting machine, invention of modern radar, and a host of other Baltimore firsts. The *S.T. Baltimore*, once the Mayor's tugboat and the only operating steam tug on the Eastern Coast, is on display. This museum is a "must visit" for all ages !!!

Great Blacks in Wax Museum. 1601 E. North Avenue. 410-563-3404. "Into the Hold: The Slave Ship Experience"

Eubie Blake National Jazz Institute and Cultural Center. 34 Market Place. 410-625-3113. Eubie Blake, Billie Holliday, and Cab Calloway have permanent displays.

Jewish Museum of Maryland. 15 Lloyd Street. 410-732-6400

The Carrollton Viaduct over Gwynns Falls was built in 1829 and was the first stone masonry bridge in the United States. The viaduct was named for Charles Carroll of Carrollton.

B&O Railroad Museum. 901 W. Pratt Street. 410-752-2490. This is the oldest railroad station in the United States. The Baltimore and Ohio Railroad left from here in 1830 to go to Ellicott's Mills.

Babe Ruth Birthplace/Baltimore Oriole Museum. 216 Emery Street. 410-727-1539

Walters Art Gallery. 600 North Charles Street. 410-547-9000. The museum is one of the very finest small art museums in the U.S. The collection was amassed by William T. and Henry Walters who made their fortune through railroads.

Johns Hopkins University. N. Charles and 34th Streets. The university was founded in 1876. Johns Hopkins at his death left an endowment to found the university and hospital. The university was opened as the U.S.' first pure research institution. The School of Medicine was the first to require a baccalaureate degree and the first to admit women.

Evergreen House. 4545 N. Charles Street. 410-516-0341. The house and gardens belonged to John Garrett of the B&O Railroad. The Garrett family owned the house from 1878 to 1943. The elegant Italianate home has 48 rooms and is on 26 acres. The house now belongs to Johns Hopkins University. Tea is served Tuesday and Thursday afternoons by appointment.

Homewood House Museum. 3400 Charles Street. On the campus of Johns Hopkins University. 410-516-5589. In 1800 Charles Carroll purchased the property as part of a 130 acre tract known as Liliendale and gave it as a present to his son Charles Carroll, Jr. upon his marriage to Harriet Chew of Philadelphia. The Federal style house was constructed 1801-06. No architect was mentioned in the records, and it is assumed Charles Carroll designed the house and worked with the carpenters Robert and William Edwards. The design is also seen in many of the buildings on the Johns Hopkins campus. An extensive orchard and gardens were once on the property. The perennial gardens contain plants are might have been representative of this region.

Behind the site was a dormitory built for a boy's school that operated at Homewood from 1897-1910. The barn was built c1809 and is now a theater. The late Robert Merrick who lived in the house as a graduate student endowed the restoration of Homewood. The original 130 acres make up the Johns Hopkins campus.

**Homewood**

Morgan State University. The university was founded in 1867 as the Biblical Institute for Blacks.

Peabody Conservatory of Music. 1 E. Mount Vernon Place. 410-659-8124. George Peabody founded the institute in 1857.

Mother Seton House. 600 N. Paca Street. The house was built in 1807 and occupied by Mother Seton 1808-09.

H.L. Mencken House. 1524 Hollins Street. The University of Maryland now owns the house. Mencken's books and papers are at the Enoch Pratt Library.

Enoch Pratt Library. 400 Cathedral Street. The library was founded in 1886 by philanthropist Enoch Pratt. The building dates from 1933.

Poe House. 203 Amity Street. Edgar Allen Poe lived here 1832-35.

Basilica of the Assumption. Cathedral and Mulberry Streets. Built in 1806, this is the oldest Catholic Cathedral in the United States.

Lloyd Street Synagogue. Lloyd and Baltimore Streets. The synagogue was built in 1845 and is the oldest synagogue in Maryland.

Old Otterbein U. M. Church. Conway Street. This church was built 1785-86 and is the oldest church in continuous use in Baltimore.

St. Paul's Church. Charles Street at Saratoga. A church was erected on this site in 1729.

Battle Monument. Calvert and Fayette Streets. A court house once stood on this site. The monument was erected in 1815-25 and was the first monument in the United States to be dedicated to those who died in the War of 1812.

Washington Monument. Mount Vernon Place and Monument Street. The monument was erected in 1815-29, and was the first monument dedicated to George Washington.

Bromo Seltzer Tower. 312-18 W. Lombard Street. The tower was built in 1911 for the Emerson Drug Company, and was the tallest building in Baltimore.

City Hall. Holiday Street at Lafayette Street. The building was built in 1867-75 in the French Revival style.

Clifton Park. This was formerly the summer estate of Johns Hopkins.

Leakin Park. This was the former estate of the Winans family that built the first railroad in Russia from Moscow to St. Petersburg.

Loudon Park Cemetery. The cemetery contains graves of Union and Confederate soldiers, Mary Pickersgill, and members of the Bonaparte family.

Greenmount Cemetery. 1501 Greenmount Avenue. Buried here are members of the Booth family, and John Wilkes Booth in an unmarked grave. Also buried here are Joseph E. Johnson, a Confederate general from Maryland; Johns Hopkins who founded the University; and the Walters family, of the Walters Art Gallery.

St. Paul's Cemetery. Fremont Avenue and W. Lombard Street. Tench Tilghman, George Washington's aide-de-camp, and Samuel Chase, a Signer of the Declaration of Independence are buried here.

Westminster Churchyard. Fayette and Green Streets. Edgar Allen Poe, his grandfather; Col. James McHenry, Washington's first secretary of war; and James Calhoun, first mayor of Baltimore are buried here.

Wyman Park. This was an estate of the grandson of Charles Carroll. Johns Hopkins University purchased it in 1902.

Federal Hill. Located on the Inner Harbor, Federal Hill has some lovely shops, restaurants and homes. A tower stood here from 1795-1895 to observe ships entering the Patapsco River and signals were sent to the owners. During the Civil War Federal Hill was occupied by Federal troops.

Fells Point. Like Federal Hill the area also has fine shops, restaurants and homes. Both areas have attracted a number of families and singles to live in such close-in habitable regions of the city. William Fell laid out Fells Point as a town in 1763, and in 1773 it became a part of Baltimore. From the mid 1700s to the 1830s Fells Point was an important shipbuilding center. Baltimore clipper ships were first built here in 1832.

Inner Harbor. For years the Inner Harbor was rather seedy and rundown. The Rouse Company initiated its renaissance and today shops, restaurants, and museums entice people of all ages to come and enjoy the scenery. Trips can be taken around the harbor by boat, or you can board the *Constellation*, a submarine, lightship, and other vessels. The Baltimore Aquarium is a highlight of any trip.

Lexington Market. The market was founded in 1782 and is probably the oldest continuously operated market in the United States.

Domino Sugars. 1100 Key Highway. 410-752-6150. The company was started in1921, and has three refineries in Baltimore, Louisiana and New York. The 1950s sign lights up the skyline with its neon lights. Most of the sugar comes from Brazil, Australia and other countries, and is unloaded at the Domino's dock.

John O'Donnell named Canton in 1785 after he arrived from China with a shipload of Chinese export goods. Mr. O'Donnell planted a peach orchard here to produce peach brandy. The Canton Company purchased the property and built wharves, a railroad, and made it into an industrial area. Today Canton is part of the Baltimore Port.

Brooklyn. The Maryland Legislature incorporated the town in 1853. R.W. Templeman, an employee of the Patapsco Company probably named the town for its resemblance to Brooklyn, NY. Brooklyn was annexed to the city of Baltimore in 1918.

Fort Holabird. Holabird Avenue. The fort was established during World War I and is named for Brig. Gen. Samuel Beckley Holabird of the Quartermaster

Department during the Civil War. The fort was the largest U.S. Army Signal Corps during World War II. Located here were the Army Intelligence Corps, the Intelligence School, and the records the records of everyone who had received clearance from the Army since the beginning of World War II. The fort was an induction center for the Baltimore-Washington area. The author's husband spent time here in the late 1960s.

Sparrows Point. Lord Baltimore granted the Patapsco River Neck to Thomas Sparrow in 1652. Solomon Sparrow, son of Thomas, built a house here called "Sparrow's Nest". The land was acquired in 1916 by Bethlehem Steel.

Fort Carroll. Off Sparrows Point. The manmade island was built in 1847 on Soldiers Flats in the Patapsco River. From 1849-52 Robert E. Lee, an engineer in the U.S. Army supervised the construction, which was never completed. In 1898 two batteries of soldiers from Ft. McHenry were stationed on the island. The fort then became a lighthouse and fog-bell station. An automatic light was installed in 1920.

## Brooklyn Park

*Dining*

El Salto. 5513 Ritchie Highway. 410-789-1621

## Catonsville

During the 1720's an area at the northern part of Catonsville was known as Johnnycake from an inn that made johnnycakes. In 1805 the county road that ran between Baltimore and Ellicott City was designated by the State legislature as the Frederick Turnpike. Charles Carroll commissioned Richard Caton, his son-in-law to lay out the new city. He had developed land and built a house called "Castle Thunder" in 1787. Because of its location on the Frederick Turnpike, the town became a popular resting spot. Also wealthy Baltimoreans came to the town to escape the heat of the city. One of the largest of these "The Summit" still stands and now is an apartment house.

St. Timothy's Church, built in 1844 is next to the site of the old Catonsville Military Academy which was founded in 1845 and burned down in 1862. Francis Scott Key studied here.

The horse-car line was established on the Frederick Road in 1862. By 1884 the Catonsville Short Line Railroad made Catonsville accessible to Baltimore. An electric trolley replaced the horse-car in the 1890s. Catonsville is home to the University of Maryland Baltimore Campus, St. Mary's Seminary, and Catonsville Community College.

**Attractions**

The Townsend House and Pullen Museum. 1824 Frederick Road. 410-744-3034. The museum has Catonsville memorabilia on display and the Catonsville Historical Society.

*Lodging*

Homestyle Inn. 6401 Baltimore National Pike. 410-744-1440
Days Inn - Baltimore West. 5801 Baltimore National Pike. 410-744-5000
Knights Inn - Catonsville. 6422 Baltimore National Pike. 410-788-3900

*Dining*

Candle Light Inn. 1835 Frederick Road. 410-788-6076
The Wharfside. 1600 Frederick Road. 410-788-1400
Dimitri's. 2205 Frederick Road. 410-747-1927
Double-T Diner. 6300 Baltimore National Pike. 410-744-4151
Indian Delight. 622 Frederick Road. 410-744-4422
Manley's Bistro. 9065 Frederick Road. 410-480-2020

# Ellicott City

Ellicott City was once known as Ellicott's Mills. Three Quaker brothers, John, Andrew and Joseph Ellicott came to this area in 1772 from Bucks County, Pennsylvania. They purchased 700 acres with adjoining water rights along the Patapsco River. They grew wheat. Power for grinding came from the Patapsco River The Ellicott brothers persuaded Charles Carroll, Signer of the Declaration of Independence, to plant wheat at his estate Doughoregan and to create Ellicott Mills, a mill town. The Ellicott brothers built roads, a bridge and wharf in Baltimore, introduced the wagon brake, erected iron works, built schools and many other buildings.

Andrew Ellicott and Benjamin Banneker, a free Black man and neighbor who had worked with the city designer L'Enfant, were commissioned to survey the boundaries for the new capital, Washington, DC in 1791. Mr. Banneker later was to build the first clock made in America and to publish Almanacs from 1792-97.

The National Road was used by the 19th c settlers to head west and as a shipping route for the Ellicott brothers. The Baltimore and Ohio Railroad's first 13 miles connected Baltimore to Ellicott City beginning in 1831. The first railroad terminal in the US was built here in 1832. The city was granted a city charter in 1867 and the name changed to Ellicott City. In 1868 a devastating flood ripped through the town. In 1972 Hurricane Agnes wreaked havoc once again. More recently the city has had to recover from a fire that destroyed some of the downtown stores.

Ellicott City still has a flour mill that produces wheat flour, stone ground corn meal, and mixes. The company was formerly called Wilkins-Rogers, Inc., and now Washington Quality Food Products.

**Attractions:**

Visitor Information Center. 8267 Main Street. 410-313-1900. The center conducts History of Ellicott Mills Guided Walking Tour April-November, Saturday and Sundays

Ellicott City B & O Railroad Station Museum. Maryland Avenue and Main Street. 410-461-1944.This is the oldest railroad station in the United States.

Howard County Historical Society. 8228 Court Avenue. 410-750-0370. The building was constructed in 1894 as a church. The library is located in a pre-1790 adjacent building.

Heritage Orientation Center. Old Court Records Building. 410-461-1944. Exhibits, photographs and diorama on Ellicott City

Firehouse Museum. Church Road. The building was constructed for $500 in 1889 and served as a fire station until 1923.

Ellicott City Colored School. Frederick Road. The one room wooden school house was built in the 1880s. On the grounds are a small building, outhouse, pump and well.

Bagpipe Music Museum. 840 Oella Avenue. 410-313-9311. Yes, there really is a museum devoted to bagpipes, the personal collection of James Coldren.

Thomas Isaac Log Cabin. Main Street and Ellicott Mills Drive. 410-750-7881. The county's oldest surviving building has living-history presentations about the

National Road. The house was moved from its original site on Merryman Street and is maintained by Historic Ellicott City, Inc.

**Thomas Isaac Log Cabin**

Patapsco Female Institute Historic Park. 3691 Sarah's Lane. 410-465-8500. The institute was built on land donated by the Ellicott brothers in 1837. Robert Carey Long, Jr. designed the Greek Revival style building. Within the park is Mount Ida built in 1828 by the Ellicott family, which serves as the Visitor Center for the park.

Patapsco Valley State Park. 8020 Baltimore National Pike. 410-461-5005. The 15,000-acre park extends along 32 miles of the Patapsco River.

Emory Methodist Church. Church Road. The church was built in 1837 and enlarged in the 1880s.

St. Paul's Catholic Church. St. Paul Street. The church was built in the 1830s and was the site of "Babe" Ruth's first wedding.

The Howard County Court House. Court Place. The court house was constructed in 1843 on Capitoline Hill, also known as Mt. Misery. The Hayden Home, later the Oaklawn Seminary, is part of the wing to the rear of the court house.

Ellicott Cemetery. Off Old Columbia Pike. The Ellicott brothers established the cemetery in 1795.

Ellicott City High School. The granite used to build the school was once part of Rock Hill College, which burned.

White Hall. Chatham Road. The early 19$^{th}$ c home is part of a land grant involving "Freeborn's Progress" and "Dorsey's Search". The main house was built between 1810 and 1820. The acreage passed from Judge Richard Ridgely to Col. Charles Worthington Dorsey, a planter and participant in the War of 1812. Mary Tolley Dorsey was born at White Hall in 1825. She married Thomas Watkins Ligon, the 33$^{rd}$ governor of Maryland. They lived at White Hall upon his retirement. The house was almost destroyed by fire in 1893, and remained unoccupied until Mr. Ligon's son, Charles Worthington Dorsey Ligon, purchased 430 acres and the house in 1900. Mr. Ligon married Harriet Ridout of Annapolis. The house was reconstructed and was passed to their daughter, Harriet Govane Ligon Hains and their son-in-law Hamilton Hains. They remained in the house until their deaths in 1988 and 1990. In 1997 the house was sold to William and Annamarie Hugel. The house was Historic Ellicott City's 1998 Annual Decorator Showhouse.

Cattail Farm. 4078 Washington Road. Cattail Farm, also known as The Farm and the Old Gaither Farm, is located on 175 acres, once part of a 2,000-acre lot owned by John Dorsey, brother of Col. Richard Dorsey. After the Revolution the Dorsey brothers founded the Roxbury Plantation and Mill near the Howard District of the Anne Arundel and Montgomery county borders. The grist mill was on Cattail Creek, a tributary of the Patuxent River. The land belonged to the Banks family during the Civil War. In 1895 Dennis Gaither bought the property and it remained in the family until 1945. The house was the 2000 HEC Annual Decorator Showhouse.

Doughoregan . Private. The Carroll family country home, is located just west of Ellicott City on the Patapsco River. The name is Gaelic for "House of Kings". The house was built in 1735-45 on 15,000 acres. Charles Carroll of Carrollton is buried here. The property is still in the Carroll family.

*Lodging*

Amanda's B&B Reservation Service. 3538 Lakeway Drive. 410-535-0008
Turf Valley Resort & Conference Center. 2700 Turf Valley Road. 410-465-1500

The Wayside Inn. 4344 Columbia Road. 410-461-4636
Brown's Motel. 8074 Baltimore National Pike. 410-465-4000
Forest Motel. 10021 Baltimore National Pike. 410-465-2090
The White Duck. 3920 College Avenue. 410-992-8994

*Dining*

Tersiguel's. 8293 Main Street. 410-465-4004.
Wayside Inn. 4344 Columbia Road. 410-461-4636.
Hunters' Lodge Cellar & Grill. 9445 Baltimore National Pike. 410-461-4990
Ellicott Mills Brewing Co. 8308 Main Street. 410-313-8141
The Trolley Stop. 6 Oella Avenue. 410-465-8546. Located in an 1830s building
Dionysus' Kitchen. 715 Pleasant Hill Road. 410-465-5989
Judge's Bench. 8385 Main Street. 410-465-3497
The Phoenix Emporium. 8049 Main Street. 410-465-566
P.J.'s Restaurant. 8307 Main Street. 410-465-0070
Crab Shanty. 3410 Plumtree Drive. 410-465-9660
Alexandria's Fine Dining Restaurant. 2700 Turf Valley Road. 410-465-1500
Bare Bones Grill & Brewery. 9150 Baltimore National Pike. 410-461-0770
Cacao Lane Restaurant. 8066 Main Street. 410-461-1378
Giovanni's. 8480 Baltimore National Pike. 410-750-7087
Sorrento's Main Street Station. 8167 Main Street. 410-465-1001
Pastano's Deli & Pizzeria. 3723 Maryland Avenue. 410-750-2302
Il Giardino Ristorante. 8809 Baltimore National Pike. 410-461-1122
RiversideRoastery & Expresso. 8059 Main Street. 410-465-0233
South Pacific. 9200 Baltimore National Pike. 410-461-2714
Shannon's Saloon. 9338 Baltimore National Pike. 410-461-4588
Sidestreets. 8069 Tiber Alley. 410-461-5577
Terrace on the Green. 2700 Turf Valley Road. 410-465-1500
Amore Italian Deli and Pizzeria. 4725 Dorsey Hall Drive. 410-740-3354
Maria's. 9065 Frederick Road. 410-461-8787
Bippy's Pub. 10194 Baltimore National Pike. 410-465-3633
Bagel Basket Café. 8450 Baltimore National Pike. 410-461-6902
The Bagel Bin. 10040 Baltimore National Pike. 410-418-8700
Little Alexander's Pasteria & Bakery. 10050 Baltimore National Pike. 410-750-7650
The Canopy. 9319 Baltimore National Pike. 410-465-5730
Cappuccino Books and Café. 8480 Baltimore National Pike. 410-461-0775
Captain's Choice. 8450 Baltimore National Pike. 410-465-6171
Carrabra's 4430 Long Gate Parkway. 410-461-5200
China Legend. 10040 Baltimore National Pike. 410-750-8880
China Village. 4882 Montgomery Road. 410-418-5855
Han Sung. 3570 St. John's Lane. 410-750-3836
The Silver Dragon. 9338 Baltimore National Pike. 410-461-1099

Uncle Y.Y.'s Szechuan Restaurant. 8601 Baltimore National Pike. 410-418-8888

Dragon Gate. 8450 Baltimore National Pike. 410-461-6744

Fisher's Bakery of Ellicott City. 8143 Main Street. 410-461-9275

Forest Diner. 10031 Baltimore National Pike. 410-465-5395

Friendly Inn. 11074 Rte. 144. 410-531-5510

Fuji. 10226 Baltimore National Pike. 410-750-2455

G.L. Shacks. 9495 Old Annapolis Road. 410-715-8500

Crossroads Café. 4900-A Waterloo Road. 410-465-9339

Jilly's. 10030 Baltimore National Pike. 410-461-3093

Johnny Star Rib Company. 4910-C Waterloo Road. 410-461-4748

House of Asia. 8815 Baltimore National Pike. 410-480-5100

# Oella

Oella was founded as a mill town in 1808. The mill closed in 1972. For years the town did not have a water or sewer system, which were put in 1984. Today the town has many restored brick and stone houses, and the mill has been converted into a shopping area. Charles L. Wagandt, great grandson of the founder, owns most of the town.

The Union Manufacturing Company was the first textile mill to be granted a corporate charter in 1808. The name commemorates the name of the first woman to spin cotton in America.

**Attractions**

Benjamin Banneker Historical Park and Museum. 300 Oella Avenue. 410-887-1087. The 142 acre park is located on the site of Mr. Banneker's birthplace and where he built the first striking clock in America. Mr. Banneker was a free-born mathematician who wrote several almanacs and surveyed the boundaries of the future capital, Washington, DC with Andrew Ellicott.

Mt. Gilboa A.M.E. Church. 300 Oella Avenue. The church was built in 1860.

# Halethorpe

Halethorpe means "Healthy Village". In 1910 the first airplane meet in the United States was held in Halethorpe. In 1927 the centennial celebration of the

Baltimore & Ohio Railroad was held on the field of the Fair of the Iron Horse.

**Attractions**

Rolling Road. The road received its name in colonial times when hogsheads of tobacco were rolled to Elkridge Landing for shipping.

# Elkridge

The Great Falls of the Patapsco River lie on the northwest side of Elkridge. The region was settled by the Patapsco Indians. Elkridge Landing was once a port where ships brought goods from England, and tobacco was shipped out. It was the largest colonial seaport north of Annapolis. Even Captain John Smith knew of the river, and wrote of the red clay in 1608. Sadly little remains of the silted up river.

In 1744 James McCubbin resurveyed the land and established a tavern on the Patapsco. The town was then known as Elk Ridge Landing. C1750 Caleb Dorsey who built the Belmont Mansion, assumed ownership of the land and built an iron smelting furnace.

In 1771 Stephen West and John Dorsey advertised goods they had imported from England. The Elkridge iron furnace produced arms for the Continental Army during the Revolutionary War. In 1781 Lafayette and his troops camped here for two nights before heading to Yorktown.

The town was a post office as early as 1815. The Thomas Viaduct, the first curved stone arch bridge built in America, opened in 1835 spanning the Patapsco River near Elkridge. During the Civil War, Union soldiers were stationed to guard the Viaduct as the plantation owners sided with the Confederacy and the mill workers with the North.

**Attractions:**

Elkridge Furnace Inn. 5745 Furnace Avenue. 410-379-9336. The inn's property was bought c1750 by Caleb Dorsey who constructed an iron smelting furnace and built slave quarters. In 1810 the property was bought by James and Andrew Ellicott who modernized the iron smelting furnace and constructed a home attached to the existing tavern. The tavern dates to c1744 and the Manor House 1810.

**Elkridge Furnace Inn**

Belmont Mansion. Montgomery Road and Rte. 103. Former home of the Dorsey family.

Historic Cider Mill Farm. 5012 Landing Road. 410-788-9595. The farm offers educational programs, cider making, hay and pony rides and other farm activities.

Thomas Viaduct. 6086 Old Lawyers Hill, Levering Avenue. 410-796-3282. The bridge built c1836 was part of the main railroad between Baltimore and Washington that transported troops during the Civil War. Benjamin H. Latrobe, the son of the architect Benjamin Latrobe, designed the bridge. On May 4, 1861 Union General Benjamin Butler's troops fortified the area above the Viaduct and on May 13th captured Federal Hill in Baltimore.

The viaduct was named for Philip Thomas the first president of the Baltimore & Ohio Railroad. In 1964 the bridge was declared a National Historic Landmark.

Patapsco State Park. River Road. The Patapsco River was the source of power for the many mills and forges that were built along its banks. In July 1868 many of these were swept away in a great flood. The state began to acquire land along

114

the river in 1912 to make into a park. In 1972 Hurricane Agnes and another flood in 1975 caused further damage.

The Elk Ridge Historical Society. 5825 Main Street. 410-796-3282. The society is located in the Brumbaugh House.

## Lodging

Boulevard Motel. 7436 Washington Boulevard. 410-799-7129
Copper Stallion Inn. 7615 Washington Boulevard. 410-799-1900
Econo Lodge. 5895 Bonnie View Lane. 410-796-1020
Exec Motel. 6265 Washington Boulevard. 410-796-4466
Halls Motel. 6775 Washington Boulevard. 410-796-2049
Hillside Motel. 6330 Washington Boulevard. 410-796-1212
Terrace Motel. 6260 Washington Boulevard. 410-796-2000
White Elk Motel. 6195 Washington Boulevard. 410-796-5151

## Dining:

Elkridge Furnace Inn. 5745 Furnace Avenue. 410-796-1578. An historic inn and truly one of Maryland's gems.

# Riviera Beach

Riviera Beach is located on the Patapsco River and became a resort in the 1920s when T.W. Pumphrey formed the Riviera Beach Development Company.

# Arundel Mills

## Attractions

Arundel Mills. Arundel Mills Boulevard. 1-866-MD.MILLS. One of the largest discount outlets recently opened in Maryland, replete with theme restaurants and Movico Theaters.

# Hanover

German families first settled Hanover in c1880.

*Lodging*

Holiday Inn Express. 7481 Ridge Road. 410-684-3388
Red Roof Inns. 7306 Parkway Drive. 410-712-4070

*Dining*

Gunning's Seafood. 7304 Parkway Drive. 410-712-9404

# Baltimore Washington Airport (BWI)

The airport was opened in 1950 as Friendship Airport. Today BWI is one of the fastest growing airports in the country.

*Lodging*

Comfort Inn at BWI. 6921 Baltimore Annapolis Boulevard. 410-789-9100
Holiday Inn Express. 7481 Ridge Road. 410-684-3388
Sheraton International Hotel. 7032 Elm Road. 410-859-3300
Sleep Inn & Suites Hotel. 6055 Belle Grove Road. 410-789-7223

# Dorsey

Dorsey was once known as Dorsey's Switch Station in 1878. The Dorsey family had settled in Maryland in the 1600s, the first being Major Edward Dorsey in 1650 who bought land on the Severn River.

*Lodging*

Best Western Hotel. 6755 Dorsey Road. 410-796-3300

# Linthicum

Thomas Linthicum came to Anne Arundel County from Wales c1658. A descendant, Abner Linthicum acquired the land now known as Linthicum, in 1801. The town is located on the 700 acre farm once owned by Sweetser Linthicum, Sr. This was platted and recorded as Linthicum Heights in 1920.

Today this town, adjacent to BWI, is home to a number of prominent companies.

**Attractions:**

Benson-Hammond House. Poplar Lane and Aviation Boulevard. 410-768-9518. The 19th c farmhouse has been restored, and is open to the public. The house is the headquarters and museum of the Anne Arrundell County Historical Society.

Historical Electronics Museum. 1745 W. Nursery Road. 410-765-0230. The museum has the nation's first operational radar. The Signal Corps Radar-270 was built in Baltimore between 1941 and 1943. This is the same technology that detected the incoming Japanese attack on Pearl Harbor.

*Lodging*

Doubletree Guest Suites. 1300 Concourse Road. 410-850-0747
Hampton Inn. 829 Elkridge Landing Road. 410-850-0600
AmeriSuites. 940 International Drive. 410-859-3366
BWI Airport Marriott Hotel. 1743 Nursery Road. 410-859-8300
Candlewood Suites. 1247 Winterston Road. 800-946-6200
Comfort Suites. 815 Elkridge Landing Road. 410-691-1000
Embassy Suites. 1300 Concourse Drive. 410-850-0747
Holiday Inn. 890 Elkridge Landing Road. 410-859-8400
Homewood Suites Hotel. 1181 Winterston Road. 410-684-6100
Marriott Residence Inn. 1160 Winterston Road. 410-690-0255
Microtel Inn and Suites. 1170 Witherston Road. 410-865-7500
SpringHill Suites. 899 Elkridge Landing Road. 410-694-0555
Susse Chalet. 1734 W. Nursery Road. 410-859-2333
Red Roof Inn. 827 Elkridge Landing Road. 410-85207600

*Dining*

G&M Restaurant. 804 N. Hammonds Ferry Road
Olive Grove Italian Restaurant. 705 N. Hammonds Ferry Road. 410-636-1385

# Glen Burnie

Glen Burnie was once known as Tracey's Station, and then Myrtle Post Office. The town became Glen Burnie in 1888, named after the estate of Judge Elias Glenn. The Glenn family had operated the Curtis Creek Mining, Furnace and Manufacturing Company which was closed in 1851. The Baltimore and Annapolis Railroad once passed through here. A tile factory also operated in the late 1890s.

## Attractions

Fort Smallwood Park. Fort Smallwood Road. The park is named in honor of General William Smallwood. The U.S. government acquired 100 acres of land in 1896 on Rock Point and erected fortifications at the mouth of Rock Creek. The government sold the property to the city of Baltimore for the use as a park in 1926.

Historical and Genealogical Research Center. Kuethe Library. 5 Crain Highway. 410-760-5206. The library has a wealth of local history and genealogical information.

## *Lodging*

Days Inn. 6600 Ritchie Highway. 410-761-8300
Hampton Inn. 6617 Governor Ritchie Highway. 410-761-7666
Holiday Inn. 6323 Ritchie Highway. 410-636-4300

## *Dining*:

Trattoria Alberto. 1660 Crain Highway. 410-761-0922. Outstanding Italian dishes
Goong Jeon. 202 Crain Highway. 410-768-9788
La Fontaine Bleu. 7541 Ritchie Highway. 410-760-4115. Banquets, weddings
Sunset Restaurant. 625 Greenway. 410-768-1417
Szechuan Café. 7400 Ritchie Highway. 410-768-8989
Michael's Eighth Avenue. 7220 Grayburn. 410-768-7901
Roy's Kwik Corner. 1002 Crain Highway. A winner in the Maryland Seafood Festival for crab soup.
Nabbs Creek Café. Nabbs Creek. 410-437-0400
The Canopy. 5 Vernon Avenue, NW
Thai-Gour Café. 7477 Baltimore Annapolis Blvd. 410-761-8399
Mo's Seafood Factory & Market. 7146 Ritchie Highway. 410-768-1000
Rocky Run Tap & Grill. 7900 Ritchie Highway. 410-760-8850

# Gibson Island

The original inhabitants on the island were Native Americans, some of whose artifacts are now on display at Salty Marks' House, a museum named for the captain who documented the history of the island. Cecil Calvert, Lord Baltimore deeded land between 1668-87 to Paul Dorrell (376 acres) on the northern part of the island; 1663-72 to Thomas Homewood (140 acres) on the southern part of the island, and to James Orrouck (190 acres) and Richard Moss (100 acres). In 1726 711 acres were patented to William Worthington. Thomas Hyde acquired this property in 1789-90. The island is named for John Gibson, whose name appeared on the patent charts in 1793-94. During the 1800s the lands were divided into three farms.

Judge W. Stuart Symington bought the farms in the 1920s and hired John Charles Olmstead and Frederick Law Olmstead to design the community and the 18 hole golf course. During the Great Depression the golf course was difficult to maintain and today is only nine holes. In 1937 the clubhouse caught fire, but was immediately rebuilt. The island was a retreat for families from Baltimore, Wilmington, Philadelphia and Washington, where they built their summer cottages.

Gibson Island has 960 acres of which only one-third is developed, and overseen by the Gibson Island Corporation. There are only 195 homes. Access to the island is through a guarded gate and is open to members and residents only.

The island for many years has been noted as a sailing haven. The Gibson Island Club once sponsored four regattas a year. The Annapolis-to-Newport Race was founded on the island. The Gibson Island Club is still a reminder of its yachting roots. The author has fond memories of sailing out of here in the late 1960s, thanks to her Baltimore friends.

**Attractions**

Please remember this is a private island and not open to the public.

Monument to Judge W. Stuart Symnington. At end of causeway to Gibson Island.

St. Christopher-by-the-Sea. Mrs. Stuart Symington, D.K. Fisher and R.E. Taylor founded the Episcopal Church in 1931.

# Pasadena

Bodkin Neck is a peninsula at the confluence of the Patapsco River and Chesapeake Bay. The earliest claim to the land was by a London merchant in 1649 for 1200 acres between the Magothy and Patapsco Rivers. Early deeds date back to 1670. Charles Carroll of Carrollton was one of the initial Bodkin Landowners. Later the property that was to become Downs Park was known as "Deer Park Farm" which produced fruit and vegetables that were sent to Baltimore by sailboat.

By the late 1800s this became the farm and summer home of H. R. Mayo Thom from Baltimore, who renamed it "Rocky Beach Farm". The farmhouse grew to a 20 room mansion and elegant Victorian gardens were planted on the property. Seven summer cottages were built and rented to other families. The Bishop family bought the property in 1937. Anne Arundel County purchased it in the 1970s.

Pasadena was settled in 1890. A silk company bought property here to grow silkworms, but the endeavor failed. The name comes from the owner's wife's hometown of Pasadena, California.

In 1999 environmentalists discovered three rare bogs along the Magothy River that are home to a number of rare plants. The plants include carnivorous species, cranberry bushes and pitcher plants. Much of the vegetation existed before the ice age 11,000 years ago. The bogs are near the proposed Magothy Greenway.

**Attractions:**

Downs Park. 8311 John Downs Loop. 410-222-6230

Hancock's Resolution. 2795 Bayside Beach Road. 410-222-7317. Open Sundays March to October. The land was patented to David Johnson in 1665, a planter from Talbot County. The tract was known as Dividing Points and had 100 acres. William Hancock is the first known person to be associated with the site. He leased 400 acres from Benjamin Hammond in 1734. The property included the 100 acres of Dividing Point and 300 adjacent acres known as Homewoods Range. In 1776 his son, Stephen Hancock, Sr. purchased a portion of Dividing Points. In the 1750s it had been resurveyed with adjacent property into two tracts known as "Heirusalem" (Fair Jerusalem) and "Peggie and Mollies Delight", a total of 135 acres. At his death in 1775 Stephen Hanock left both his tracts to his son Stephen, Jr.

Stephen, Jr. constructed a one and one-half story stone house on the Fair Jerusalem tract. He did not live in the house, but maintained it as a tenant farm.

120

In 1793 he acquired land to the west of the two original tracts and named it Hancock's Resolution. By 1806 he had amassed 409.5 acres and then called it Long Meadows.

Upon Stephen, Jr.'s death in 1809 Long Meadows passed to his eldest son, Francis who continued to farm the land, but did not live in the house. In 1828 his son, John Hancock, purchased 100 acres of Long Meadow and lived in the house. He farmed the land and shipped goods to Baltimore by boat from the family wharf on Bodkin's Creek. When he died in 1853 his eldest son, Henry Alfred Hancock took over the 100 acre farm. A one and one-half story addition was added to the house. Henry married Matilda Wilkinson in 1861 and they had four children. Two of the children, John Henry and Mary Adeline were the last Hancock's to live the house, without modernizing it – no electricity or plumbing.

John Henry died in 1962. In his will the house, outbuildings and 10 acres was to be given to an historical society. The family cemetery was placed in a perpetual trust. In 1964 the Historic Annapolis Foundation took formal deed to the property. In 1989 Anna Arundel County signed a 25 year lease to develop the site as an historic park. Archeological work has been done on the site. The projects were underwritten with a $50,000 grant by the county.

*Dining:*

Clarks Bayside Inn. 410-437-5711
Cheshire Crab. 1701 Poplar Ridge Road. 410-360-2220.
Windows on the Bay. White Rocks Marina. 1402 Colony Road. 410-255-1413.
Riverdale Restaurant. 143 Inverness Road. 410-647-9830
The Canopy. 8125-P Ritchie Highway. 410-647-7722
Double-T Diner. 1 Mountain Road. 410-766-9669
Stonebridge Restaurant. 8238 Fort Smallwood Road
Sakura. 34 Mountain Road
Anchor Inn. 7617 Water Oak Point Road. 410-437-0696
Cesare's. 8359 Baltimore-Annapolis Boulevard. 410-647-6100
Granny's Café. 2412 Mountain Road. 410-439-8200

# Odenton

Odenton was founded in 1867 and is named for Governor Oden Bowie. Odenton was the crossing for two railroads - the Baltimore & Potomac and the Washington, Baltimore and Annapolis.

Odenton is home of the Piney Orchard Ice Forum, the training facility for the Washington Capitals. The Piney Orchard Visitor's Center operates a Farmer's Market, March through October each Wednesday afternoon.

Odenton was the birthplace of Babe Phelps who played for the Brooklyn Dodgers 1935-41 and Chicago Cubs 1933-34.

**Attractions**

Epiphany Episcopal Church. 1417 Odenton Road. 410-269-6543. This is believed to be the only World War I military chapel in the United States. Doughboys were welcomed here in the spring 1918 before they were sent off to the front in France. The Bishops of Maryland, Washington and Pennsylvania planned the chapel in 1918. An $11,000 donation came from two parishioners of Epiphany Episcopal Church in Washington. Other parishes furnished rooms for $150.

The church was built as a home away from home for soldiers who were passing through Camp Meade, now Fort George C. Meade. The church had a sanctuary and nave, offices for the chaplain and living space for parents who came to see the young men off. Over 100,000 men and women passed through Fort Meade. Women were members of the Signal Corps "Hello Girls" who worked in communications behind the lines. The first 33 were sent to France in the spring of 1918.

Odenton Heritage Society Museum. Citizen's State Bank. 1402 Odenton Road. The bank was constructed in 1917 and has served as a bank, grocery store, canteen during World II and now a museum The bank building kept accounts and valuables for Camp Meade personnel and provided cash for the payroll.

*Dining:*

Hunan L'Rose. 1131 Annapolis Road. 410-672-2928

# Fort Meade

Just west of Odenton is Fort Meade/NSA. The Fort Meade Museum, Medal of Honor Library and the National Cryptologic Museum with old cipher machines and other cryptologic materials are open to the public. Ft. Meade was erected 1917 during World War I and is named after the Commander of the Army of the Potomac during the Civil War, Gen. George Meade. His troops defeated Gen. Lee at the Battle of Gettysburg.

**Attractions:**

<u>Fort George C. Meade Museum</u>. Building 4674 Griffin Avenue. 410-677-6966. The museum has exhibits on the history of Ft. Meade and the US Army from World War I to present.

<u>National Cryptyologic Museum.</u> Colony 7 Road. 410-688-5849. The museum contains articles on the history of cryptology. Included are early books dating back to 1526, a 1930s Hebern machine used for security, and the German Enigma.

# Laurel

Laurel was settled by Richard Snowden in 1658. Laurel was originally a mill town located on the Patuxent River, and called "Laurel Factory" for all the mountain laurel that grew in the area. The Snowden family also owned iron smelters and Montpelier Mansion. The Baltimore and Ohio Railroad began service in 1835 with Laurel a major station between Baltimore and Washington The Laurel Race Track opened in 1911.

*Attractions*

<u>Snow Hill Manor</u>. 3301 Laurel-Bowie Road. 301-725-6037. The Maryland-National Capital Park purchased this beautiful brick plantation home in 1992. The Manor is available for rental for special events.

<u>St. Mary of the Mills Roman Catholic Church</u>. St. Mary's Place. The original part of the church was built in 1843 with stone hauled by oxen. The 1846 bell once hung in the belfry of the Laurel Cotton Mill.

<u>Montpelier Cultural Arts Center</u>. 12826 Laurel-Bowie Road. 301-953-1993. Galleries, artists' studios, and special programs

<u>Laurel Museum</u>. 817 Main Street. 301-725-7975 The mill worker's house dates from c 1840.

<u>Fairland Regional Center.</u> 13820 Old Gunpowder Road. 301-206-2359. This sports complex is comprised of the Fairland Aquatics Center and Fairland Regional Park.

National Wildlife Visitors Center. Patuxent Research Refuge. 10901 Scarlet Tangier Loop. 301-497-5760. Open daily. Explore wildlife habitats, endangered species and hike along the trails.

Montpelier Mansion. Rte. 197 and Muirkirk Road. 301-953-1376. The house was built for Major Thomas Snowden in 1774. This beautiful Georgian home resembles some of Annapolis' lovely mansions such as the Hammond Harwood and William Paca Houses. The Snowden family established many of the Patuxent River mills. Montpelier is a National Historic Landmark and is located on 70 acres with gardens, including boxwood.

**Montpelier Mansion**

McCeney House. 402 Main Street. The house was built c1825 and was part of the original Talbott plantation. The house has a rare "gib" door.

St. Philip's Episcopal Church. 522 Main Street. The church was built in 1848. The bell came from St. Paul's Church in Baltimore and rang to warn of the approach of the British in 1814.

First United Methodist Church. 424 Main Street. The sanctuary was built in 1884 and was first known as Centenary Methodist Episcopal Church.

Dr. Sadler's Pharmacy. 420 Main Street. The building was constructed in 1871, and used as a home, office and pharmacy. The home belonged to Robert H. Sadler, Jr. whose early photographs of Laurel are in the Laurel Museum.

Citizens National Bank. Corner of 4th and Main Streets. The bank is the oldest in Prince George's County and opened in 1890.

FCNB Bank. 380 Main Street. The building was originally the Laurel Building Association, established in 1868.

Baltimore & Ohio Railroad Depot. Laurel Train Station. 101 Lafayette Avenue. 301-725-5300. The building was constructed in 1894 in the Queen Anne style, and is listed on the National Register of Historic Places. The depot was designed by the architect, E. Francis Baldwin.

The Old Cotton Mill Dam Ruins. Main Street. The Laurel Cotton Mill, which operated from 1811-1940s, is located where the swimming pool now is. The mill was built by Richard Snowden and employed over 500 workers.

The Avondale Mill. Avondale Street. The mill was built c1845 and called the Avondale Flour Mill. During World War I it operated as a lace factory.

"The Lovely Old Ladies of Main Street". Main Street between 7th and 9th Streets. The brick, stone and stucco mill company tenements were built between 1836-45.

Oliver's Saloon. 531 Main Street. The saloon is a made-over Electric Car Station, once the end of the line for the trolleys running between Laurel and Washington.

Laurel High School. 8th and Montgomery Streets. The school was built c1899 and was the first high school in Prince George's County. It is now the Laurel Boys and Girls Club.

Tapscott House. 429 Main Street. The house was built pre-Civil War and has windows topped by elliptical arches.

Odd Fellows Hall. 419 Main Street. The hall was built in 1860. The ornate 2nd floor has projecting brick pilasters that support paired brackets under a low hip roof.

Stone Factory Building. 612-14 Main Street. The building was constructed in 1895 of "twice-used" hand-quarried stones from a demolished 1840 machine shop.

## Lodging

Best Western Maryland Inn. 15101 Sweitzer Lane. 301-776-5300
Comfort Suites. 14402 Laurel Place. 1-800-628-776
Budget Host-Valencia. 10131 Washington Boulevard. 410-725-4200
Econo Lodge. 9700 Washington Boulevard. 301-776-8008
Fairfield Inn by Marriott. 13700 Baltimore Avenue. 301-498-8900
Holiday Inn. 3400 Fort Meade Road. 301-498-0900
Quality Inn & Suites. One Second Street. 301-725-8800
Ramada Inn. 9920 Washington Boulevard. 410-498-7750
Red Roof Inn. 12525 Laurel-Bowie Road. 301-498-8811

## Dining

Café de Paris. 14252 Baltimore Avenue (Rte. 1). 301-490-8111
Pasta Plus Restaurant & Market. 209 Gorham Avenue. 301-498-5100.
Oliver's Saloon. 531 Main Street. 301-490-9200
Linny's Deli. 643 Main Street. 301-953-1068
C.J. Ferrari's Italian Restaurant. 14311 Baltimore Avenue. 301-725-1772
Bay 'n Surf. 14411 Baltimore Avenue. 410-776-7021

# Savage Mill

Joseph White was known to have owned land here in 1753. The land was sold to John Savage from Philadelphia in 1823. Amos Williams and his three brothers established Savage Mill in 1822 with $20,000 borrowed from John Savage. The water flowed over a 30-foot water wheel on the Little Patuxent River to power the machines that wove the cloth. The mill wove mainly canvas for sails used by clipper ships. From the Civil War through World War II the canvas was used for tents, cots, bags, cannon and truck covers. From 1890 to 1900 the mill wove painted backdrops for the first silent movies filmed in Hollywood. The mill operated from 1822 to 1947.

Harry Heim bought the 12 building complex in 1947 and operated the buildings as the Christmas Display Village until 1950.

With the opening of the Baltimore and Ohio Railroad a station was established one mile southeast of Savage. The Bollman Truss Bridge was brought to Savage Mill in 1860 and was an early bridge for the B & O Railroad line.

Today Savage Mill has nine remaining buildings. The mill houses around the complex are privately owned and are included as part of the surrounding historic district. The Mill, a Historic Landmark, was placed on the National Register of Historic Places in 1974. Howard County owns and maintains Savage Park.

**Savage Mill and Bollman Truss Bridge**

*Attractions*

Bollman Truss Bridge. This iron truss bridge spans the Middle Patuxent River and was designed by Wendel Bollman. The design of the bridge was used throughout the United States and Europe. Rust however, destroyed most of the bridges. This is one of the few still remaining.

Historic Savage Mill. The mill was built 1821-22 and used until 1947. From 1948-51 Christmas ornaments were made here. It now has very nice shops and restaurants.

Savage Manor House. The house was built in 1840 for the cotton mill's first manager.

*Dining:*

Ma's Kettle. 8949 Baltimore Street. 301-725-8838
Ruby Buttons. Historic Savage Mill. 301-776-9057
Savage Mill Café. Historic Savage Mill. 301-724-0060

# Annapolis Junction

This town is not adjacent to Annapolis, but 3½ miles northeast of Laurel. A line of the B&O Railroad passed through here to Annapolis. Annapolis Junction was once called Centralia as it was midway between Washington, Annapolis and Baltimore.

# Dobbins Island

Dobbins Island, located in the Magothy River, was once home to Native Americans, whose artifacts have been dated back 8,000 years. The island may have been a summer camp for them. Later the island was called Dutch Ship Island because of a wreck visible on its shores. In the 1800s the island was a working tobacco plantation. During Prohibition the island was a drop spot for bootleggers. Presently the island is privately owned, but preservationists have been working to preserve it as part of the Magothy River Greenway. Over the years the island has eroded, but people still return to anchor or hike and enjoy the scenery.

# Millersville

*Dining*

Mediterranean Deli. 489 Old Mill Road. 410-987-6004

# Severna Park

In 1648 Christopher Randall acquired a land grant of 2600 acres, named "Randall's Purchase", that was later to become Severna Park. The area is surrounded by the Chesapeake Bay, the Magothy and Severn Rivers. In the early 1900's Baltimoreans came here as a summer retreat. Severna Park had a post office, general store, railroad station, truck farms and a few residents. The town now has a population of over 34,000, many of whom commute to Baltimore or Washington. Many of the homes were built prior to the 1960s, although it has been popular recently with very large homes going up.

## Attractions

Severna Park Railroad Station. Riggs Avenue. The earliest station was a small shed. In 1896 Elizabeth and Tom Boone sold a piece of their land to the Baltimore and Annapolis Short Line Railroad which became Boone Station, completed in 1919. In 1921 the name was changed to Severna Park. Many homes grew up around this area. In 1950 the last train made its run, and the Severna Park Post Office remained in the building until 1951. The station was then used for classrooms from the overfilled elementary school. In 1956 it became the Severna Park Public Library and today is home to the Severna Park Model Railroad Club.

## *Dining:*

O'Shea's Pub. Benfield and Jumpers Hole Roads. 410-315-8055
Moulin de Paris. 578 Benfield Road. 410-647-7699
The Big Bean coffee shop. Riggs Road
Café Boulevard. 548 Baltimore Annapolis Boulevard
Szechuan Inn. 550 Benfield Road. 410-544-0227.
Woodfire. 580 P Ritchie Highway. 410-315-8100.
Garry's Grill. 553 B&A Blvd. 410-544-0499
Café Bretton. 849 Baltimore-Annapolis Blvd. 410-647-8222
Chocolates from the Heart. 562 B Ritchie Highway. 410-544-4240.
Romilo's. 478 Ritchie Highway. 410-544-6188
Café Mezzanotte. 760 Ritchie Highway. 410-647-1100
Rivera's Mexican Café. 594 Benfield Road. 410-544-4102
Kyoto Steak House. 568 Ritchie Highway. 410-647-4500
Vince's Italian Deli & Catering Service. 550 B&A Boulevard. 410-721-1101
Adam's Rib. 589 Annapolis-Baltimore Blvd. 410-647-5757
Hunan Annapolis. 8151 Gov. Ritchie Highway. 410-544-5604

# Beltsville

Beltsville was by the B&O Railroad for Truman Belt in 1839.

**Attractions**

Beltsville Agricultural Research Center of the U.S. Department of Agriculture. 10300 Baltimore Avenue. 301-504-9403. The center was founded in 1910 and has over 7,000 acres. The National Agricultural Library is the largest agricultural library in the world. The library was opened in 1862 and is one of only four national libraries in the United States. Guided tours are by appointment only.

Abraham Hall. 7612 Old Muirkirk Road. 301-210-3788. The building was constructed in 1889 as the Benevolent society lodge for the African-American community of Rossville. The hall has served as a school and Methodist Church, and is presently the office of Anacostia Trails Heritage Area.


# Greenbelt

Greenbelt is a planned community developed by the Resettlement Administration during the New Deal. Houses, apartments, schools, a shopping center, and community center were built on the 3,300 acres

**Attractions**

NASA/Goodard Space Flight Center/Museum. Explorer Road. 301-286-8981 The center was established in 1959 and named after Dr. Robert Goddard who invented the liquid fuel rocket. NASA scientists design, test and build satellites. There are exhibits on NASA programs and model rocket launches.

Greenbelt Regional Park. 6565 Greenbelt Road. 301-344-3948. The 1,100-acre park opened in 1964. Guided walks and programs are provided by National Park Service Rangers.

Greenbelt Museum. 10-B Crescent Road. 301-474-1936. Open Sundays. The house is one of the original planned homes and has Art-Deco and Depression-era furnishings. A walking tour is offered around the planned community.

*Lodging*

Courtyard by Marriott-Greenbelt. 6301 Golden Triangle Drive. 301-441-3311
Holiday Inn-Greenbelt. 7200 Hanover Drive. 301-982-7000

# College Park

The University of Maryland, founded in 1856 by Charles Benedict Calvert, is located on about 500 acres that once were part of the Riversdale estate owned by Mr. Calvert. The buildings are built in the Georgian-Colonial style. This was one of the first agricultural colleges in America. In 1920 the state legislature made the college a state university.

The Maryland Agricultural Experimental Station, the Cooperative Extension Service, U.S. Bureau of Mines, and U.S. Bureau of Commercial Fisheries are located here. Over the years many of the university's sports teams have been nationally ranked. The football stadium was named for Harry Clifton Byrd, former President of the university.

**Attractions**

The University of Maryland. Rte.1. Turner Hall Visitor Center. 301-314-7777. The university was formed in 1920 with the merger of Maryland State College, founded at College Park in 1856, and the University of Maryland in Baltimore.

College Park Aviation Museum. 1985 Corporal Frank Scott Drive. 301-864-6029. Open daily. Wilbur and Orville Wright built the museum in 1909. The College Park Airport was the first airport in the U.S. and the first military training ground.

Lake Artemesia Natural Area Park. 600 Cleveland Avenue. 301-927-2163 The park was developed at the time of the Metro line as an adaptive land use project.

National Archives at College Park – Archives II. 8601 Adelphi Road. 202-501-5205. Monday-Friday. Tours are available of the research center, office areas, laboratories and record storage areas. The National Archives II houses all U.S. military records from World War I to the present and also has a collection of microfilm and still pictures.

Rossborough Tavern. U.S.1. The brick tavern was built in 1799 and renovated in 1954. The tavern is now used as a faculty club.

*Lodging*

Best Western Maryland Inn and Fundome. 8601 Baltimore Blvd. 301-474-2800
Comfort Inn and Suites. 9020 Baltimore Avenue. 301-441-8110
Days Inn- College Park. 9137 Baltimore Boulevard. 301-345-5000
Hillcrest Motor Court. 9122 Baltimore Boulevard. 301-441-2211
Holiday Inn-College Park. 10000 Baltimore Boulevard. 301-345-6700
Quality Inn & Suites. 7200 Baltimore Boulevard. 301-864-5820
Ramada Limited. 9113 Baltimore Boulevard. 301-345-4900
Super 8 Motel. 9150 Baltimore Boulevard. 301-474-0894
Howard Johnson. 9113 A Baltimore Boulevard. 301-513-0002

*Dining*

94 Aero Squadron Restaurant. 5240 Paint Branch Parkway. 301-699-9400
Calvert House Inn. 6211 Baltimore Avenue. 301-864-5220

# Riverdale

**Attractions**

Riversdale. 4811 Riverdale Road. 301-864-0420. Riversdale was the home of Rosalie and George Calvert. Their son Charles Benedict Calvert, was one of the founders of the University of Maryland and the creation of a federal Department of Agriculture under President Abraham Lincoln. Her father, Henri Stier built the mansion between 1801-03. Mr. and Mrs. Calvert completed the mansion after Mr. Stier's return to Belgium. Before moving to Riversdale the family lived in Annapolis and at nearby "Bostwick". The five-part stucco mansion is a combination of European and American architecture, influenced by Mr. Stier's Flemish heritage.

George Calvert was the grandson of the fifth Lord Baltimore. He maintained several plantations, and was actively involved in the State of Maryland, including serving in the state legislature.

The mansion and land were sold in 1887 to the Riverdale Park Company. The company developed the land and the house was sold to private owners. Senator Hiram Johnson rented the mansion from 1912-1929. He was a founder of the Progressive (Bull-Moose) Party and President Theodore Roosevelt's running mate in 1912. Senator Thaddeus Carraway rented the house from 1929-33. The senator died in 1931 and his wife, Hattie, completed his Senate term and then became the first woman in her own right to be elected to the United States Senate.

In 1949 the Maryland - National Capital and Planning Commission acquired the site. Riversdale is a National Historic Landmark. The *Mistress of Riversdale* is a compilation of Rosalie Stier Calvert's letters, and a wonderful book to read about the history of her era. Restoration of the house was begun in 1987 using Rosalie Calvert's letters as a guide.

**Riversdale Mansion**

Calvert Memorial Park. The park is maintained by the Riversdale Historical Society and surrounds the Calvert Family Cemetery, the burial site of Rosalie and George Calvert, their infant children, and Charles Benedict Calvert and his infant son.

## Hyattsville

Hyattsville, located on the Anacostia River, was originally called Chittam's Addition to Beall Town. The area may have been a seaport. It is named for

Christopher Hyatt who settled here in 1860. James Harrison Rogers, the inventor, lived here.

# Bladensburg

Bladensburg was once a port on the Anacostia River in the 18th c called Garrison's Landing, founded in 1742. The town was renamed for Gov. Baden. As the river silted the town lost its prominence as a port, but because it was located on the coach road, commerce continued. For a while Bladensburg was a terminus on the Baltimore & Ohio Railroad until it was moved to Washington.

On August 24, 1814 the British defeated the American troops under Com. Joshua Barney, and then moved on to burn Washington. Many duels were fought in Bladensburg and the Dueling Ground is now a park.

The first school for black children in Prince George's County, the Union Institute, was established in Bladensburg in 1866 and was sponsored by the Freedman's Bureau. The first teacher was Sallie Cadwallader, a Quaker.

**Attractions**

Bostwick. 3901 48th Street. Private. The Georgian style home was built in 1746 for Town Commissioner Christopher Lowndes. Later his son-in-law Benjamin Stoddert, Secretary of the Navy, owned the house, which was purchased by the town of Bladensburg in 1997. The Stiers of Riversdale briefly lived here.

Bladensburg Waterfront Park. The Battle of Bladensburg was fought here in August 1814.

Market Master's House. 4006 Forty-Eighth Street. Private. Christopher Lowndes, a merchant built the house, before the Revolution.

Indian Queen Tavern. Alt. U.S. 1. The house was also known as the George Washington House and was built between 1755-65. The building was used as a store and tavern when Bladensburg was a port. Jacob Wirt may have built the house. His son, William Wirt, was a lawyer, Attorney General of the United States and the anti-Masonic candidate for President in 1832.

Fort Lincoln Cemetery. Alt. U.S. 1. Several duels were held here including when General Armistead T. Mason, a Senator from Virginia challenged and was killed by Col. John M. McCarty in 1819. Com. James Barron shot and killed Stephen Decatur in 1820

# New Carrollton

New Carrollton is conveniently located between Baltimore, Annapolis and Washington. Amtrak and the Metro stop here avoiding the larger cities. The town was developed by Albert Turner who named it after Charles Carroll of Carrollton.

## *Lodging*

Ramada Conference & Exhibition Center. 8500 Annapolis Road. 301-459-6700

# Largo

## **Attractions**

<u>Northampton Slave Quarters Site</u>. 1000 block of Overlook Drive. Northampton was once a large tobacco plantation. The site contains two slave cabins, a partially reconstructed brick building, and the foundations of a log cabin. Self-guided tours are offered.

<u>Six Flags America</u>. 13710 Central Avenue. 301-249-1500. The family theme park has rides, roller coasters, a water park and other attractions.

## *Lodging*

Doubletree Club Hotel. 9100 Basil Court. 301-773-0700

# Glenn Dale

The property was bought by John Glenn of Baltimore in 1872. The town was called Glennville and then Glendale.

## **Attractions**

<u>Marietta</u>. 5626 Bell Station Road. 301-464-5291. Sundays, March to December. Gabriel Duvall built this Federal style house in 1811, the year he was appointed an Associate Justice on the U.S. Supreme Court. The 650 acre estate had a

number of outbuildings, but only his house, office and root cellar remain. Mr. Duvall was also a member of the Maryland House of Delegates, the U.S. Congress, the Maryland State Supreme Court, and Comptroller of the U.S. Treasury. Marietta remained in the Duvall family until 1902.

**Marietta – Justice Duvall's Office**

Dorsey Chapel. 10704 Brookland Road. 301-464-5291. Open by appointment. The African-American meeting house dates to c1900.

# Bowie

The town is named for Oden Bowie, Governor of Maryland 1867-72 and President of the Baltimore & Potomac Railroad. In 1870 Ben M. Plumb sold building lots around the station. The city was first known as Huntington City at the junction of two rail lines, and the station was known as Bowie Station in 1880. C1902 the Baltimore & Potomac Railroad was purchased by the Pennsylvania Railroad. The town was incorporated in 1916 and as a city in 1961.

Much of the town is on the tobacco fields of Belair Plantation patented in 1683. The first Catholic Church in Prince George's County, Sacred Heart-Whitemarsh was established in 1741. William Levitt & Sons, Inc. built many of the existing homes in the 1960s.

Old Town Bowie has number of antique shops.

**Attractions**

Bowie Railroad Station - Huntington Railroad Museum. 8614 Chestnut Avenue. 310-809-3088. Open Saturday and Sunday. The rail depot and tower operated from 1872 to 1989.

Harmel House. 2608 Mitchellville Road. 301-390-1020. The 1906 shopkeeper's house is located in t, now South Bowie. The house had been the residence and shop store for the Edlavitch family, Russian Jews who immigrated in 1888. The house was later owned by the Harmel family who operated an African-American store on the site. The building burned in 1985. The city of Bowie bought the property and restored the structure which is now used as the Radio-Television Museum. The museum has early broadcasting equipment and technology.

Prince George's County Genealogy Library. 12219 Tulip Grove Drive. 301-262-2063. The library contains over 4,000 volumes of genealogical data.

Belair Mansion. 12207 Tulip Grove Drive. 301-805-5029. The home of Governor Samuel Ogle was built in 1745. Governor Ogle arrived in Maryland in 1731 at the request of Charles Calvert, fifth Lord Baltimore. Gov. Ogle owned a home on Prince George Street in Annapolis, which is now the headquarters of the Naval Academy Alumni Association. Mr. Tasker and Mr. Ogle bought the property in 1737 on five hundred acres, which they increased to 2,000 as a working tobacco plantation. Mr. Ogle lived there with his wife, Anne Tasker Ogle, who moved to the Slayton House on Duke of Gloucester Street, Annapolis after his death. Benjamin Ogle, son of Samuel Ogle, was governor of Maryland 1798-1801and owned the house after Col. Benjamin Tasker.

Gov. Ogle was the first to import thoroughbred horses from England, two famous ones being *Spark* and *Queen Mab*. His brother-in-law Benjamin Tasker, later owner of the house, also owned the mare, Selima. In 1898 the house was sold to William Woodward of New York, president of the Hanover National Bank, whose son was to inherit the house and from whose stable came *Gallant Fox* and *Omaha*, two horses who won the Triple Crown. The Woodward Cup Race is named for this family. The stables and house are open to the public. The Woodward portraits of horses hang in the Woodward Wing of the Baltimore Museum of Art. William J. Levitt purchased the property in 1957.

137

The house has 34 rooms and is one of Maryland's truly elegant 18th c mansions. Belair was added to the National Register of Historic Places in 1977. From 1964 to 1978 the house was the Bowie City Hall. It was restored over a period of eight years at a cost of $4 million.

**Belair Mansion**

Belair Stable Museum. 2835 Belair Drive. 301-809-3088. April to October, Sundays only. The stables were built in 1907 and were home to several of Maryland's most famous thoroughbreds.

Fairview was the home of Gov. Oden Bowie, founding president of the Baltimore and Potomac Railroad.

*Lodging*

Comfort Inn Hotel & Conference Center. U.S. 50 and Rte. 301. 301-464-0089
Rip's Country Inn. 3809 N. Crain Highway. 301-262-0900

*Dining:*

Mare e Monti. 15554-B Annapolis Road. 301-262-9179.
Elliott's Restaurant. Bowie Plaza. 301-262-6282

# Crofton

Crofton was once the site of several large plantations. Jesuits who later sold 600 acres called "AynoBrightseat" to the Duvall family inhabited some of the land. Mareen Duvall, a French aristocrat, was granted a charter by Lord Baltimore to found a plantation on the South River. This became known as Middle Plantation, and still exists on Davidsonville Road. Later Barton Duvall was to buy other plantations in the Crofton area. His son, Ferdinand Duvall, was a Confederate infantry captain during the Civil War, commanding a company of Maryland secessionists. After the war he lost the land. He is buried on a site off Harrow Lane. His son, Robert E. Lee Duvall moved to Portland, Oregon and became a railroad executive. He came back to Maryland in 1900 to claim his family grave site, and then returned to Portland. There are still Duvall descendants in this area. Crofton was established in 1964.

*Dining:*

Sly Horse Tavern. 1678 Village Green. 410-721-4550
Christopher's. 1286 Rt. 3 South. 410-451-1602.
Jasper's. 1651 N. Rte. 3. 410-261-3505
Coconuts Bar & Grill. 1629 Crofton Center
The Dough Roller. 1260 S. Crain Highway. 410-451-3133
Crystal Hunan. 2225A Defense Highway. 410-721-7800
Pachanga Grill. Piney Orchard Parkway
Lucky Luciano's. 2205 Defense Highway. 410-721-7995
Vince's Italian Deli & Catering Service. 1268 Rte. 3, South. 410-721-7300
Hunan Express. 1153 Rte. 3. 301-261-0484
Hunan Express. Crofton Station Shopping Mall. 410-721-1199
Fortune Cookie Express. 1286 Rte. 3. 410-721-8188

# Arnold

During the 17th and 18th c tobacco and produce were grown here. By 1783 over 500 slaves were known to have lived on Broadneck Peninsula, and following their freedom many stayed on and bought property. This used to be an area of large farms and summer cottages, now mainly permanent residences.

The area is named for Thomas H. Arnold, born in 1825, and who bought land in the area. He was Treasurer of the Annapolis Court House and a farmer. His family donated land for a school, church, cemetery and other buildings, plus managed Arnold's Store.

**Dining:**

Deep Creek Restaurant and Marina. 1050 Deep Creek Avenue. 410-974-1408
Magothy Seafood Crab Deck & Tiki Bar. 700 Mill Creek Road. 410-647-5793.
O'Loughlin's. College Parkway Center. 410-349-0200
George's Restaurant. 1274 Bay Dale Drive. 410-757-3400
Texas Steaks. 969 Ritchie Highway. 410-975-9662

## St. Margaret's

This town is named for St. Margaret's, Westminster, London and was founded in 1692. The present St. Margaret's Church built in 1895, was the parish church for all of Broad Neck Peninsula. The property was bought from Dr. Zachary Ridout, a member of the Annapolis Ridout family.

## Crownsville

Crownsville was once home to tobacco and grain plantations. George Washington and his troops passed through here on their way to his resignation of his commission, and Generals Highway is named in his honor. It was the site of the Crownsville Post Office in 1851.

The Crownsville State Hospital is located on 1,217 acres. The hospital was originally a mental hospital for African Americans, and was integrated in 1962. The hospital is now a residential treatment facility for delinquent boys. During the mid to late 1800s part of the site was a train station on the Annapolis and Elkridge train line. A county census map shows that Thomas Crown owned property in the area and may have owned the white house on the property that was the superintendent's home when the hospital opened in 1911.

The Scottish brown plants (which bloom bright yellow in spring) found along General's Highway are found wild only in this local area. When Gen. Rochembeau arrived during the Revolutionary War with his horses, the food for them was laden with Scottish broom. The horses ate the plants, the seeds were sown, and the plants still thrive.

**Attractions:**

Generals Highway. The highway was named for General George Washington who passed through here in 1783 on his way to Annapolis.

The Rising Sun Inn. 1090 Generals Highway. The inn is owned by the Daughters of the American Revolution, but was used by Gen. Rochambeau during the Revolutionary War as one of his headquarters. The inn was built c1753 and has massive hand-hewn beams. The boxwood hedges are over two hundred years old. The inn has artifacts including colonial paper money printed in Annapolis and a Virginia half-penny bearing the likeness of King George III.

Belvoir. Off Wyatts Ridge Road. Private. The manor dates to 1690. Belvoir was built c 1730 for John Ross, great-grandfather of Francis Scott Key. Mr. Ross married Ann Arnold, a relative of the Calverts. In 1720 he arrived in Maryland as deputy agent to Lord Baltimore. His wife joined him in 1723.

Ann Arnold Key is buried on the property. Also in the same plot is Lilibet, a child, who perished in the manor house fire. The site was used for a French troop encampment during the Revolutionary War.

St. Stephen's Church of Severn Parish. St. Stephen's Road. The church was built for settlers in the Severn Parish area who could not travel the distance to St. Anne's in Annapolis or All Hallow's in Davidsonville. The original part of the church was built in the early 1800s using bricks made from clay found on the site. The Rev. Harry Aisquith became the first rector in 1839. Bishop Whittingham consecrated the church in 1845.

The church has been renovated, but still contains many symbols of the past. The narthex contains the original kerosene lamps wired with electricity. The stained glass windows are hand-painted. Woodward Hall was built in 1863 and contains many old family Bibles.

St. Paul's Chapel. Dubois Rd. The chapel was built in 1865 and is now the Annapolis Friends Meeting.

Baldwin Hall. Generals Highway. The building was constructed in 1861 where Baldwin Memorial United Methodist Church is now, located across the street. The church was built in 1897 and named for Charles Baldwin, a Methodist minister. After the completion of the church Baldwin Hall was moved to a location on Indian Landing Road. In 1982 it was moved again to its present location. The Baldwin family bequeathed $50,000 to the building for recent renovations. Baldwin Hall now serves as a center for community events.

*Dining*

Trifles Restaurant. 1397 Generals Highway. 410-923-3775
Rudy's Tavern. General's Highway. 410-849-8058

# Gambrills

From 1869-1885 Gambills was known as Sappington. It was then named for Dr. Steven Gambrill whose house was at Gambrills and Maple Road. The dairy farm, once operated as the Naval Academy Dairy Farm, is located here. The Hammond Manor House dates c1700 and was owned by the Hammond family until 1913 when it was sold to the Navy. The original owner was thought to be Philip Hammond of Annapolis.

## Attractions

Linthicum Walks. 2295 Davidsonville Road. Open by appointment. The property was named by Thomas Linthicum II in 1701. The original one and one-half story house was built in the 18th c and expanded c1840. The orchards and gardens were added in the 1920's by Benjamin and Olive Warfield King.

## *Dining*

Kaufmann's Tavern. 329 Gambrills Road. 410-923-2005. The Kaufmann family has run this restaurant for over 60 years.
Brick House Bar & Grill. 1534 Cedarhurst Road. 410-867-3400
Java Joint. 750 Route 3 South. 410-923-2221
Rick's American Grill. 1334 Defense Highway. 410-721-3500

# Annapolis

Please refer to "Annapolis: The Guidebook" by Katie Moose for information on Annapolis.

# Highland Beach

The town was founded in 1893 by Charles R. Douglass, son of abolitionist Frederick Douglass as a summer retreat for African-Americans. Mr. Douglass and his wife had been turned away from the Bay Ridge Resort because of their color. Mr. and Mrs. Douglass crossed a creek just south of Bay Ridge where they met Daniel Brashears. Mr. Brashears recognized Mr. Douglass and offered to sell him 26 acres of his farm.

The first cottage was built in 1894. The town was incorporated in 1922 and was the first chartered African-American township in Maryland. The town had its own governing body and post office. The first mayor was Haley Douglass. Besides cottages, the town had a horse stable, guest house, hotel and tennis courts. The guest house built by George Bowen in 1902 became an important center of the community as lectures were given here and informal gatherings. The hotel was built by Richard Ware in the 1920s, and converted into a private home in the 1970s.

A number of prominent Africa-Americans visited Highland Beach including the singer Paul Robeson, poet Paul Laurence Dunbar, Justice Thurgood Marshall, Alex Haley, and Booker T. Washington. Other beach communities for African-Americans sprang up after this, including Venice Beach founded by Osborne T. Taylor in 1922, Sparrow's Point and Carr's Beach. Many of the original families still return to Highland Beach and Venice Beach, but developers have bought the other two.

## Attractions

Frederick Douglass Museum and Cultural Center. 3200 Wayman Avenue. 410-267-6960. Open by appointment. The elder Mr. Douglass began building the cottage "Twin Oaks" but did not complete it because of his death. The house has now been restored. Homestead Gardens of Davidsonville donated its landscape design and building services to landscape the grounds.

# London Town/Edgewater

## Attractions

Historic London Town and Gardens. 839 London Town Road. 410-222-1919. The house was built in 1760 for William Brown, a cabinet maker and planter who also ran the ferry across the South River and a tavern (1752-1780s). The site is set on 23 acres and has lovely gardens and a rolling lawn down to the South River.

London Town was a tobacco port on the South River beginning in the 17th c, and was considered as a site for the capitol of Maryland. The town was established in 1683 on land given by William Burgess for All Hallow's Parish, which became the local church in Davidsonville. This was the site of the Arundel Court House, built in the mid 1690's and later moved to Annapolis. The community was an agricultural one, and not centered around public buildings or a church.

With recent excavations the site was discovered to date back hundreds of years earlier, having been settled by Native Americans of the Woodland Period (AD800-1600). The peninsula was used to harvest oysters, which were preserved by drying in the sun.

**London Town**

Most of the archeological work had centered around the William Brown House completed in 1764, but more recently on London Town. The ravine was known as Scott Street, and at least three more buildings are now known to have existed. Edward and Elinor Rumney operated a tavern as early as the 1690s. Stephen West took over the tavern in 1720.

Taverns may have been operating here prior to 1703. David and Alice Mackelfish married sometime before 1695 and lived on Lot 49. He had purchased the lot from the original patentee, Henry Ridgely in 1698. Mr. Mackelfish ran an ordinary and may also have run the ferry authorized by the Maryland Assembly in 1695 to carry passengers across the South River. It is known that he died in 1711 and his wife approached the court to renew the ferry license. When she remarried, she and her new husband, Richard Dixon operated the ferry and she applied to keep the tavern. Mrs. Dixon and her son, David sold Lot 49 in 1727 to the innkeeper, William Wootton. He operated the ordinary and ferry until 1744. A tailor, Alexander Ferguson and his wife purchased Lot 49 in 1757 and other lots in London Town. He obtained an ordinary license in 1756.

Otho Holland and his wife, Metable lived in London Town before 1699. After his death Metable married John Peirpont. He requested a license in 1705 to keep an ordinary. In 1703 Hester Grace (Groce?) renewed her license. Innkeeper Thomas Davis who lived on London Town Lot 24 might have owned one of the earliest. He first applied for an ordinary license in 1706 and renewed it every year until the lot was sold to Patrick Sympson, a merchant, in 1715. Unfortunately Anne Arundel County court records are missing from 1723-34 and 1773-1783, thus making it difficult to trace the earliest taverns here.

A second ferry, 'the new ferry", was operated by William Brown from near his house. When he died in 1718, his wife Elinor was granted an ordinary and ferry license. In 1719 the provincial government revoked both licenses. Mrs. Brown and her son Edward moved to Annapolis where they operated a tavern.

Stephen West, Sr. also obtained an ordinary license in 1713 and was a tavern keeper until his death. He purchased Rumney's lot and probably took over the tavern's operations. William Brown ran the tavern after West's death. With the archeological work being done all may have operated in the same building on Lot 87.

The Maryland Assembly passed a law in 1747 limiting tobacco exports to specific export stations. Annapolis and London Town were not included. Between this and the economic depression caused during the Revolution, and the silting up of the South River, London Town lost its prominence as a port around 1800.

The main street in London Town was Scott Street along which was built shops. William Brown's carpenter's shop was found dating to the 1740s-50s, along with window leads that formed a diamond-shaped window lists in casement windows that dates to 1757 and may be the oldest example of a dated window lead in the Americas. In 1828 the Anne Arundel County government purchased the house and operated it as an almshouse until 1965.

In 1998 a book was published on Dr. Richard Hill, a physician in London Town from 1720-40. He experimented with medicinal plants, some of which are again planted at London Town.

The London Town Foundation is a non-profit organization that operates Historic London Town and Gardens. In the spring of 2001 London Town began a $2.5 million project to build a new visitor center and museum to house an orientation center, classrooms and archeology lab. Included in the project is the reconstruction of the tenement house of the Lord Mayor of London, David Mackelfish. Rumney's Tavern, a storehouse and Ann Lambeth's home and garden that were part of William Brown's carpentry shop will also be reconstructed. An existing log tobacco barn will display the processes of growing, picking, curing and selling the tobacco leaf. The grant is part of a federal program focusing on historic transportation-related sites throughout the United States. The crossing of the South River at London Town was important for north-south travel.

The original settlement comprised about 100 acres. Archeological work is proceeding on neighboring properties also. A Native American campsite has been found, probably used by the Algonquin Indians from about 1000 to 1200, and the remains of a shipyard dating to the 1730s.

South River Club. South River Road. Private. The club house was built in 1742 and is thought to be oldest social club in continuous use. Gentlemen met here every two weeks for dinner. The silver punchbowl has been in use since 1746. Today the club has 25 members who meet four times a year for a traditional Maryland dinner.

Java History Trail. 647 Contees Wharf Road. 410-798-2648. Open Sundays. The outdoor exhibit is located on the grounds of the Smithsonian Environmental Research Center. There is a recreated Piscataway Indian village, tobacco plantation exhibit, dairy farm implements, and a marsh walkway.

Smithsonian Environmental Research Center. Contees Wharf Road. 301-261-4190. The area has self-guided trails, lectures, and guided tours by appointment.

## Dining

Adam's Ribs. 169 Mayo Road. 410-956-2995
Bayside Inn. Rte. 214. 410-798-0201
Surfside 7. 48 S. River Road. Good music in the evening.
Dragon House. 101 Mayo Road. 410-956-2121
Jake's Steaks. 3275 B Solomons Island Road. 410-956-4420
Edgewater Restaurant. 148 Mayo Road. 410-956-3202

The Greene Turtle. 3213A Solomons Island Road. 410-956-1144
Hayman's Crab House. 3105 Solomons Island Road. 410-956-2023

# Riva

Riva was once known as Waterview or Riverview.

## *Dining*

Mike's. 3030 Riva Road. 410-956-2784
Paul's. 3027 Riva Road. 410-956-3410

## *Chocolates*

The Chocolate Box. 126-B Mayo Road. 410-721-2282

# Davidsonville

James Davidson came to Pennsylvania from England in 1775. He served in a
Maryland regiment under General Smallwood during the Revolutionary War and
died in Davidsonville in 1841. Thomas Davidson was known to be the
postmaster in 1834.

## Attractions

All Hallow's Episcopal Church. 3604 Solomons Island Road. 410-798-0808.
All Hallow's Episcopal Church is one of the oldest parishes in Maryland and
was registered as early as 1657. The original parish was comprised of about 80
square miles bounded by the South, Patuxent and West Rivers. The main crop
was tobacco. William Burgess, a planter, provided the establishment in 1683 of
the new town for the parish to be located on the South River, which later became
London Town.

The official charter was bestowed on May 10, 1692 when William and Mary
established the Church of England in the English Colonies with 30 parishes. This
was one of four parishes established in Anne Arundel County. The Rev. Joseph
Colebatch, rector 1698-1734, was designated as the first bishop of Maryland by
the bishop of London. However the Maryland courts issued a writ of *ne exeat*
and he was not permitted to go to London to be consecrated. He occupied

Larkins Hundred, built c 1704. Queen Anne succeeded King William in 1702 and presented the parish the silver communion set. The first recorded baptism in South County was Thomas Cheney in 1669. Some of his descendants still live near here.

The present church is a lovely brick built in 1729. From 1784-1792 Mason Locke Weems, the biographer of George Washington was rector. He wrote "The Life and Memorable Actions of George Washington" in 1800. Rev. Weems concocted some of the stories (fictitious) such as George cutting down the apple tree.

Larkins Hills. Rte.2. This private home was built by John Gassaway who served in the Maryland State Legislature and was a member of the South River Club. He purchased the land in 1753.

The original patent on the property dates to 1663. Charles Calvert, Lord Baltimore and his council attended a meeting here in 1683. Thirty-one towns and ports-of-entry were established in the counties along the Bay.

Just south of Larkins Hundred and Larkins Hills is Etowah Farm, built c 1824, and once owned by Anna Lee Marshall, sister of Robert E. Lee.

Obligation Farm. Rte. 2. Private. The house was built in the 17$^{th}$ c and enlarged in the 1730s.

Middle Plantation Marker. Route 424. The 600 acre tract presented in 1664 to Mareen Duvall, Esq., a French Hugenot and Commissioner for Advancement of Trade, 1683. He died here in 1694. The plantation remained in the Duvall family for many years.

Annearrundell Free School. 1290 Lavall Drive. 410-222-5050. Open Sunday afternoons and by appointment. One of the oldest schoolhouses mandated by the colonial government was built in 1723. The school is owned by the Board of Education of Anne Arundel County.

Roedown Farm. Harwood Road. This home was built in the 1740s. Jerome Bonaparte and Betsy Patterson spent their honeymoon here (see Baltimore).

Hal Contee Bowie Clagett II presently owns the farm and is a well-known breeder of race horses. Five of his horses have won the Maryland Million. The farm now encompasses 134 acres and is the site of the annually held Roedown races.

# Mayo

The town was probably named for Commodore Isaac Mayo who served in the War of 1812 and lived at 'Gresham". There were Mayos here earlier, including Joshua Mayo who married Hannah Learson in 1770.

In 1975 Mayo Beach, a private resort for foreign diplomats, was auctioned off for $225,000. The owner of the resort, the Jaycees International Foundation, could not make the mortgage payments.

## *Dining*

Old Stein Inn. 1143 Central Avenue. 410-798-6807

# Harwood

## Attractions

Oakwood. Off Rte. 2. The private house was built in the mid 1800s by Thomas Richard Sprigg Harwood. Mr. Harwood purchased 241 acres in 1847 from the Cherry Hill plantation owned by his father, Osborn Sprigg Harwood. Mr. Harwood was a tobacco farmer and active in the Democratic Party. At the time of the Civil War he was a secessionist, and led the failed attempt to have Maryland withdraw from the Union. He owned slaves and had sharecropping tenant farmers on the property. He served as a state senator and state treasurer.

In 1866 the property was sold to Jacob Rodger Woolen and Mr. Harwood moved Annapolis. Mr. Woolen was a gentleman farmer but opposed slavery. The farm remained in the Woolen family until 1937.

Rawlings' Tavern Marker. Rte. 2 and Harwood Road. Jonathan Rawlings was given a license to keep an "ordinary" in 1771. George Washington stopped here on his way to the Annapolis races in 1773.

# Galesville

Just a few miles south of Annapolis on the West River and nearby Rhode River is the charming town of Galesville. Settled in 1649 by Quakers it was then called West River Landing. The town was an "Official Port of Entry" beginning in

1684. In 1699 Francis Wayson settled in Galesville, buying property and building a restaurant and inn. For most of the last three centuries a member of the Wayson family has run an inn, including the present one, the Topside Inn.

The only military action in Anne Arundel County during the Revolutionary War in 1781occurred in Galesville when a party from a British ship went up the West River to the property of Stephen Steward. Mr. Steward built fast and durable ships, and the British burned his shipyard and a 20 gun ship that was almost completed.

In 1832 Henry Hartge, a German émigré who had settled in Baltimore, purchased 467 acres on the West River in what is now Shady Side with many walnut trees to provide wood for his piano manufacturing business. He died before the beginning of the Civil War, and because most of his customers were wealthy Southerners the piano business died also. His grandson, Emile Alexander Hartge was to purchase 17 acres on the other side of the river 1879 at White Stake Point. The Hartge Yacht Yard is located on that site. They became renowned boatbuilders of the Chesapeake 20s (designed by Capt. Dick Hartge in 1934), bateaux, log canoes, bugeyes and other boats native to the Chesapeake Bay. In 1934 the State of Maryland asked Dick Hartge to convert two boats into replicas of the *Ark* and *Dove* to celebrate the 300th anniversary of their landing in St. Mary's City,

For many years the town was called Browntown until 1879 when the post office changed the name to Galloway. The name was changed to Galesville in 1924 in honor of Richard Gale, a Quaker planter. George Gale settled here in the 1800s and was the proprietor of Belle Grove and Brownton plantations.

Woodfield's Fish and Ice Company is now run by the fourth generation of Woodfield's.

Steamboat Landing was a place of call for Chesapeake Bay boats, including the "Emma Giles" in the 1930s.

Today the town is filled with antique shops and boutiques. Good seafood restaurants entice many people to travel down from Annapolis. The Fourth of July parade couldn't be more American, followed by a band concert and fireworks.

**Attractions**

Tulip Hill. Rte. 255. The land was patented to Richard Talbott as "Poplar Knowle" in 1659. The brick house was built c1756 for Samuel Galloway, a wealthy merchant and Quaker. The property was named for the tulip poplar trees, some believed to be over 400 years old. Samuel Galloway owned *Selim*, a famous horse during the 18th c. George Washington was a visitor several times. Today the magnificent brick home is owned by "Sonny" Wayson, a descendant of Francis Wayson.

Cedar Park. Cumberstone Road. The private house is on a tract of land bought by Richard Galloway in 1697.The property had been patented to Richard Ewen in 1666 as "Ewen upon Ewenton". Col. John Francis Mercer, Governor of Maryland 1801-03, later lived in the house, then known as "West River Farm". His daughter, Margaret, later operated Miss Mercer's School, a girl's boarding school from 1825-34.

West River Quaker Burial Ground. Rte. 255. The West River Meeting was founded 1672. Many Quakers lived in this area, but later joined the Protestant Episcopal Church. The West River Meeting merged with the Baltimore Yearly Meeting of Friends in 1785.

In 1999 The Ann of Arrundell Chapter of the National Society of The Colonial Dames 17th c memorialized the "Site of the First Quaker Regional Gathering in Maryland Convened by George Fox in 1672" with a bronze plaque. Mr. Fox founded Quakerism and refused to accept the Church of England. He traveled throughout Europe preaching his principles of nonviolence, equality, obedience to God, and simplicity and conviction of the Divine Presence within every individual.

The Steward Colonial Shipyard Foundation, Inc. Chalk Point Road. 410-867-7995. The foundation was founded to preserve the tradition of colonial shipbuilding and the maritime history of the 18[th]c. on the site of the Stephen Steward Shipyard. The shipyard served as Maryland's first naval base.

Hartge Homestead/Museum. Church Lane. 410-268-1837. Monday- Saturday 10-4. Laurence Hartge opened the museum in the house built by his grandfather Emile Hartge in 1879 on the grounds of the Hartge Yacht Yard. The museum has a piano made by Henry Hartge in 1836 and much family memorabilia, including sailing trophies.

Heritage House. Behind the West River Market. Sundays 1-4 PM. The Galesville Heritage Society has antique boat building tools, boat models, and memorabilia of the area, plus the original land grant from England dated 1652.

Parkhurst. Cumberstone Road. This private home was built c1848 by Richard Mercer, a grandson of John Francis Mercer, 10th governor of Maryland, and nephew of Thomas Swann, the 33rd governor of Maryland. Mr. Mercer's brother, William established the Mercer complex in Doylestown, PA.

Parkhurst is built on land patented to Richard Ewen, a Puritan, in 1656. The land was called Ewen upon Ewenton, later "West River Farm" and "Cedar Park". Many of the antiques in the house came from the Kitty Knight House in Georgetown, MD.

Norman's Retreat. Plantation Boulevard. The private house was built about the same time as the Stephen Steward Shipyard. William Norman, a Captain in the 3rd Maryland Militia, purchased the property. The house was patented in 1811 and remained in the Norman family for over 100 years.

William Penn Marker. Rte. 255. William Penn attended a meeting of the Friends (Quakers) at Thomas Hooker's in December 1682 on a tract known as "Brownton", which was patented in 1652 on 660 acres. From here Mr. Penn sailed across the Bay to the Choptank River and a meeting of the Friends there.

*Lodging*

Inn at Pirates Cove. 4718 Riverside Drive. 410-867-2300
Topside Inn. 1004 Galesville Road. 410-867-1321. Located in an historic tavern

*Dining*

The Inn at Pirate's Cove. 4718 Riverside Drive. 410-867-2300. Music on weekends, and specials during the week.
Topside Inn. 1004 Galesville Road. 410-867-1321
Wagner's Steamboat Landing Restaurant. 4851 Riverside Drive. 410-867-7200.
West River Market & Deli. 410-867-4844. The general store and gourmet shop is located in the heart of Galesville.

# Shady Side

The official post office opened here in 1886. Earlier the town was known as Parrishe's Choice and Rural Felicity. It once was a resort with steamboats calling from Baltimore.

## Attractions

Capt. Salem Avery House. 1418 E.W. Shady Side Road. 410-867-4486. The house was built in 1860 on the West River as a waterman's home. The museum has a good collection of furniture, memorabilia, pictures, and watermen's equipment On the property are historic boats, examples of boats used on the Bay and rivers. During the fall the Shady Side Heritage Society sponsors one of the best oyster festivals in Maryland.

**Captain Salem Avery House**

Black Watermen of the Chesapeake Living History Museum. Discovery Village: "Where Science and Technology Met the Bay". (410) 867-2100 x102. Discovery Village is a 9-acre peninsula located at the confluence of Parrish Creek, West River and the Chesapeake Bay. The Black Watermen of the Chesapeake Museum was established to preserve the oral histories of African-Americans whose lives have been shaped by the waters of the Bay. Their stories are shared through a multi-media presentation which uses the actual voices of the men and women who have made enormous contributions to the maritime and seafood industry in the region. The tools they used to harvest crabs, fish, oysters and clams are on display along with photographic and other archival materials. Historically, Parrish Creek has been the home to the highest numbers of African Americans who owned and operated their fishing boats on the western shore of the Bay. The Blacks of the Chesapeake Foundation, Inc., is a historical, cultural and environmental organization committed to sharing the legacy of African-American achievement; fostering preservation and conservation of the environmental; and facilitating the economic success of the Chesapeake Bay maritime trade and seafood-related industries.

*Dining*

Restaurant Peninsule. Cedarhurst Road. 410-867-8664
Snug Harbor Inn. 1484 Snug Harbor Road. 301-261-9771
Richard's Corner Grill. 6127 Shady Side Road. 301-261-5655
Shannon's. 1468 Snug Harbor Road. 410-867-1502

# Deale

James Deale bought three tracts of land here in 1736.

## Attractions

St. Mark's Chapel. This chapel was founded by St. James Church, Lothian and built in 1924.

Herrington Harbor North Historic Village. 389 Deale Road. 410-867-4343. At the entrance to Herrington Harbour North, Tracey's Landing are several historic buildings preserved by Steuert Chaney, owner of the Herrington Harbour marinas. They include:

- the Holland United Brothers and Sisters Meeting House moved from Franklin Gibson Road about two miles away. African American families around Nutwell paid 25 cents in dues each month to belong to the society which took care of families struck by illness or injury
- the Nutwell School, a one-room schoolhouse, first for white, then African American children also brought over from Franklin Gibson Road. Mr. Chaney's great aunt, Nelly Chaney Watts, once taught in the schoolhouse
- ancestral home of William Parran, a 2 story house built in the 1880s near Prince Frederick
- a small dairy building, c1830 from the farm of Joseph Emerich, an uncle of Mr. Chaney, that was moved from Bayard Road in Lothian
- a carriage house from Charles County
- a corn crib donated by Mark Childs in Lothian

*Dining*

Calypso Bay Restaurant & Dock Bar. Tracy's Landing. 410-867-9787
Happy Harbor Inn. 533 Deale Road. 410-867-0949.
Bay Harbor Marina. 6031 Herrington Bay. 410-867-2392
Skipper's Pier. Drum Point Road. 410-867-7110.
Jake's Steaks. 5720 Deale-Churchton Road. 410-867-8368

# Lothian

Lothian is a Scottish name, as are several of the roads located in the village. Lothian was settled in the early 1700's. In 1878 the post office was known as Mt. Zion.

## Attractions

St. James Church. 5757 Solomons Island Road. St. James Parish, Old Herring Creek, was established in 1692, although there were people worshipping in the area prior to that time. However, the exact location of the church is unknown.

**St. James Church**

In 1695 a church was built on the present site. Rev. Henry Hall was the first rector until his death in 1722. In 1704 Robert Montague, chief of the Patuxent Indians, was baptized as an adult at the church, and is remembered in one of the church's stained glass windows. In 1763 the old church was deemed inadequate, and the vestry ordered a new church built. The present church dates from 1763-65. The vestry room and bell tower were added later. Stained glass windows replaced clear glass windows.

In 1792 the seventh rector, Rev. Thomas John Claggett resigned to become the first Episcopal Bishop to be consecrated on American soil. The present rector, Rev. William H.C.Ticknor, is the fourth great-grandson of Bishop Claggett.

The church's Eucharistic service set dates to the1700's and is still in use. On the grounds is the first parochial lending library of the American parishes of the Church of England. The Rev. Dr. Thomas Bray founded the library in 1698 and donated 118 books.

In the churchyard are many old gravestones, one dating back to 1665, and probably the oldest tombstone in Maryland.

The church also founded several chapels: St. Mark's Chapel at Friendship which was consecrated in 1850 and sold in 1915; the Chapel of St. James the Less in Owensville in 1853 (now Christ Church, West River); St. James Chapel in Tracey's Landing in 1876; and St. Mark's Chapel built in 1924. St. James and St. Mark's now serve this community.

Portland Manor. Off Rte. 258. Private. In 1667 Lord Baltimore granted 1,000 acres to Jerome White, the surveyor general of Maryland. Col. Henry Darnall, who was a cousin to Charles Calvert, the third Lord Baltimore, bought the property in 1709, and it remained in the Darnall family until the mid 1800's. The left portion of the house was built in 1754 and the large rear two story section added in 1852. The house is listed on the National Register of Historic Places.

Lothian. Rte. 408. This elegant brick private home was built in 1804 for Phillip Thomas, a Quaker, for his bride Cornelia Landsdale. When their daughter, Mary, married Dr. James Cheston the house was enlarged. The house has four chimneys and nine fireplaces.

Birkhead's Parcel. Rte. 258. The private home is on property acquired in 1799 by Jerningham Drury. Tobacco is still grown on the property. The house was built in 1994, but the property is still owned by Mr. Drury's descendants.

Some Day Farm. Rte. 258. The house was known as Birkhead's Choice and was built in the late 1600s. The property was acquired by Jerningham Drury inn 1799, and remained in the family until 1952. On the property is the Drury graveyard dating from 1823. The original house burned in 1897, and was rebuilt in 1898.

# Upper Marlboro

Upper Marlboro was named in 1721 for John Churchill Marlborough, the first Duke of Marlborough, and an ancestor of Winston Churchill. The town was laid out in 1706. The town is the county seat for Prince George's County.

Upper Marlboro attracted a number of well-to-do families, including the Carroll family, who participated in theater and horse racing. Many fortunes were made from growing tobacco. From 1748-1818 Upper Marlboro maintained the public warehouse for tobacco in this area. Hogsheads were carried down the West Branch to the Patuxent River in shallow boats. In 1939 local auctions were used to market the tobacco.

**Attractions**

Courthouse. The courthouse was built in 1881 on a lot deeded by Daniel Carroll in 1730.

Trinity Church. Church Street. The church was designed by Robert Cary Long, Jr., a Baltimore architect. Rev. Thomas John Claggett founded the congregation in 1810. The present building dates from 1846.

Content. Church Street. Private. The house was built c1787 with a pair of brick chimneys.

Tomb of Dr. Beane. Academy Hill. In 1814 Dr. William Beane was arrested by the British and held in Baltimore Harbor. While negotiating for his release lawyer, Francis Scott Key wrote the "Star-Spangled Banner".

W.H. Duvall Tool Museum. Patuxent River Park. 16000 Croom Airport Road. 301-627-6074. The museum has 19th c tools and implements.

Merkle Wildlife Sanctuary and Visitor Center. 11704 Fenno Road. 301-888-1410. This is a fall feeding ground for thousands of Canadian geese.

Billingsley Manor. 6900 Green Landing. 301-627-0730. Open Sunday and by appointment. The 1740 house overlooks the Patuxent River.

Darnall's Chance. 14800 Governor Oden Bowie Drive. 301-952-8010. Open Sunday afternoons. This home was constructed between 1694 and 1713 for Col. Henry Darnall on a 105 acre tract. The house may have been the birthplace of Daniel Carroll II, a Signer of the U.S. Constitution and his brother John Carroll, the first Bishop of the Roman Catholic Church in the U.S. and founder of Georgetown University.

**Darnall's Chance**

Daniel Carroll came to Upper Marlboro c1720. He married Eleanor Darnall, who was related to the Calvert family. The house was formerly known as the Harry Buck House. In 1858 the house was rebuilt in the Italianate style. The house was restored during the 1980s and is open to the public.

Old Maryland Farm. 301 Watkins Park Drive. 301-249-6202

Patuxent River Park. 16000 Croom Airport Drive. 301-627-6074. The park has guided tours, canoe and kayak rentals, fishing, boat ramps, hiking and riding trails.

Melwood Park. Old Marlboro Pike. Private. Ignatius Digges owned this property and entertained George Washington.

Compton Bassett. Old Marlboro Pke. This private home was the residence of Clement Hill, once Surveyor General of Maryland. A chapel was built on the property when Catholic services were not permitted, except in private homes, 1704 to the Revolutionary War.

Mount Carmel Cemetery. Old Marlboro Pike. Governor Thomas Sim Lee, the second elected governor (1779-83) is buried here.

Claggett Family Burying Ground. Near Old Crain Highway and Rte. 301.

Claggett House. Church Street, Rte. 408 and Old Crain Highway. Private. The house is believed to have been built before the Revolutionary War by David Craufurd, a founder of Upper Marlboro.

Weston. Old Crain Highway. Private. The property has been owned by the Claggetts since the 17th c. The house was built between 1805-10.

Antique Carousel at Watkins Regional Park. 301 Watkins Park Drive. 301-390-9224. The 80+ year old Dentzel carousel is hand-carved and painted.

# Croom

The town is named for an estate patented to the coroner of Calvert County in 1789. Croom is mentioned in the will of Christopher Rousby in 1684 as Crome.

**Attractions**

St. Thomas Episcopal Church. Rte. 382 and St. Thomas Church Road. The church was completed in 1745 as a chapel for St. Paul's Parish in Baden. Bishop Thomas Claggett was a rector and buried here. His and his wife's remains are now at the Washington National Cathedral. The bell tower was erected in 1888 as a memorial to Bishop Claggett. Other famous people buried here include members of the Oden, Bowie, Sim and Calvert families.

Mount Calvert. Mount Calvert Road. This private home is on the site of Charles Town, the county seat for Prince George's County 1696-1721. In 1685 Elizabeth Fowler, who lived on the manor, was the only person executed for witchcraft in the state of Maryland.

Bellefields. Duley Station Road. This private home was once known as Sim's Delight. The house is believed to have been built by Dr. Patrick Sim, who had fought in the Scottish rebellion of 1715, and fled Scotland for America.

Mattaponi. St. Thomas Church Road. William Bowie is thought to have constructed this private home in 1745. The house was altered in 1820 in the Federal style.

Croom Vocational School. Mt. Calvert Road Spur. The school is located on the site of the Croom Nike Site, a former missile installation to protect the Washington-Baltimore region.

# Rosaryville

The town received its name from the Holy Rosary Church, a Catholic Church that was built in the 1850s and destroyed by a storm in the 1920s.

**His Lordship's Kindness**

## Attractions

His Lordship's Kindness. 7606 Woodyard Road. 301-856-0358. Tours are by appointment. The property is also known as Poplar Hill. This Georgian mansion was built in the 1780s for Robert Darnall and is in five sections. The property remained in the Darnall, Sewall, and Daingerfield families until 1928. There are beautiful barns, horses and special events held on the property. A private foundation runs His Lordship's Kindness.

Rosaryville State Park. Rte. 301. 301-888-1410. Mount Airy plantation, built in c1740 for the Calvert family, is located in the park. The home remained in Calvert hands until 1903 when Eleanora Calvert died. The house was destroyed by fire in 1931, but rebuilt. It was later a country inn, and is now open to the public.

# Cheltenham

**Attractions**

Boys Village of Maryland. Rte. 301. Once a private institution for delinquent boys, Boys Village opened in 1870 and became a state institution in 1937.

Globecom Radio Station. Rte. 381. This was once called the Naval Communications Station. The 560 acre site began operations in 1938.

# Clinton

The post office was known as Surratts in 1854 and later Surrattsville. The town became Clinton in 1878.

**Attractions**

**Surratt House**

Surratt House and Tavern. 9118 Brandywine Road. 301-868-1121. Open Thursday to Sunday. The house was built in 1852 for John and Mary Surratt. During the Civil War it was a safehouse for the Confederate underground. In

1864 John Wilkes Booth left some of his possessions here. On fleeing from Washington after President Lincoln's assassination, he stopped here for them. Mary Surratt was tried as a co-conspirator and on July 7, 1865 became the first woman to be executed by the federal government.

Clearwater Nature Center. 11000 Thrift Road. 301-297-4575. Live animal displays, hiking trails, nature programs

Chesapeake Bay Critical Area Driving Tour. Patuxent River Park & Merkle Wildlife. 16000 Croom Airport Road. 302-627-6074. Four mile auto tour with exhibits along the Patuxent

*Lodging*

Colony South Hotel and Conference Center. 7401 Surratts Road. 301-856-4500
Comfort Inn. 7979 Malcolm Road. 301-856-5200
Econo lodge. 7851 Malcolm Road. 301-856-2800

# Highview on the Bay

**Attractions**

Marshes Seat. Highview Road. The private home was surveyed in 1651 for Thomas Marsh, a Separatist, who settled in Annapolis in 1649. By 1684 the home belonged to the Thomas Knighton family. David Weems purchased the property in 1733. Mason Locke Weems (see Davidsonville), who wrote the tale of George Washington cutting down the cherry tree, was born here. George Nutwell purchased the property in 1860 and built the present house.

# Fairhaven

This was once a port on Herring Bay. Peaches, vegetables and tobacco were transported from here to Baltimore. Later steamboats ran between here and Baltimore.

**Attractions**

Gravelly Hill. Fairhaven Road. The private house is believed to have been built by Capt. Samuel Gover who fought in the War of 1812. The Prout family of

Southern Anne Arundel County owned the house for more than a century. The property once was more than 4,000 acres, but is now only 6 acres.

# Friendship

Originally known as "Greenhead", Friendship was founded in 1804 by Isaac Simmons.

**Attractions**

Methodist Church. The church dates from 1834.

Holly Hill. Friendship Road. This private home was built beginning in 1698 probably by Richard Harrison.

# Rose Haven

*Lodging and Dining*

Herrington Harhour South Marina Resort. Rte. 261. 410-741-5100

# Owings

**Attractions**

Maidstone. Rte. 260. Dr. Samuel Chew lived in this private home until 1735 when he moved to Dover, Delaware. In 1741 he was appointed Chief Justice of Pennsylvania. His son, Benjamin, who was raised at Maidstone, also became Chief Justice and President of the High Court of Errors in Pennsylvania.

# Dunkirk

Dunkirk is named for the estate of William Groome, a lawyer, and dates to c 1661.

**Attractions**

Smithville United Methodist Church. Ferry Landing Road. 410-257-3160. The two and half story church was constructed in 1843 in the Greek Revival Style.

*Lodging*:

Haven's Rest B&B. 1961 Haven Lane. 301-855-2232

*Dining*

Penwick House. Rte. 4 at Ferry Landing Road. 410-855-5388. Victorian restaurant with Maryland specialties.
Rusty's Restaurant & Carry-out. Dunkirk Village Shopping Center. 410-257-6966
Bernie's Restaurant. Country Plaza Shopping Center. 410-257-2446
Chessie's. 10363 Southern Maryland Boulevard. 410-257-2290
Great Wall Restaurant. 10020 Southern Maryland Boulevard. 410-257-0185
Hong Kong. 10318 Southern Maryland Boulevard. 410-257-5745
Jerry's Subs. 10290 Southern Maryland Boulevard. 410-257-9480
Mama Lucia Italian Restaurant. 10136 Southern Maryland Boulevard. 410-257-5667
Pap's Pit Bar-B-Que. 10094 Southern Maryland Boulevard. 410-257-4477

# North Beach

North Beach and its neighbor Chesapeake Beach were once resort towns. North Beach was a cottage community and known as North Chesapeake Beach, later shortening its name. "Cadydid" dates from 1909 and is one of the original summer homes. Pop's Furniture Company dates from 1920.

*Lodging*

Angels in the Attic's Westlawn Inn (B&B). Chesapeake Avenue and 7th Street. 301-855-2607.

*Dining*

Neptune's Seafood Pub. 8800 Chesapeake Avenue .410-257-7899
Thursday's Bar & Grill. 9200 Bay Avenue. 410-286-8695
Franchi's Italian Restaurant. Third Street and Chesapeake Avenue. 301-855-6410
Surfside South. 2149 Lakeside Drive. 410-741-5006

# Chesapeake Beach

The State of Maryland granted a charter to the Washington and Chesapeake Beach Railway Company in 1891. The town was incorporated in 1894. Chesapeake Beach was once a popular resort town, designed by Otto Mears and group of associates from Denver. By 1900 a 1600 foot boardwalk had been built, with a band shell, carousel, dance pavilion, roller coaster, and booths. A mile long pier was built for passengers arriving by steamer. Trains brought visitors from Washington and Baltimore.

In 1930 the amusements were moved to land and Seaside Park opened. In the 1940s the name was changed to Chesapeake Beach Amusement Park until it was closed in 1972. Chesapeake Beach still attracts people who have now basically retired here and winterized the cottages and new homes were built. The railway station is the museum.

## Attractions

St. Edmonds United Methodist Church. 3000 Dalyrmple Road. Built of logs in 1865 with assistance from the Freedman's Bureau, the church served freed blacks as a church and school. The church burned in 1882 and was rebuilt in 1928.

Chesapeake Beach Water Park. 4079 Gordon Stinnett Avenue. 410-257-1404. Beach, pools.

Breezy Point Beach & Campground. Breezy Point Road. Chesapeake Beach. 410-535-0259

Chesapeake Beach Railway Museum. Mears and C Streets. 410-257-3892. Open daily May-September, and week-ends in April and October. A railway once ran from Washington and Baltimore to the beach, built by Otto Mears, a Colorado railroad builder. He wanted a "Monte Carlo on the Bay", but most often it was frequented by working class people from Washington. The railroad folded during the Depression, and the town was to suffer from gas rationing during World War II and the closing of the amusement park. The final train left on April 15, 1935.

**Chesapeake Beach Railway Museum**

## *Lodging*

Chesapeake Beach Hotel & Spa. Rte. 261 and Mears Avenue. 1-877- Rod-N-Reel
Tidewater Treasures. 7315 Bayside Road. 410-257-0785
Breezy Point Beach & Campground. Breezy Point Road. 410-535-0259

## *Dining*

Rod 'n Reel Restaurant. Rte. 261 & Mears Avenue. 410-257-2735
Sea Breeze Restaurant. 8132 Bayside Road. 410-257-6126
Abner's Seaside Crab House. 3748 Harbor Road. 410-257-3689
Adam's The Place for Ribs. Rte. 261 and Mears Avenue. 410-257-2427
Bayhill Accents. 7628 Bayside Road. 410-257-2349. Gourmet and gift shop
Chaney's Seafood. 8323 Bayside Road. 301-855-2323
Tudie's Place. 3737 East Chesapeake Avenue. 301-855-2599

Smokey Joe's Grill. Rte. 261 and Mears Avenue. 410-257-2427
Stinnett's Restaurant. 8617 Bayside Road. 410-257-6100
Dunphy's Restaurant. 3800 Harbor Road. 301-855-5020
Vic's By the Bay. 3800 Harbor Road. 410-257-1601. Pizza, pasta
Lagoons Island Grille. 8416 Bayside Road. 301-855-0025
Ledo Pizza. 3737 Chesapeake Beach Road. 410-257-0909
Little Panda Restaurant. 7863 Bayside Road. 410-257-2545
One of a Kind Gallery & Espresso Bar. 3725 East Chesapeake Beach Road. 410-257-7580
Peking, Inc. 3801 Chesapeake Beach Road. 410-257-3333

# Sunderland

The name Sunderland was changed to Chestnut Hill in 1848. John Sunderland came to Calvert County in 1669 and settled at "Hopewell". Other members of the Sunderland family also owned property here.

**Attractions**

All Saints Episcopal Church. Rte. 2,4, 262. 410-257-6306. A log church was built near here in 1693. This brick church was built 1774-77, remodeled in 1850 and restored in 1950. Bishop Thomas Claggett was rector here 1767-76 and presented the sundial upon his consecration as the first Episcopal Bishop of Maryland.

St. Edmund's United Methodist Church. 3000 Dalrymple Road. 410-535-2506. The church was built of logs in 1865 and served as a church and school for African-Americans. The church burned in 1882 and was rebuilt in 1928.

# Lower Marlboro

Lower Marlborough was established in 1683 on the Patuxent River and was called Coxtown. The Patuxent River was navigable to the town and a ferry once operated here. The town was later named for John Churchill, the Duke of Marlborough. The Lower Marlborough Academy operated c1775-1860.

During the War of 1812, a cyclone in 1913 and a fire in 1936 much of the town was destroyed. Today several lovely buildings remain in one of the oldest towns in Maryland.

**Attractions**

Harbor Master's House. Rte. 262.

Graham House. Malcolm Graham built this private house c1744 on land that was once part of Patuxent Manor. The paneling is now at the Winterthur Museum.


# Cedarville

**Attractions**

Cedarville State Forest. Rte. 301. There are over 3,000 acres of woods and swampland. The Zekiah Swamp is located on the winter camp of the Piscataway Indians.


# Baden

Baden was named for the Baden family. Lt. Nehemiah Baden was the first commandant of the Maryland Line Confederate Soldier's Home in Pikesville.

**Attractions**

St. Paul's Church. The church was built in 1732-35. Bishop Clagettg was rector 1780-86 and 1793-1806. The east window is a memorial to Bishop Claggett.


# Horsehead

The town was a post office in 1819. The name probably comes from the Horsehead Tavern, a tavern visited several times by John Wilkes Booth.

**Attractions**

William Schmidt Environmental Education Center. Rte. 381

# Aquasco

The village originally was named Woodville and has a number of Victorian buildings.

**Attractions**

Aquasco Speedway. Rte. 381

St. Mary's Episcopal Church. St. Mary's Church Road. There are a number of Confederate crosses in the graveyard.

# Huntingtown

Huntingtown lies at the head of Hunting Creek and was founded in 1683. Old Huntingtown was attacked by the British in 1814 and completely destroyed. The creek later silted up and was not navigable. The town had been a tobacco port.

**Attractions**

Kings Landing Park. End of Kings Landing Road. 410-535-2661. The 260 acre park is located on the Patuxent River and Cocktown Creek. Activities include picnicking, trails, canoes and kayaks, and swimming.

Emmanuel United Methodist Church. 1250 Emmanuel Church Drive. 410-535-3177. The church was founded in 1867 and the present building constructed in 1903.

*Lodging*

Back Woods B&B. 2135 Deer Run Court. 410-535-4627
Ches'Bayvu B&B. 4720 Paul Hance Road. 410-535-0123. Has winery on property
Serenity Acres B&B. 4270 Hardesty Road. 410-535-3744

*Dining*

Chessie's. Huntingtown Plaza Shopping Center. 410-535-3130
China King. 6200 Solomons Island Road. 410-257-2588
John's Open Pit. 3930 Old Town Road. 410-535-5995
Surrey Inn Restaurant. 2520 Solomons Island Road. 410-535-0989

# Waldorf

Waldorf was a station on the Baltimore and Potomac railway line in 1872, and a post office in 1880. Waldorf means "Town in the woods". It was one of the four Maryland tobacco auction centers. 1949 Charles County legalized slot machine and Waldorf ended up with many gambling spots. These were all closed in 1968.

**Attractions**

**Dr. Samuel Mudd House**

Dr. Samuel Mudd House. Off Rte 5 South. 301-934-8464. Open April to November, Saturday, Sunday, Wednesday. The house was built c1754. Dr. Mudd was the doctor that set John Wilkes Booth's leg, which he had fractured, after leaping from the Presidential Box at Ford's Theater on April 14, 1865 after shooting President Abraham Lincoln. Mr. Booth and David Herrold arrived on April 15th at Dr. Mudd's house. Dr. Mudd did not realize who they were or that Lincoln had been assassinated. The two men left later that day.

Dr. Mudd was tried and convicted by a Military Court for setting Mr. Booth's leg and harboring him for a few hours. He was sent to Fort Jefferson Prison, Florida for life. However, he was pardoned and released by President Andrew Jackson on February 8, 1969 for caring for the sick during an outbreak of yellow fever at the prison. He died on January 10, 1883 at the age of 49.

American Indian Cultural Center. 16816 Country Lane. 301-372-1932. By appointment. The museum educates the public on the Pre-European Native Americans.

Linden. Rte. 227. Private. The house is believed to have been built by John Mitchell in the 18th c.

*Lodging*

Comfort Suites. 11765 Business Park Drive. 301-932-4000
Days Inn. 11370 Days Ct. 301-932-9200
Econo Lodge. Rte. 301 at Acton Road. 301-645-0022
Hampton Inn. 3750 Crain Highway. 301-632-9600
Holiday Inn. 45 St. Patrick's Drive. 301-645-8277
Howard Johnson's Express Inn. 3125 Crain Highway. 301-932-5090
MasterSuites. 2228 Old Washington Road. 301-870-5500
Super 8. 5050 Rte. 301. 301-932-8957
Waldorf Motel. 2125 Crain Highway. 301-645-5555

*Dining*

Wall's Bakery. 2805 Crain Highway. 301-645-2833.
Lisa's Carry-out. 2571 Old Washington Road. 301-705-7965
Eddie's Diner. 2708 Crain Highway. 301-870-1600

# Bryantown Historic District

Bryantown is located along the Zeikiah Swamp where Federal troops searched for John Wilkes Booth after he assassinated President Lincoln. The town was named for the proprietor of a local inn. Old Bryantown Tavern and St. Mary's

Catholic Church which contains the grave of Dr. Samuel Mudd can still be visited.

## Attractions

St. Mary's Catholic Church. Notre Dame Place. 301-870-2220. The original church was a frame chapel attached to the home of Major William Boarman and run by Jesuit missionaries. Father David erected a church in 1793. In 1845 Father Courtney erected a brick church which is now the middle section of the present building. Fire destroyed all but the walls in 1963. The church was rebuilt and dedicated in 1966. St. Mary's was established as a separate parish from Waldorf, Aquasco and Benedict in 1851.

Mount Eagle. Rte. 232. Private. The brick farmhouse was built in 1796 and the wings added in 1940.

## *Lodging*

Shady Oaks B&B. 7490 Serenity Drive. 301-597-0924
Wiltshire Plains B&B. 4710 Bryantown Road. 301-638-7773

# Hughesville

Tobacco is still a major crop grown in Charles County. Each spring auctions are held at the Hughesville Tobacco Warehouses.

## Attractions

Trinity Church, Newport; Oldfields Chapel, Hughesville (Trinity Parish, 1744). Rte. 231. 301-934-1424. Trinity Parish was created in 1744 and consisted of portions of King and Queen Parish (Chaptico) and All Faith Parish (Charlotte Hall). The original church was brought from the Chaptico Parish. A new church and vestry house were built 1771-75. The Chapel of Ease was completed in 1769 and is still used. The bricks were used as ballast on ships from England.

During the War of 1812 Oldfields Chapel was used as a campground for the British. Two of the soldiers are buried in the cemetery. (See Benedict).

In 1856 the Vestry House was used as a schoolhouse. William Wirt, the U.S. Attorney General who prosecuted Aaron Burr, attended school here.

Patuxent Friends Cemetery, 1871. Luke's Lane. 301-855-7048. This is Southern Maryland's only Quaker cemetery. There are 31 graves that have been here since about 1871.

# Beantown

Beantown is named for the Bean family. Edith Bean (Bayne) was recorded as marrying a Charles County minister in 1669. In 1683 John Bayne, a commissioner, bought the town lands.

In 1870 when the Pope's Creek Railroad was built the Beantown post office was moved to the railroad and called Waldorf.

**Attractions**

Zekiah Swamp Run. MD Rte.5. The Department of the Interior has designated the swamp area as a "Wild and Scenic River".

# Mount Carmel

**Attractions**

Mount Carmel. Mitchell Road. In 1790 four nuns established the first nunnery in the United States. The women joined the Carmelite order in Belgium, and came to stay at Chandler's Hope, the family home of Father Charles Neale, and then built their own residence. By the 1820s the farm was no longer profitable and the order moved to Baltimore in 1831. In 1954 the Restorers of Mount Carmel built the Pilgrim's Chapel. Two of the original buildings have been joined to make a frame house.

# Windcliff

In 2000 the State of Maryland announced plans to purchase 755 acres for $5.4 million along the Chesapeake Bay in an area once called Warrington. In 1679 Augustine Herman drew a map that showed Warrington, close by Dares Beach and part of the estate owned by Louis L. Goldstein, former state comptroller. However, traces of Warrington have never been found. Some county records were also lost in the fire at the Calvert County Court House in the late 1800s. Erosion also may have changed the landscape. The property is part of the Parkers Creek watershed, a state-preserved area of more than 7,300 acres. Native Americans and early colonists had lived in the area.

# Stoakley

**Attractions**

Cedar Hill. Barstow Road. Private. Cedar Hill otherwise known as the Gantt House was built c1730 with a pitched roof and tall chimneys. The house is cross-shaped.

# Dares Beach

Patents were granted in the 17th c to some of the early Puritan colonists. By the 1670's Quakers had moved into the area. Now a resort the beach has good views towards the Calvert Cliffs.

# Prince Frederick

Prince Frederick was originally called Williams Old Fields and became the county seat for Calvert County in 1722. Prince Frederick was named for the oldest son of George I. In 1814 the British burned the town. After being rebuilt, a fire destroyed most of the town again in 1882. The courthouse is the fifth erected, and was built in 1916.

Louis L. Goldstein was born in Prince Frederick in 1913. He became a lawyer, was elected a member of the House of Delegates in 1939, state senator in 1947, and state comptroller from 1958-98.

**Attractions**

Battle Creek Cypress Swamp Sanctuary. Grays Road. 410-535-5327.Open Tuesday to Sunday. The 100 acre nature sanctuary has the largest number of bald cypress this far north in North America.

Calvert County Farmers Market. Route 4 North. 410-535-9567. Open July to December Saturday and Sunday.

Taney Place. Just south of Prince Frederick. Richard Brooke Taney lived in this private home. He was a lawyer, Attorney General under President Andrew Jackson, Secretary of the Treasury, and later U.S. Supreme Court Justice 1836-64. One of his most famous cases was the Dred Scott case in 1857. He married the sister of Francis Scott Key. The British destroyed the home in 1814.

St. Paul's Episcopal Church. 25 Church Street. 410-535-2897. The church was organized in 1841 and the church built in 1842 from brick fired in a kiln on the property.

Hallowing Point Park Tobacco Barn. 4755 Hallowing Point Road. 410-535-1600. Open daily. The barn is thought to be about 150 years old. It is listed on the Maryland Inventory of Historic Sites and included in the Calvert County tobacco barn survey. An exhibit highlights raising tobacco and the implements used.

*Lodging*

Baycliff B&B. 168 Windcliff Road. 410-535-2278. Overlooks Chesapeake Bay.
The Cliff House. 156 Windcliff Road. 410-535-4839. Also overlooks Bay.
Hutchins Heritage B&B. 2860 Adelina Road. 410-535-1759
Holiday Inn Express. 355 Merrimac Court. 410-535-6800
Super 8 Motel. 40 Commerce Lane. 410-535-8668
Lyle Simmons House. 455 Sixes Street. 410-535-5393

*Dining*

Old Field Inn. 485 Main Street. 301-855-1054. Victorian inn
Adam's The Place for Ribs. 2200 Solomons Island Road North. 410-586-0001
International Buffet. Prince Frederick Shopping Center. 410-535-5500
Chesapeake Bagel Bakery. 100 Harrow Lane. 410-535-4913
Common Grounds. 738 North Prince Frederick Boulevard. 410-414-2100
The Corner Shoppe. Calvert Village Shopping Centre. 410-535-3944
Courthouse Café. 305 Main Street. 410-535-9110
Crystal Palace Mongolian Buffet. Chapline Place Shopping Center. 410-535-7557
Donn & Doug's. 1541 Solomons Island Road. 410-535-3242
Emperor's Delight Chinese Restaurant. Calvert Village Shopping Center. 410-535-3530
Finger Lick'n Chick'n. Calvert Village Shopping Center. 410-535-3551
Fortune Cookie Chinese Restaurant. 74 Solomons Island Road 410-535-3255

Four Star Pizza. 605 Solomons Island Road. 410-414-5565
Golden Chicken. 537 Solomons Island Road. 410-535-5984
Hong Kong Chinese Restaurant. 641 Solomons Island Road. 410-535-6818
King Street Blues. 545 Solomons Island Road. 410-535-1888
Ledo Pizza. 147 Central Square Drive. 410-535-6084
Pizza Oven. 198 West Dares Beach Road. 410-535-3434
Little Caesars. Fox run Shopping Center. 410-535-6000
Log Cabin Inn. 2200 Solomons Island road. 410-586-9100
Pizza Oven. Calvert Village Shopping Center. 410-535-3434
Prince Frederick Café. 1541 Solomons Island Road. 410-535-4773
Robert's Fresh Baked Deli and Mom's in the Kitchen Catering. 135 West Dares Beach Road. 410-535-3944
Romano's Italian Restaurant. Prince Frederick Shopping Center. 410-535-3337
Ruby Tuesday. 815 Prince Frederick Boulevard North. 410-414-5797
Stoney's Seafood House of Fox Run. 545 Solomons Island Road North. 410-535-1888
DuPaul's Catering & Gourmet. 130 West Dares Beach Road. 410-535-0866
Smokin' Joe's BBQ. 2190 Sixes Road. 410-535-8664 (catering)

# Benedict

Benedict was one of the first ports established by the 1683 Act for Advancement of Trade. The port had a customs house and from here tobacco was shipped. In 1695 Benedict was known as Benedict-Leonard Town and in 1747 the name was changed to Benedict Town for Benedict Leonard Calvert, the fourth Lord Baltimore and Lord Proprietor.

General James Wilkinson was born in Benedict. He joined the Continental Army at age 19 and served as adjutant to General Horatio Gates. After the Revolutionary War he headed West and took part in the negotiations with the Spanish to open the Mississippi River to American commerce. However he was to become a Spanish agent, while still serving in the U.S. Army. He became the Army commander of the West succeeding General Anthony Wayne, and then Governor of the northern part of the Louisiana Territory. With Aaron Burr he conspired to seize Spanish lands near the Louisiana Territory. However, he did inform President Thomas Jefferson of Burr and placed New Orleans under martial law. Later he was to serve in the War of 1812, and then died in Mexico City. A traitor or an American!!!

The British landed 5,000 troops in 1814 to march on Washington. The British marched up the west side of the Patuxent River. When Comm. Joshua Barney realized he was outnumbered he blew up his flotilla to escape capture. Two of the wounded British soldiers died and were buried at Old Fields Chapel in Hughesville.

From 1817 to 1937 steamboats carrying freight and passengers stopped at Benedict on their routes between Baltimore and the Rappahannock and Potomac Rivers. Camp Stanton was set up during the Civil War to recruit and train black infantry to serve in the Union Army.

# Port Republic

It is not known how Port Republic received its name, though it may once have been a port of entry.

**Attractions**

American Chestnut Land Trust. Scientists Cliffs Road. 410-586-1570. Hiking trails, an arboretum, and historic buildings.

One-Room School House. Broomes Island Road. 410-586-0482. The schoolroom is over 100 years old and was restored in 1977 by the Calvert Retired Teachers Association. The school was known as School Number 7.

Christ Episcopal Church. 3100 Broomes Island Road. 410-586-0565. The first church was a log church built in 1672. The present brick church dates from 1772.

*Lodging*

Yowell House. Governor's Run Road. 703-620-4408
The Cottages of Governor's Run. 2847 Governor's Run Road. 410-586-1793
Enchanted Bayfront House. 10 Governor's Run Road. 703-620-4408

*Dining*

Gateway Restaurant. 5455 Broome's Island Road. 301-586-1870

# St. Leonard

St. Leonard was founded in 1683 at the mouth of the St. Leonard River and was probably named for Leonard Calvert. An act of the Maryland Assembly enlarged the size of the town to handle the shipments of tobacco.

Joshua Barney was one of the heroes of the War of 1812. He also lobbied the Maryland legislature in Annapolis to build a fleet of boats to harass the British in the Chesapeake, but the legislature refused. He instead received money from the U.S. Congress. In 1814 the British cornered Joshua Barney's barges on St. Leonard's Creek during a naval battle. The barges were burned rather than allowed to fall into British hands. Recent discoveries by archeologists have found what they believe are the remains of a gunboat used by Capt. Barney.

**Attractions**

Jefferson Patterson Park & Museum. 10515 Mackall Road. 410-586-8500. The 512 acre park on the Patuxent River and St. Leonard Creek was created through the generosity of Marvin Breckinridge Patterson who gave Point Farm to the state in 1983. The property has trails, archeological exhibits, special events, picnic areas, an Indian village site, and a teaching laboratory.

Much archeological work has taken place on this property. For over 9,000 years Native Americans camped in the area and hunted along the river. John Smith mapped the villages in 1608. The village of Quomocac may be within the park. Among the 17th c Colonial sites in the park are the buried remains of St. Leonard Town. Records trace the ownership of the property to about 1651 when William Stone patented it as St. Leonards.

 Sometime in the late 1650s Richard Smith, Lord Baltimore's first attorney general acquired St Leonard's plantation. His son Richard Smith, Jr., surveyor general of Maryland, built King's Reach 1690-1714. Walter Smith, his grandson later inherited the properties. His daughter Margaret Mackall Smith was born here and married General Zachary Taylor, 12th President. The property was sold to John Stuart Skinner in 1814.

During the War of 1812 the American Flotilla and the British Royal Navy were engaged in the Battle of St. Leonard Creek for more than two weeks. Two cannon batteries that were constructed on the grounds of the park were used during the night of June 25, 1814 to assist the American boats to force the British to retreat.

In 1932 Jefferson Patterson bought the property and hired Gertrude Sawyer to design the buildings for Point Farm. Ms. Sawyer, a Washington architect was the

178

first female member of the American Institute of Architects. In 1940 Mr. Patterson married Mary Marvin Breckinridge, a war correspondent and who appeared with Edward R. Murrow on CBS in London. Mrs. Patterson's foundation in Washington continues to support writers and awards special grants each year.

The Academy of Natural Sciences Estuarine Research Center. 10545 Mackall Road. 410-586-9700. The Center has spent over 30 years researching the interrelationships of the aquatic ecosystems and human activities of the Patuxent River.

Chesapeake Market Place. 5015 St. Leonard Road. 410-586-3725. This is Southern Maryland's largest market. Auctions take place every Wednesday and Friday.

*Lodging*

Patuxent Camp Sites. 4770 Williams Wharf Road. 410-586-9880
Matoaka Beach Cabins. Calvert Beach Drive. 410-586-0269
Jeff's Bed & Fix Your Own Breakfast. 6040 Bayview Road. 410-535-5308
The Cliffs Motor Inn. 4985 St. Leonard Road. 410-586-1514

*Dining*

Chessie's. Rte. 765 and Calvert Beach Road. 410-586-9137

# Broomes Island

Broomes Island was named for the Broome family.

## Attractions

Christ Episcopal Church. Rte. 264. The original church was built prior to 1692 and another later in 1735. Bricks from this church were used to construct the present structure in 1769.

Brooke Manor Place. Rte. 264. This private home was named for the first family to settle in Calvert County. Robert Brooke arrived in 1650 with his wife, 10 children, and 28 servants.

*Lodging*

Island Creek B&B. 9435 River View Road. 410-586-0576

*Dining*

Stoney's Seafood House. Oyster House Road. 410-586-1888. Excellent crab cakes!

# Mutual

**Attractions**

The Cage. Rte. 265. Private. The brick house on the Patuxent may date back to 1652.

# Lusby

**Attractions**

Calvert Cliffs Nuclear Power Plant. 1650 Calvert Cliffs Parkway. 410-495-4673. 19th c tobacco barn has exhibits on archeological and agricultural products from area, and on nuclear power. BG & E now owns the first nuclear power plant in Maryland. At the end of Calvert Cliffs is Cove Point Park.

Calvert Cliffs State Park. Rte. 765. Almost 1600 acres. Trails. Cliff formed over 15 million years ago. Fossils

Flag Ponds Nature Park. Solomons Island Road North. 410-586-1477. Hiking trails, fishing pier, beach, visitors' center and wildlife exhibits.

Middleham Episcopal Church. Rte. 765. 410-326-4948. The church was established in 1684. In 1746 the vestry of Christ Church petitioned the Assembly to levy the sum of 80,000 pounds of tobacco to build a new church. The present church was built in 1748 and is the oldest cruciform church in Maryland. The bell was given by John Holdsworth of Middleham, England and the communion service received from Queen Anne in 1714.

**Middleham Chapel**

Morgan Hill Farm. Rte. 2. Private. The frame house was built c1670.

Spout Farm. Sollers Road. Private. The house is located on St. Leonard Creek and was built in 1700. The house is named for the "spout" or spring located on Sollers Wharf.

## Dining

Vera's White Sands Restaurant and Marina. White Sands Drive. 410-586-1182. Vera's is one of those places that seems so out of place in this small town, but it is the personality of Vera that makes it a landmark. The setting is Polynesian and pink predominates. Effie and Vera Freeman came here from California in 1953 to open the White Sands Yacht Club. She had given up an acting career and their stay was to be short term, and now still here.

Calvert Café. Rte. 765 and Coster Road. 410-326-2010
Frying Pan Restaurant. 9895 H.G. Trueman Road. 410-326-1125
Guido's. 11735 H. G. Trueman Road. 410-326-0040
Jethro's Bar-B-Que. 12601 Corral Drive. 410-394-6700

# Solomons

Solomons was once known as Somerville Island. Solomons lies one mile from the mouth of the Patuxent River on the north shore. The island was a plantation once owned by Dr. James Somervell, and was known as Somervell's Island. Dr. Somervell was a supporter of "Bonnie Prince Charlie" in Scotland. The English captured him in 1715 and sent him to the American colonies as an indentured servant. He settled in this area about 1719 and became High Sheriff in 1747.

Capt. Isaac Solomon established an oyster business in 1867. The area once had a large oyster fleet. Deep water oyster tongs and bugeyes were invented here. The J.C. Lore Oyster Processing Plant operated from 1888 to 1978. The causeway is built on a bed of oyster shells.

In 1879 two men from Connecticut, Thomas R. Moore and John H. Farren , bought Solomons Island for $6,225 and operated the Solomons Cannery. Mr. Moore operated a shipyard from 1880-1906.

The Patuxent enters the Bay, and though only a few watermen still work out of here, Solomons has become a very popular boating haven, and many homes have sprung up with Washington only sixty miles away and Annapolis a bit closer.

The Navy has had an active presence on Solomons for many years. In 1905 the drydock *Dewey* was tested here before being sent to the Philippines. During World War II (1942-45) troops were trained for amphibious landings adjacent to the Calvert Marina. The Naval Surface Weapons Center is just north of Solomons.

The Patuxent River is very deep, often over 100 feet. The British blocked the river and Bay here during the War of 1812. The Governor Thomas Johnson Bridge crosses the river to St. Mary's County and is named for the state's first governor. Gov. Johnson was also a member of the Continental Congress and an associate of the U.S. Supreme Court. He nominated George Washington to be Commander-in-Chief of the Continental Army in 1776. The bridge was completed in 1977.

**Attractions**

Calvert Marine Museum. Rte. 2/4. 410-326-2042. The museum has much history of the area, and particularly its relationship with watermen, and fossils from Calvert Cliffs. Drum Point Lighthouse was first commissioned in 1883 to guard the entrance to the Patuxent River, and is a screwpile lighthouse. It was moved and restored to Solomons in 1975. The *Wm. B. Tennison* is the oldest Coast Guard-licensed passenger carrying vessel on the Chesapeake. The nine-log chunk-built bugeye built in 1899, was converted from sail to power and served as an oyster buyboat until 1978. One hour cruises are offered on the Patuxent River.

The Small Craft Building is home to 19 historic boats, including a dugout canoe and a 48 foot Hooper Island "Drake Tail" deadrise. Also on the grounds are the Boat-building Skills Preservation Center and the Woodcarving and Model Boat Shop. Nearby is the Cove Point Lighthouse.

Joseph C. Lore & Sons Oyster House. 14430 Solomons Island Road. 410-326-2878. The building dates back to 1934, replacing an earlier structure destroyed by a storm. The building was a seafood-packing and shipping house. J.C. Lore & Sons closed in 1978. In 1984 the oyster house was named to the National Register of Historic Places.

Chesapeake Biological Laboratory Visitor Center. Charles Street. 410-326-7282. The laboratory was founded in 1925 by Reginald Truitt, a zoologist, and is now part of the University of Maryland Center for Environmental Science.

Annmarie Garden on St. John's Creek. Dowell Road. 410-326-4640. Located three miles north of Solomons Island is a magnificent garden donated by Francis and Ann Koenig to Calvert County in 1993. The gardens have a collection of Glen Dale Azaleas that began in 1997 with over 113 varieties.

**Annmarie Garden**

The gateposts entering the garden are elaborate ceramic sections comprising over 630 pieces. In the gardens is a statue, "Tribute to the Oyster Tonger" that symbolizes a tonger's existence. Other works of art include the Council Ring, The Surveyor's Map, the Generations Room, Thirteen Talking Benches, and Rooms to Rest and Refresh.

Rousby Hall. The home once belonged to John Rousby who died in 1750. His widow married Col. William Fitzhugh, who was to become a planter and political activist. He befriended Gov. Robert Eden, the royal governor, who visited Rousby Hall. In 1776 Mr. Rousby was a member of the 1776 convention that enacted the first state Constitution and in 1778 became Speaker of the House of Delegates. The British burned the main house in 1780. The property was laid out in lots in 1890 for a new city, which was never built.

Our Lady Star of the Sea. 14400 Solomons Island Road. 410-326-3535. The church was established in 1888 and is the oldest Catholic Church and parish in Calvert County. The present building was constructed in 1927.

Solomons United Methodist Church. 14454 Solomons Island Road South. 410-326-3848. The church was constructed in 1870 and is the oldest church on Solomons.

St. Peter's Episcopal Church. 14590 Solomons Island Road South. 410-326-4948. The church was established in 1889.

Solomons Pier Restaurant. The pier was built in 1919 by Perry Evans and was called Evans Pavilion. This had an ice cream parlor and confectionery. A waterslide for small boats to slide into the Patuxent River was built from the roof in 1920. The movie house, now the restaurant was added later.

*Lodging*

Holiday Inn Select Conference Center & Marina. 155 Holiday Road. 410-326-2009
Davis House. Charles and Maltby Streets. 410-326-4811
Myrtle Point Bed and Breakfast. Over Thomas Johnson Bridge. 301-862-3090. C1860
Bowens Inn. 14630 Solomon's Island Road South. 410-326-9814
Grey Fox Inn. 14560 Solomons Island Road. 410-326-6826
Adina's Guest House. 14236 South Solomons Island Road. 410-326-4895
Back Creek Inn. Calvert and Alexander Streets. 410-326-2022. Lovely gardens
By-the-Bay B&B. 14374 Calvert Street. 410-326-3428. Victorian house
Solomons Victorian Inn. 125 Charles Street. 410-326-4811. On harbor
Webster House. 14364 Sedgwick Avenue. 410-326-0454
Captain's Quarters. 14368 Calvert Street. 410-326-6470
Locust Inn Rooms. 14478 Solomons Island Road South. 410-326-9817. On Patuxent River.
Comfort Inn Solomons. Lore Road. 410-326-6303
Island Manor Motel. 77 Charles Street. 410-326-3700

*Restaurants*

Lighthouse Inn. Solomons Island Road. 410-326-2444. On harbor
Maryland Way Restaurant & Mallard Café. 155 Holiday Drive. 410-326-6311
Solomons Crabhouse. 103880 Old Rte.4. 410-326-2800
Solomons Pier. 14575 Solomons Island Road. 410-326-2424
Harbor Sounds Restaurant. 120 Charles Street. 410-326-9522
Dry Dock Restaurant. Zahniser's Yachting Center. 410-326-4817

185

The Naughty Gull Pub & Restaurant. Lore Road. 410-326-4855
*Anticipation II.* 14470 Solomons Island Road. 410-326-3303. Friday night
dinner cruises
The Tiki Bar. Island Manor Hotel. 410-326-4075
Rhumbline Inn & Restaurant. 14442 Main Street. 410-326-3261
Harbor Island Family Restaurant. 120 Charles Street. 410-326-9522
Capt. Smith's Seafood Market. Patuxent Plaza Shopping Center. 410-326-1134
CD Café. 14350 Solomons Island Road. 410-326-3877
Riverside Restaurant. Calvert Marina, Dowell Road. 410-326-4251
DiGiovannia's Dock of the Bay. 14556 Solomons Island Road. 410-394-6400
Boomerangs Original Ribs. 13820 Solomons Island Road South. 410-326-6050
Bowen's Inn. 14630 Solomons Island Road. 410-326-9814
Captain's Table. 275 Lore Road. 410-326-6600
Robert's Deli at Carmen's. 410-326-9331
Catamaran's Seafood & Steaks. 14470 Solomons Island Road South. 410-326-
8379
Woodburn's Market. Rte. 2/4 Patuxent Plaza. 410-326-3284
Jerry's Subs & Pizza of Solomons. Patuxent Plaza Shopping Center. 410-326-
4820
China Harbor Seafood Restaurant. 77 Charles Street. 410-326-6888
Swann's Country Café & Collectibles. 14640 Solomons Island Road. 410-394-
6825
Adam's The Place for Ribs. 13830 Solomons Island Road. 410-326-6050
Captain Seaweed's Crab House. 14470 Patuxent Avenue. 410-326-0766

# Hollywood

*Attractions*

Sotterley Plantation. Rte. 245. 1-800-681-0850. Open Tuesday to Sunday, year
round 10-4.This magnificent home on the banks of the Patuxent River was once
part of a 4,000 acre grant given to Thomas Cornwallis by Lord Baltimore in
1650 and called Resurrection Manor. It was subdivided in 1710 with 890 acres,
and was purchased by James Bowles. He began construction on the main house
but died in 1727. His widow married George Plater II, a lawyer, who with his
son George Plater III (sixth governor of Maryland) completed the house. His
widow was later to marry Edward Lloyd of Wye House (see Eastern Shore of
Maryland: The Guidebook).

**Sotterley Plantation**

George Plater V lost the home in a game of chance in 1822 to Col. Sommerville. Col. Sommerville sold the estate to Thomas Barber and his stepdaughter Emeline Dallam, who married Dr. Walter Briscoe. Herbert Satterlee, a New York lawyer bought the plantation, in 1910. Sotterley was the name of the Satterlee family home in Suffolk, England c 1066. Mabel Satterlee Ingalls deeded the property to the Sotterley Manor Foundation in 1961.

St. John's Church. This Catholic frame church was built in 1898. William H. Barnes, a member of the United States Colored Troops who won a Congressional Medal of Honor in 1864, is buried in an unmarked grave.

Greenwell State Park. Steer Horn Neck Lane. This was originally known as Resurrection Manor, a tract of 4,000 acres owned by Cecil Calvert, second Lord Baltimore in 1650. The house was built 1718. The Civil War contributed to the depletion of wealth for the family and the property was sold several times. The Greenwell family purchased the property and named it Rosedale. During World War II the house fell into disrepair. After the war the restoration of the house was started. Philip Greenwell and his sister Mary donated the property to the State of Maryland. The park is now only 596 acres.

*Dining*

Clarkes Landing Restaurant. Clarkes Landing Road. 301-373-8468
The Early Bird. Mervell Dean Road. 301-373-2828

# Oraville

The name Oraville comes from Ora, the daughter of a town milliner, Mr. Hopkins.

**Attractions**

All Faith Church. Off Rte. 6. Samuel Abell, Jr., built the church with plans by Richard Boulton. The same two men also built St. Andrew's Church near California.

# Mechanicsville

The Adams brothers owned a tavern, forge and blacksmith shop, thus the name.

**Attractions**

Maryland International Raceway at Budd's Creek. 13 Budds Creek Road. 310-884-4624

Potomac Speedway. Rte. 234. 301-884-4624

*Lodging*

Wide Bay Cottage at Dameron B&B. 997 Old Rte. 5. 301-884-3254

*Dining*

Seafood Corner. 301-884-5251. Seafood carry-out
Bert's 50's Diner. 28760 Three Notch Road. 301-884-3837
Cape St. Mary's Marina. Rte. 472. 301-373-2001
Captain Leonards. Rte. 235. 301-884-3701
Copsey's Seafood. Rte. 5. 301-884-4235
Drift Inn. Della Brook Road. 301-884-3470

Hills Club. Rte. 5. 301-884-8499
Hills Halfway House. Rte. 5. 301-884-3287
Sandgates Inn. Rte. 472. 301-373-5100
Seabreeze Restaurant & Crab House. Rte. 472. 301-373-5217

# Preston on Patuxent

This town was the capital of Maryland 1654-1659. The land was patented to Richard Preston in 1652. Richard Preston century built a house that served as the provincial seat of government from 1654-57.Capt. Richard Ladd purchased the house in 1676 and left it to Christ's Church. It was later bought by the Johnson family (Governor Thomas Johnson was first Governor of Maryland, and his niece married President John Quincy Adams).

The author Hulbert Footner bought an 18th century house on Mears Creek and the Patuxent River in 1915. The house inspired a book about the 17th century called "Charles' Gift".

# California

The town was on Martinet's Map of 1866 with the original name of Benita. One story relates that the town received its name from lumber shipped from California. The other says that there were so many California natives stationed at the Patuxent Naval air Warfare Center that they named the town.

**Attractions**

St. Andrew's Episcopal Church. Rte. 4. The Parish was created by the Maryland Provincial Assembly in 1744 and began functioning in 1753. In 1766 two acres were purchased for 5 pounds. Richard Boulton 1776-78 built the brick church. The church has an inset portico, large Palladian window and original box pews. The hand-lettered altarpiece was painted in 1771.

Gov. Thomas Johnson Memorial Bridge. The bridge is named in honor of Maryland's first state governor (1777-79).

St. Joseph's Manor. Town Creek Drive. Private. Cecilius Calvert in London issued the 1,000 acre patent in 1641 to Nicholas Harvey, who asked that it be named "the Manor of St. Joseph's". In 1645 Richard Ingle's Raiders burned the manor. In 1657 George Beckwith became the "Second Lord of the Manor" by his marriage to Francis Harvey, the sole heiress and daughter of Nicholas Harvey. In 1800 the second manor house was destroyed by fire. The present house was built in 1975.

### Lodging

Best Western/Patuxent Inn. Rte. 235. 301-862-4100
Super 8. Rte. 235. 301-862-922
Myrtle Point B&B. Patuxent Blvd. 301-862-3090

### Dining

Lenny's Restaurant. 23418 Three Notch Road. 301-737-0777
The Tavern at the Village. 23154 Wetstone Lane. 301-863-3219
Western Steer. Rt. 4 & Rt. 235
Wildwood Pastry Shop. 2031 Wildwood Center. 301-862-4177

# Great Mills

### Attractions

Cecil's Old Mill. Off Rte. 5. 301-994-1510. This was one of Maryland's first industrial districts. The building now has craft shops.

St. Mary's River State Park. Camp Cosoma Road. 301-872-5688. 250 acre lake with good bass fishing.

# Lexington Park

The village was once known as Cedar Point, then Jarboesville, for its first postmaster, Mr. Jarsboe. In 1943 the Navy appropriated 6,000 acres. Lexington Park was named for the World War II aircraft carrier *Lexington* (lost at the Battle of Coral Sea).

### Attractions

Patuxent Naval Air Station. Rte. 235 and Rte. 246. This is the U.S.' only center dedicated to testing and evaluation of naval aviation .Alan Shepard served two tours at the Patuxent River Naval Air Station. He arrived in 1950 to attend the US Naval Test Pilot School, and later in the 1950's to test aircraft and teach at the school. He was one of the original seven Mercury astronauts, the first to go into space and one of only 12 men to walk on the moon. Alan Shepard was a graduate of the Naval Academy, and died July 1998.

Among the other naval aviators to serve here was Maj. Gen. Marion E. Carl, one of the Marine Corps' most decorated aviators, an ace who flew during World War II. Sadly he was killed during a burglary at his home in Roseburg, OR. He made one of the first carrier landings and takeoff with the F-80 Shooting Star. While serving at the air station he set a world speed record in the Douglas Skystreak, winning a fourth Distinguished Flying Cross. He shot down 11 enemy aircraft at Guadacanal.

The Patuxent Naval Air Museum. Rte.235. 301-863-7418. The museum has numerous models, photographs and memorabilia. The museum has been undergoing a capital campaign to expand and move the museum to a larger location. On the ground are Naval aircraft, including F-18 Hornet, F-14 Tomcat, Sea Stallion helicopter and S-2 tracker. The model collection should not be missed.

Mattapany. This brick 19th c house is on the grounds of the center and is the residence for the commandant. In the 1630s the Jesuits acquired a mission and storehouse from the Mattapany tribe. Lord Baltimore was to reclaim the land in 1641. In 1663 the land was granted to Henry Sewall, secretary of the province. In 1666 his widow, Jane Sewall married Governor Charles Calvert. Gov. Calvert was to build a larger house and magazine here.

*Lodging*

A & E Motel. Great Mills Road. 301-863-7411
Days Inn. Three Notch Road. 800-428-2871
Hampton Inn. Rte. 235. 301-863-3200
Best Western. 22769 Three Notch Road. 301-862-4100
Extended Stay America. Rte. 235. 1-800-EXT-STAY

*Dining*

Mattie's Seafood & Steaks. 19661 Three Notch Road. 301-863-2718
The Roost Restaurant. 21736 Great Mills Road. 301-863-5051
Linda's Café. 27 Tulagi Place. 301-862-3544
Aloha Restaurant. Rte. 235. 301-862-4838
Northridge Restaurant & Pub. Rte. 235. 301-862-3644
Nocolletti's Pizza. Rte. 235. 301-863-2233

Peking Restaurant. Great Mills Road. 301-863-6190
Showtime Deli. Coral Drive. 301-863-2555
Hong Kong Chinese Restaurant. N. Shangri-La Drive. 301-862-4776


## Pope's Freehold

Pope's Freehold lies just north of St. Mary's City. Nathaniel Pope, a maternal ancestor of George Washington patented 100 acres in 1641. Later Thomas Hatton and Philip Calvert were to settle here. Thomas Hatton was a Protestant supporter of Lord Baltimore and Secretary of Maryland. He died at the Battle of the Severn in 1655. Philip Calvert was the youngest son of George Calvert and served as Chancellor of the Province. Moses Tabbs, rector of the William and Mary Parish purchased the property in 1763. Archeological excavations are presently in process.


## St. Mary's City

Leonard Calvert, who arrived on board the Dove and the Ark with 140 people, including Mathias De Sousa, the first Black to arrive in Maryland, founded the original Catholic capital of Maryland in 1634. The town was named for the Virgin Mary. A fort was known to have been built c1634, along with the home of Leonard Calvert. In 1636 Lord Baltimore granted 1,200 acres to the settlers.

A courthouse was built in 1676. In 1662 the Calvert house was purchased as the state house and an ordinary, and was known as the Country's House. William Smith took over the ordinary and built Smith's Ordinary in 1664. In 1672 the building "Two Messages" was built nearby. (Presently the buildings are being reconstructed). Aldermanbury Street was laid out along the river in 1672. The State House of 1676 was built where the street started.

In 1688 the British Parliament deposed King James II, a Catholic and placed on the throne William III and Mary, daughter of King James. St. Mary's City served as a tobacco plantation and capital of Maryland until 1695 when the capital was moved to Annapolis and St. Mary's almost became a ghost town.

### Attractions

A number of buildings and sites have offered archeologists an insight into the earliest Maryland settlers. This is an ongoing project, and one in which the public can participate. Several sites that are presently being excavated may contain the fort built in 1634. Ghost frames have been erected over archeological sites where funds are not yet available to reconstruct buildings. The museum is open Wednesday through Sunday mid-March through the last Saturday in November. For further information please call 301-862-0990.

Visitor Center. Rosecroft Road off Route 5. Tickets and an orientation are available.

Godiah Spray Tobacco Plantation. This plantation has been recreated on the property of Godiah Spray, who had acquired over two hundred acres of land, growing tobacco.

**Godiah Spray Tobacco Plantation**
(Courtesy of Historic St. Mary's City – Katie Moose Photo)

Woodland Indian Hamlet. Explore the Woodland Indians culture and their relationship to the colonists. This includes a Long House, similar to what the Indians would have lived in when the first white settlers arrived.

The Governor's Field Town Center. The field contains sites and structures such as Calvert House, home of the Maryland's first governor, Leonard Calvert. Leonard Calvert was the brother of Lord Baltimore and built one of the earliest homes in St. Mary's City. The home was later leased to Nathaniel Pope, an anti-Catholic, in 1645. Also included here are Cordea's Hope, the Lawyer's Lodging, and Smith's Ordinary, and William Nuthead's Print House. Mr. Nuthead left Virginia in 1685 to become the first printer, having been banned by royal order from printing in that state.

The Van Sweringen Inn & Coffee House are the remains of inns dating to the 1680s.

The Margaret Brent Memorial Garden. The gazebo and garden were constructed during the 1984 celebration of Maryland's 350th anniversary.

One of the more famous people from St. Mary's was Margaret Brent (c 1601-1671) who grew up in Gloucestershire, England, and in 1619 converted to Roman Catholicism. Her father lost most of his estate, due to his non-Anglican stance, and Margaret and three of her siblings decided to move to the Maryland colony with thousands of acres through land grants. Margaret and her sister Mary lived on 70 acres in St. Mary's called "Sisters Freehold". Their brother, Giles Brent, lived on an adjacent property known as the "White House". Margaret became very involved in community affairs, and was eventually asked to act as the sole executor of Leonard Calvert's estate. Lord Calvert was governor of Maryland, and the younger brother of Lord Baltimore. She has been titled "America's first litigator". The American Bar Association's Commission on Women in the Profession has named The Women Lawyers of Achievement Award for her.

1667 Brick Chapel and the Chapel Field. This archeological site is the founding site of the American Catholic Church and includes the cross-shaped brick foundations of the 1667 Brick Chapel. Three lead coffins were found buried in 1990 and have now been identified as the remains of Chancellor Philip Calvert, his first wife Anne Wolseley Calvert, and an infant thought to be the daughter of Philip Calvert by his second wife. A Capital Campaign is underway to rebuild the 1667 Brick Chapel.

Calvert Hall. Reconstruction of the first school building in 1844 and destroyed by fire in 1924.

*Maryland Dove.* (See Cover) The *Dove* is a replica of the original boat the settlers arrived on Maryland shores. The boat was designed by William Baker and built by James Richardson of Dorchester County (See Eastern Shore of Maryland: The Guidebook)

Mathias de Sousa Monument. This is a memorial to the first non-white settler who arrived aboard the *Ark*. He was also the first man of African descent to serve and vote in a colonial American legislature in 1642.

State House of 1676. (See page 24) The reconstructed Statehouse was built in 1934, during the 300<sup>th</sup> anniversary celebration of Maryland. Capt. John Quigley built the Original State House of 1676 for 300,000 pounds of tobacco. The site is marked in the churchyard of Trinity Church.

The Father White Memorial was erected to honor Jesuit priest who traveled with the first settlers on board the *Ark* and *Dove*.

Freedom of Conscience Monument. Rte. 5 and Rte. 584.

Trinity Episcopal Church. Church Point. The church was built from bricks that came from the original Courthouse 1676. Behind the church is the Copley Vault, which is believed to contain the remains of Sir Lionel Copley and his wife. Mr. Copley became the first royal Governor of Maryland after the crown suspended the Calvert's right to rule the Province after the Glorious Revolution of 1689. The Leonard Calvert Monument (1890) marks the site where the Maryland colonists gathered to establish their new government and freedom of worship.

William Farthing's Ordinary. Reconstruction of an 17<sup>th</sup> century inn. The building is modeled after the Third Haven Meetinghouse in Easton, Maryland. During the sessions of the courts and Assembly, guests resided at the various inns in St. Mary's City. Today the inn interprets 17<sup>th</sup> c life and provides cooking demonstrations.

St. Mary's College is rated one of the "best small schools in the U.S." The college was established in 1840. Lucille Clifton, Poet Laureate of Maryland (1979-1985) serves on the faculty. On the campus is St. John's, a house built in 1638 by John Lewgar, an Anglican minister who converted to Catholicism, and was also the first Secretary of the Province. Rev. Lewgar was to leave Maryland c1649 and Simon Overzee, a Dutch merchant, bought the house. Governor Charles Calvert, the third Lord Baltimore acquired the house in 1661. The John Hicks House belonged to John Hicks, a sea captain from Whitehaven, England. The house was built c1723. Mr. Hicks became a planter, merchant, sheriff and sat on the Provincial Court.

## Lodging

Brome-Howard Inn. 18281 Rosecroft Road. 301-866-0656. The Greek revival house was built in 1840 for Dr. John M. Brome. The house was moved in 1994 to a site overlooking the St. Mary's River.

**Brome-Howard Inn**
(Courtesy of Historic St. Mary's City –Katie Moose Photo)

*Dining*

Brome-Howard Country Inn & Restaurant. 301-866-0656.
Farthing's Ordinary. Governor's Field. 301-862-0988. Dine in a reconstructed inn dating from the 17th c.
St. Mary's College. Great Room

# St. Inigoes

A colonial estate once occupied the land, now known as Webster Field. Inigo was the baptismal name of St. Ignatius of Loyola, founder of the Society of Jesuits. St. Inigoes Manor was patented to Thomas Copley, a Catholic priest (1594-1653). Cuthbert Fenwick and Ralph Crouch held the trust for the Jesuits.

Within five years of their arrival, the Jesuits who settled in Southern Maryland had established large plantations where indentured servants harvested their crops. The 2,000 acre St. Inigoes Plantation mainly raised tobacco.

Mathias de Sousa, an African Portuguese Jew and one of nine indentured servants, arrived with the first colonists, most of whom were Catholics. He earned his freedom from indentured servitude and went to work for the Jesuit priests as captain of a trading fleet. He is thought to have lived at Inigoes Plantation and then went on to serve in the Colonial legislature, the first person of color to do so.

**Attractions**

Cross Manor. Grayson Road. This private 18th c home is located on a grant made to Thomas Cornwallis in 1638.

St. Ignatius Catholic Church. Villa Road. 301-872-2247. The church was erected in 1788 on the site of a church dating back to 1641. The church was restored in 1953 and has beautiful stained glass windows and altar. On the grounds is one of the oldest cemeteries in America.

St. Inigoes Manor. The land was patented in 1641 and 1651 to Cuthbert Fenwick and Ralph Crouch. Father Thomas Copley who came to Maryland in 1636 served as superior of the Jesuits and moved his headquarters from St. Mary's City to St. Inigoes in 1644.

The site is on the property of the Patuxent River Naval Air Station. Beginning in 1996 the tract where the house stood has been combed by archeologists, work that was originally commissioned by the station for an historical inventory of the 800 acres.

Naval Air Warfare Center – Aircraft Division. Villa Road. This is part of the Patuxent Naval Air Station. Webster Field was built on this site during World War II.

## Chancellor's Point

The point, 2 miles SW of St. Mary's City on the St. Mary's River, is named for Philip Calvert, brother of the Second Lord Baltimore, chancellor of this province 1661-82.

St. Peter's. Near Rte. 5 and Rosecroft Road lies the ruins of St. Peter's property. In 1658 Philip Calvert settled in Maryland and built a grand house on this property in 1679. Lionel Copley and Francis Nicholson, the first royal governors lived here.

## Ridge

### Attractions

St. Mary's Episcopal Church. Rte. 5. 301-862-4596. The church was built in 1884 and is thought to be the third chapel to serve Episcopalians in southern St. Mary's County.

### *Lodging*

Bard's Field in Trinity Manor B&B. 15671 Pratt Road. 301-872-5989
Scheible's. Wynne Road. 301-872-5185
Longpoint Cottage. 301-872-0057

### *Dining*

Scheible's Crab Pot Restaurant. Wynne Road. 301-872-5185
Spinnakers Restaurant. Point Lookout Marina. 301-872-4340
Courtney's Restaurant & Seafood. Wynne Road. 301-872-4403

# Scotland/Scotland Beach

*Lodging*

St. Michael's Manor B&B. Rte. 5. 301-872-4025. The 1805 inn is located on Long Neck Creek and has a vineyard.

Hale House B&B. 49644 Potomac River Drive. 301-872-4558. On the water with dock

Wide Bay Cottage. Rte. 5. 301-872-0057

# Point Lookout

This area was named St. Michael's Point and was one of three manors owned by Leonard Calvert. In 1862 the government built the Hammond General Hospital. Camp Hoffman was originally designed to house 10,000 prisoners. However, after the Battle of Gettysburg the prison held 52,264 Confederate prisoners, of whom 3,384 died. The poet Sidney Lanier was one of those held here. Fort Lincoln is one of the three remaining forts. A federal and a state monument are dedicated to those that died.

In the 1850s this became a popular resort area. A hotel was located here from 1930-60. A railroad had been planned to connect the resort to Washington, but was never completed.

**Attractions**

St. Michael's Manor is located near Point Lookout. 301-872-4025. It was one of three manors granted to Leonard Calvert in 1639. The present house was built by James I. Richardson c 1805.

Point Lookout State Park. Junction of the Chesapeake Bay and Potomac River. In 1962 the State of Maryland began to acquire land for the park. There are now 514 acres.

Point Lookout Confederate Cemetery. Located in the park. Many Confederate soldiers are buried here. There had been some controversy over flying the Confederate flag, but because of the number of Confederates buried here, the flag remains.

**Point Lookout Confederate Cemetery**

<u>Fort Lincoln</u>. The fort was built in 1865 and has now been restored as a museum and with special exhibits.

## Callaway

*Dining*

Bear Creek Open Pit BBQ. 21030 Point Lookout Road. 301-994-1030

## Valley Lee

**Attractions**

<u>St. George's Episcopal Church</u>. Rte. 249. 301-994-0585. The first church was founded in the 1650s. The first Anglican rector was Rev. William Wilkinson. Francis Sourton who is buried near the church, succeeded him. Also buried here is Leigh Massey, another rector. The present church was built in the mid 1750s. The church burned c1799, but a new church was constructed immediately. The

interior was restored in 1958.

Mulberry Fields. Off Rte. 244. John Anthony Clarke home built this private home in 1765. Mulberry trees were planted for their silk.

Porto Bello. Off Rte. 244. This private home was built by William Hebb c1740.

*Dining*

Cedar Cove Inn. Rte. 249. 301-994-1155. On the water.

# Drayden

**Attractions**

West St. Mary's Road. This private property was part of a 2,000 manor granted to Capt. Henry Fleet in 1634. Capt. Fleet, a Protestant, had come from Virginia and had acted as a guide for Leonard Calvert and the Maryland settlers.

*Dining*

Still Anchors Restaurant. Dennis Point Marina. 301-994-2288

# Piney Point

Piney Point was a post office in 1855 and later a resort for Washingtonians. President James Monroe maintained a cottage here, the first "Summer White House". The house was swept away in a gale in 1933.

**Attractions**

Piney Point Lighthouse Museum and Park. Rte. 249. This lighthouse is located on the Potomac River. The lighthouse was constructed in 1836, and became part of the museum division in 1990. The lighthouse is one of only four in existence along the Potomac.

Black Panther U-1105 Shipwreck Preserve. Lighthouse Road. 301-769-2222. Towards the end of World War II a German submarine became a possession of the U.S. Navy and sank in the Potomac River. This was designated Maryland's first historic shipwreck preserve in 1994.

Harry Lundeberg School of Seamanship. Rte. 249. This school established in 1953 to train men and women for the merchant marine is located on the site of a former navy torpedo station, and is named for the first president of the Seafarers International Union.

*Lodging*

Swanns Resort Properties. 17220 Piney Point Road. 301-994-0774

*Dining*

Oakwood Lodge. Lighthouse Road. 301-994-2271

# Tall Timbers

*Lodging*

Potomac View Farm Bed & Breakfast. 44477 Tall Timbers Road. 301-994-2311

# St. George Island

The island is at the confluence of the Potomac and St. Mary's Rivers. The British fleet captured the island in July 1776 under Lord Dunsmore. It belonged to St. Inigoes Manor, a group of Jesuits until 1850. The island is now a resort.

*Lodging*

Potomac View Farm B&B. Rte. 249. 301-994-2311
Camp Merryelande Vacation Cottages. Rte. 249. 1-800-382-1073

*Dining*

Evans Seafood. Rte. 249. 301-994-2299

# Leonardtown

Leonardtown may have been founded as early as 1652, and was called "Sheppard's Old Fields". In 1708 Philip Lynes, mayor of St. Mary's City, gave the Maryland colony 50 acres at the head of Breton Bay to lay out the county seat. The seven commissioners were to lay out the town and a courthouse not to cost more than 12,000 pounds of tobacco. The name was changed to Seymour Town, in honor of Governor John Seymour. In 1728 new commissioners named the town Leonardtown in honor of Benedict Leonard Calvert, fourth Lord Baltimore. The first courthouse was built in 1710, rebuilt in 1910 and 1957.

In 1744 1,096 acres were patented to Col. Abraham Barnes, who was to become the tobacco inspector for Leonardtown and built his house, Tudor Hall, overlooking Breton Bay. His home was later sold the Key family, which included Francis Scott Key. During the War of 1812 the town was raided and during the Civil War Union troops occupied it. Leonardtown was incorporated in 1858.

## Attractions

The town sits on a bluff at the head of Breton's Bay and is situated around a village green.

Old Jail Museum.11 Courthouse Drive. 301-475-2467 The building was built c1876.

St. Mary's County Historical Society. 41625 Courthouse Drive. 301-475-2467

Tudor Hall. Library Place. The original land grant was extended to Bartram Obert and Dominick and named "Little St. Lawrence". Abraham Barnes acquired the property in 1744. He was a delegate to the Provincial Assembly and 1744 Chairman of the Committee of Observation of St. Mary's County. In 1814 Philip Barton Key, an uncle of Francis Scott Key bought the property. He raised the roof and squared the house out into a fourteen room mansion. The house was restored by the late Mrs. Howard C. Davidson and in 1950 donated to the St. Mary's County Memorial Library Association. Today the first floor contains offices for the Leonardtown Commissioners and on the second floors the St. Mary's Historical Society.

Beacon. John Franklin King, then thirteen years old founded the paper in 1839, and funded the paper with money from the Orphan's Court. During the Civil War the paper sympathized with the South and for a while was suppressed. Mr. King founded the St. Mary's Reading Room and Debating Society, which now has book centers and a book mobile to deliver books around the county. His son

Francis Vernon King and later grandson Aloysius Fenwick King succeeded him. The paper today remains in the King family and the printing shop is located in a King building that dates back to 1704.

St. Francis Xavier Church. 21370 Newtown Neck Road. 301-475-9885. Compton Newtown Manor House c1789 is the oldest Catholic Church in continuous use in English-speaking America. The church is listed on the National Register of Historic Places.

*Lodging*

Relax Inn. Park Avenue. 301-475-3011

*Dining*

The Willow Restaurant & Tavern. 23154 Whetstone Lane. 301-475-6553
Café des Artistes. Washington & Fenwick Streets. 301-997-0500
Country Kitchen. 41566 Medley Neck. 301-475-3821
Happy Dragon Chinese Restaurant. Rte.5. 301-475-9695
Perkins Family Restaurant & Bakery. Rte. 5. 301-475-1906
The English Tea Room. Rte. 5. 301-475-1960
Willows Restaurant. Rte. 5. 301-475-6553

# Charlotte Hall

Charlotte Hall was established in 1698 and later became a health resort "Ye Cool Springs of St. Marie's". A school was built here in 1774 and named for Queen Charlotte of England who married George III in 1761. The school became a military academy in 1850. Most of the buildings were demolished in 1983. The Charlotte Hall Veteran's Home was built on the site.

**Attractions**

All Faith Episcopal Church. Charlotte Hall Road. 301-884-3773. The church dates to 1776 and has a rose window, barrel-shaped ceiling, and slave gallery.

Old White House. This was erected as a classroom building and headmaster's residence in 1830 for the school.

Dent Chapel. Old Route 5. Dent Chapel is located on the grounds of the Veteran's Home. The church was erected in 1883 and named for the Rev. Hatch Dent, the first principal of the military academy. The chapel is built of granite with a decorative brick belt. It is considered one of the best examples of Victorian Gothic architecture in Maryland.

St. Mary's Church, Newport, 1674. 11555 St. Mary's Church Road. 301-934-8825. The church was the first Franciscan church in the colonies. The only remaining building was built c1800.

*Lodging*

Charlotte Hall Motel. Rte. 5. 301-884-3172

*Dining*

Charlotte Hall House of Ribs. Rte. 5. 301-884-6125
Hensons Charcoal Steakhouse. Rte. 5. 301-884-3820

# Newmarket

**Attractions**

Ebenezer African Methodist Episcopal Church. Rte. 5 and Rte. 6. The wooden cabin dates to before the Civil War and was used by the Black population.

# Chaptico

The village was named for the Chaptico or Choptico Indians. Chaptico became a river port in 1683, lying on Chaptico Run which empties into the Wicomico River. In 1689 John Coode organized a rebellion against Lord Baltimore here. The British burned the town in 1813. The creek was later to silt in and was no longer navigable.

**Attractions**

Christ Church. Rte. 238. 301-884-3451. A church existed on the site in 1642. The present church was built in 1736 according to a Christopher Wren design. The tower was added in 1913. During the War of 1812 British troops occupied the church. The cemetery contains the vault of the Francis Scott Key family.

*Dining*

Wicomico Shores Bar & Grill. Wicomico Shore Subdivision. 301-884-4601

# Morganza

The post office was established here between 1875-80. The town was named for the Morgan family. George Morgan owned "Goodrick Farm".

**Attractions**

St. Joseph's Church. The church was built in 1858 in the Italianate style.

# Bushwood

**Attractions**

Ocean Hall. This private home was built by Robert Slye, a merchant who died in 1671. He married Susannah Gerard, daughter of Dr. Thomas Gerard of St. Clement's Manor. Her second husband was John Coode of Chaptico. The gable roof dates from c1703.

# St. Clement's Island

The original settlers brought over by the second Lord Baltimore landed March 25, 1634 on St. Clement's Island in the Potomac, and celebrated the first Roman Catholic Mass here. The island was once about 400 acres and is now about one-tenth that size. A later proprietor changed the name of the island to Blakistone Island. During the Revolutionary War the British occupied the island and burned Mr. Blakistone's house. In 1919 the island was assigned to the U.S. Navy for use as an observation point, and returned to the State of Maryland in 1962. Today the island is a state park. The 40 foot cross was built in 1934 to commemorate the landing of the Maryland colonists.

# Colton's Point

## Attractions

St. Clement's Island-Potomac River Museum. 301-769-2222. The museum, founded in 1975, traces the history of Maryland's early colonists, the Potomac River and the Chesapeake Bay. The three flags represent the United States, the State of Maryland, and St. Mary's County. On the grounds are the Little Red Schoolhouse (Charlotte Hall School) c 1820 and two Potomac dory boats.

**Little Red Schoolhouse**

The Mother of Light Shrine, otherwise known as Our Lady of St. Mary's County was recently constructed from bricks and rocks brought from throughout the world, and including the Holy Land. The statue is to remind all that the settlers named the county for the Mother of Jesus.

# Avenue

Avenue is located on the site of St. Clement's Manor, owned by Dr. Thomas Gerard. Dr.Thomas Gerard patented St. Clement's Manor in 1639. In 1652 Robert Cole built a plantation on St. Clement's Bay. In 1660 Josias Fendall whom Lord Baltimore had appointed Governor in 1657 gave up his proprietary commission and started the "pigmie rebellion" (Protestant) against the Lord. His accomplice was John Coode. Lord Baltimore left for England, but while there, William and Mary became rulers of England, thus establishing a Protestant monarchy.

**Attractions**

All Saints Episcopal Church. Oakley Road. 301-769-4288. The church was formerly known as Tomakoken Episcopal Church. Dr. Thomas Gerard, a Catholic, built the church for his wife in 1642.

*Lodging*

Enfield's B&B. 21400 Colton's Point Road. 301-769-4755

# LaPlata

The Pope's Creek section of the Baltimore and Potomac Railroad came through in 1873 with the stop known as La Plata Station. This was located on the Chapman farm, which was named "Le Plateau", French for flat terrain. Robert F. Chapman was the first postmaster. The station consisted of a warehouse and passenger waiting room.

The town was incorporated in 1888. In 1895 La Plata became the county seat for Charles County, when the river silted up at Port Tobacco and the court house burned. The original courthouse was built in 1896 and the present one dates from 1956.

**Attractions**

Christ Church, La Plata (Port Tobacco Parish, 1692). 110 E. Charles Street. 301-932-1051. The church was among the first 30 original parishes. The original building was constructed in 1683 on Port Tobacco Creek. New structures followed in 1709 and 1815. A stone church was built on Port Tobacco Square in 1884. The church was dismantled and moved here from Port Tobacco in 1904.

The narthex windows celebrate Maryland, the Episcopal Church, and the parish history. The marble altar commemorates Lemeul Wilmer, rector (1822-69), and a Unionist who continued to pray for Abraham Lincoln in this parish which still had slaves.

Friendship House. Charles County Community College. Mitchell Road. 301-934-9177. The house was built by the Dent family in 1740.

La Grange. Rte. 6 This private home was built on property bought by Dr. James Craik in 1763. The house is named for the Marquis de Lafayette's chateau near Paris. Dr. Craik was a very close friend of George Washington and was one of his attending physicians when he died in 1799.

Archbishop Neale School. Rte. 6. This school is on the site of the McDonough Institute which opened in 1903 to educate poor children. This was the only high school in the county until 1924 when public high schools were established.

African-American Heritage Society Museum. 7485 Crain Highway. 301-843-0371. By Appointment. The museum contains artifacts used during the time of slavery and the contributions of Black Americans on life in southern Maryland.

Mount Carmel Monastery, (1790). Mount Carmel Drive. 301-934-1654. The monastery was founded by four Carmelite nuns in 1790 and was the first monastery of religious women in Colonial America. Three of the four founding nuns, Ann Matthew and her two nieces, Ann Theresa and Susanna Matthews and their chaplain, Rev. Charles Neale, were all natives of Charles County. The four of them set up temporary quarters at Chandler's Hope owned by the Neale family. Father Neale donated 860 acres to the Carmelites for the establishment of the monastery. Two of the convent buildings have been restored and open to the public.

*Lodging*

Best Western. 6900 Crain Highway. 301-934-4900
Deluxe Inn. 6705 Crain Highway. 301-934-1400
Super 8 Motel. 9400 Chesapeake Street. 301-934-3465
Patuxent Inn. Rte. 301. 301-934-3465

# Bel Alton

Bel Alton grew as a village after the Pope's Creek Railroad was built.

*Lodging*

Bel Alton Motel. Rte. 301. 301-934-9505

# Pope's Creek

Pope's Creek was named for Francis Pope, who settled in the area in the 17<sup>th</sup>c and was the first person in the county to import slaves. Archeological work has revealed that the Indians made huge heaps of oysters. Not much is left of the town, except for a few crab houses.

John Wilkes Booth crossed the Potomac River at Pope's Creek after assassinating President Lincoln.

Pope's Creek was the terminus of the Pope's Creek branch of the railroad which ran from Bowie to the Potomac River.

In 1958, the Charles County Tercentenary Year, the Catholic Church erected the Loyola-on-the-Potomac Retreat House.

# Faulkner

*Lodging*

Town & Country Motel. 10870 Crain Highway. 301-934-8252

# Newport

Newport was a post office in 1806. The village was located on a tributary of the Wicomico River, which might have silted up.

**Attractions**

Sarum. Rte. 234. Private. Sarum was granted to Joseph Pile, Esq. in 1680 and is a 1,150 acre estate.

# Newburg

Just south of Newburg is the Harry W. Nice Bridge which crosses the Potomac to Virginia. The bridge is named for one of the few Republican governors of Maryland, and opened in 1940.

**Attractions**

Christ Church, Wayside (William and Mary Parish, 1692) Rte. 257. 301-259-4327. William and Mary is one of the 30 original parishes created by the Establishment Act of 1692. A church was already in existence in 1694 and was known as Picawaxon Parish. The present church was constructed before 1750 and remodeled in 1871. The communion service was brought from England in 1700.

Society Hill. Mt.Victoria Road. Private. The 18th c house overlooks the Wicomico River area.

West Hatton. West Hatton Road. Private. Maj. William Truman Stoddert built the house overlooking the Wicomico River. His brother, Benjamin Stoddert, was the first Secretary of the U.S. Navy.

Mount Republican. Rte. 257. Private. The house was built in 1792 by Theophilus Yates and overlooks the Potomac River. Franklin Weems later lived in the house.

# Cobb Island

Cobb Island, located on a peninsula at the confluence of the Potomac and Wicomico Rivers, is a resort.

*Dining*

Capt. John's Crab House & Marina. 16215 Cobb Island Road. 301-259-2315

# Port Tobacco

Port Tobacco was located where the Potomac River meets the Port Tobacco River. Capt. John Smith sailed up the Potomac in 1608 and marked the Indian village of Potopaco, which was colonized by the English in 1634. Potopaco means the "jutting of water inland". The town was originally named Chandler's Town for Job Chandler, the earliest white settler. A Jesuit missionary, Father Andrew White, converted the Indians and translated the catechism and other English works into the Indian language in 1638. The Jesuits had been given four thousand acres in this region. Father White was later tried in England for being a Catholic priest. He was acquitted, but never returned to Maryland. At one time Port Tobacco was Maryland's second largest port.

A 1727 Act of the Maryland Assembly planned for the building of a courthouse and village in the vicinity, and named the town "Charles Town". This was the county seat of Charles County, before it was moved to La Plata. Port Tobacco received its name in 1821 from the thousands of pounds of tobacco annually shipped from here .This was the second largest river port until the Revolutionary War.

Saint Thomas Manor on Chapel Point is home to the beautiful church of St. Ignatius with its historic cemetery, built in 1798. The cornerstone of the church was laid by Bishop John Carroll, first Bishop of the United States. The Manor House next door was built in 1741 and had quarters for slaves given to the Jesuit priests. Slavery ended here in 1839. Pastor Francis Neale brought the Carmelite nuns to the U.S. and settled them in this parish. The first religious community for women was founded at the Mount Carmel Monastery in 1790.

In 1808 the courthouse and Episcopal Church were blown down in a windstorm. The courthouse was rebuilt, but burned in 1892. With the silting of the river the county seat was moved to La Plata in 1895. The courthouse was restored with state funds starting in 1965. Other places of note are the Chimney House (1765), Stag Hall (1732), The Charles County Museum of Port Tobacco, and the Birch House c 1700. The Society for the Restoration of Port Tobacco continues its work to preserve this charming place.

Among the famous people who lived here were Thomas Stone, a Signer of the Declaration of Independence at "Habre de Venture" (built 1771-73) - now Thomas Stone National Historic Site; John Hanson, first elected President in Congress Assembled at "Mulberry Grove"; Major-General William Smallwood (Revolutionary War) at "Smallwood's Retreat"; Daniel of St. Thomas Jenifer, signer of the U.S. Constitution at "Retreat"; Dr. Gustavus Brown, the Washington family physician at "Rose Hill"; and Dr. James Craik, Surgeon General of the Continental Army at "La Grange".

The story of the "Blue Dog" has been around this area for more than one hundred years. Supposedly the spirit of a large bluetick hound dog protects his murdered master's treasure buried on Rose Hill Road. According to the story,

Charles Thomas Sims on February 8th during the Revolution, and his dog were killed while returning from a tavern in Port Tobacco. Henry Hanos of Port Tobacco killed him and his dog for his gold and deed to his property. He then buried the gold and deed under a tree on Rose Hill Road. When Hanos returned for the treasure he was scared away by the ghost of the blue dog and suddenly became ill and died. The legend dates back to 1897 when Olivia Floyd, owner of the property, saw the ghost.

**Port Tobacco Courthouse**

### Attractions

Around the public square are several historic private homes. These include Chimney House, built c1770; Stagg Hall; Quinnsell House; and the Cat Slide House.

Port Tobacco One-Room School. 7215 Chapel Point Road. 301-932-6064. The school was built in 1876 and was used for 77 years. White students were enrolled until 1924, and from 1924-53 the school housed black students, grades one through seven. In the 1990s the Charles County Retired Teachers Association began to restore the school.

Port Tobacco Courthouse. Chapel Point Road. 301-934-4313. April to October, Wednesday to Sunday. The first county courthouse was completed in 1729, and the second in 1819. The courthouse burned in 1892, and was rebuilt.

Charles County Museum. Courthouse 2nd floor. 301-934-4313 On display are pictures of Charles County's oldest homes, artifacts and history of the area. The Union army surrendered at the Courthouse in 1864.

Catslide Hill. Originally known as the Burch House, built in 1720 this house has been going through extensive renovations. The name comes from the steep slope in the roof.

Rose Hill. Rose Hill Road. This private home was built by Dr. Gustavus Richard Brown c1730 on land known as Betty's Delight. The house has an incredible view down the Port Tobacco River to the Potomac. The house has brick ends and clapboard sides. The boxwood gardens are said to be the finest in Maryland.

**Thomas Stone National Historic Site**

Thomas Stone National Historic Site. 6655 Rose Hill Road. 301-934-6027. Thomas Stone and his wife Margaret Brown built "Habre de Venture" c1771 of brick. They had two daughters and a son. The main product of the farm was tobacco. Mr. Stone was one of four Maryland Signers of the Declaration of Independence, a Continental Congressman, and a Framer of the Articles of Confederation. Mr. Stone and his wife died within five months of each other in 1787 and are buried on the property. A frame wing was added in 1840. The house remained in the Stone family until 1936. A fire nearly destroyed the house in 1977, but was restored beginning in 1992. The paneling, corner cupboards and family portraits are now in the Colonial Room at the Baltimore Museum of Art. The house is open to the public and is part of the National Park Service.

Chandler's Hope. Chapel Point Road. Job Chandler acquired property on both sides of the Port Tobacco River in 1651. Later the prominent Catholic Neale family was to occupy the house. Father Leonard Neale became Archbishop of Baltimore after John Carroll and later President of Georgetown University. His brother Francis Neale was also to become President of Georgetown. Father Charles Neale was a founder of Mount Carmel Convent and then Superior of the Jesuit Mission in America.

Mulberry Grove. Chapel Point Road. Private. In 1747 John Hanson, whom the Congress elected as President in 1781, bought this private home.

St. Ignatius Roman Catholic Church and St. Thomas Manor House. 8855 Chapel Point Road. The church is the nation's oldest active parish with a continual pastorate. The Rev. Andrew S. White who accompanied the settlers to Maryland founded St. Ignatius in 1641. This was part of a Jesuit mission established in 1662. The property once included over 3,500 acres on both sides of the Port Tobacco River and was a working farm with slaves.

The church building dates from 1790. A hyphen, which was used as a chapel, connects the church and house and were built 1741-90. The original manor house was burned by the British in 1781 and rebuilt. Another fire in 1866 destroyed the interior and hipped roof. During the Civil War the property was occupied by Union Troops. After the war the Jesuits maintained the property once again as a working farm and ran a ferry boat along the Potomac. In 1970 the state of Maryland purchased 828 acres for a state park.

On the property is a servant house that has a basement with an empty well. The well is part of an underground tunnel that goes down to the river. There are a variety of legends about the use of the tunnel. Included are a place for Jesuits to be smuggled into the colonies; a hiding place for priests from the British; a place to bring goods up during inclement weather; and it may have been part of the Underground Railroad. The church and manor house are located on a 120 foot bluff overlooking the mouth of the Port Tobacco River where it joins the Potomac River. The sight is incredible and well worth the trip to visit.

# Ironsides

## Attractions

Araby. Rte. 425. This restored private home was built c1760 and belonged to the widow Elbeck whose daughter married George Mason of Gunston Hall in Virginia. The garden has a blue rambler rose, the only one in Maryland.

# Nanjemoy

The town was called Nanjemoy Cross Roads before 1890.

## Attractions

Christ Church, Ironsides (Durham Parish, 1692). 8685 Ironsides Road. 301-743-7099. The church is one of the 30 original parishes in Maryland and one of the oldest churches. The present brick church was constructed in 1732, replacing the original log church. Near the front gate is a replica of a sundial which determined the time of the service.

The communion service, chalice and paten of London Silver dating from 1707, are among the oldest in use in this country. William Dent, the owner and builder of Friendship House, built in 1680, bequeathed the chalice to the church in 1708.

The church was visited several times by George Washington. The building was restored in 1932 as a memorial to General Smallwood, a vestryman. The Smallwood Bell Tower was constructed from bricks that had been part of Gen. Smallwood's sister's house. One of the gravestones dates back to 1692.

Nanjemoy Baptist Church, 1791. 2975 Baptist Church Road. 301-246-4926. The church is one of the oldest Baptist churches in continuous use in Maryland. The church is the mother of Southern Baptist Churches in the Tri-County area. In 1791 one acre was purchased to build a meeting house.

# Marbury

Marbury was named for Frances Marbury who came from Cheshire, England and settled near Piscataway. He received a deed for "Carroll's Kindness" on

Piscataway Creek. He obtained a second grant in 1698 called "Marbury's Chance".

**Attractions**

General Smallwood State Park. Smallwood's Retreat. Rte. 224. 301-743-7613. The plantation home of General William Smallwood (1732-92) was built c1760. In 1776 Gen. Smallwood marched from Annapolis to defend Long Island against the British. About two hundred of his men fought under Maj. Mordecai Gist at the Battle of Long Island, losing 37 men. Maryland received its name "Old Line State" from Gen. Washington who knew they had held the line.

General Smallwood was promoted to brigadier and in 1780 a major general at the Battle of Camden, South Carolina. In 1785 the General Assembly of Maryland appointed him Governor until 1788. He retired to this house in 1785.

# Indian Head

Indian Head was incorporated in 1920. The name may have come from a Native American legend, or that it resembles an Indian head from the air.

**Attractions**

U.S. Naval Ordnance Station. Ensign Robert Brooke Dashiell built the station in 1890. During World War I torpedoes were manufactured here. In the 1920s Robert Goddard experimented with propellants for his rockets. Across the creek an Explosive Ordnance Disposal School was built in the 1940s.

*Lodging*

Indian Head Inn. 301-743-5405

# Purse State Park

The park is just east of Indian Head. Rte 224 and Liverpool Point Road. Dr. Purse deeded the 100 acre park to the State. The park is a treasure trove for fossil hunters, which includes shark's teeth that are 15 million years old. The park has pileated and hairy woodpeckers, titmouse and black and white warblers among its bird population, and at least seven different types of butterflies.

# Chapman Point

The Chapman family occupied the plantation "Mount Aventine" during the 19<sup>th</sup> c. A ferry crossed from here to Virginia.

# Accokeek

**Attractions:**

<u>Piscataway National Park</u>. Farmington Road. Piscataway was named for the Piscataway Indian tribe. During the 18<sup>th</sup> c the town was a port exporting mainly tobacco. Piscataway Creek is located almost directly across the Potomac River from George Washington's "Mount Vernon". By the 1830s the creek had silted in and Piscataway lost its importance as a port.

The park has many trails, an excellent view of Mount Vernon. On the property are The National Colonial Farm Museum and Ecosystem Farm.

**National Colonial Farm Museum**

The Accokeek Foundation at Piscataway Park. National Colonial Farm Museum. Bryan Point Road. 301-283-2113. This is a restored c1775 farm and offers a hands-on tour of a tobacco farm.

The Ecosystem Farm. 3400 Bryan Point Road. 201-283-2113. The eight acre organic vegetable farm is located on former tobacco fields overlooking the Potomac River. Two solar panels power the irrigation system and the electric fence to deter deer and other animals from entering the garden.

St. James Hill. Livingston Road. Private. The house was built c1740.

Christ Church. Farmington Road. A chapel was built here in 1698. The church was built in 1745, destroyed by fire in 1856, and rebuilt in 1857.

Site of Mayaone. Bryan Point Road. This was an Indian village marked on John Smith's map. The house was burned in 1622 following an Indian uprising in Virginia. The Piscataway that survived moved along Piscataway Creek.

# Marshall Hall

Marshall Hall was a five hundred acre tract surveyed for William Marshall in 1651. Thomas Hanson Marshall represented Charles County at the provincial convention in Annapolis in 1775. John Marshall was First Major of the Lower Battalion in 1776.

**Attractions**

Marshall Hall. Rte. 227. Thomas Marshall purchased the property in 1728. From 1949-68 it became a legal gambling spot for slot machines.

# Fort Washington

Warburton Manor was patented in 1661 and was the home of the Digges family. They were descended from Edward Digges, Governor of Virginia 1652-89.

**Attractions**

Fort Washington. Fort Washington Road. 301-763-4600. Open daily. This was the first fort built to defend Washington. George Washington chose the location on the Potomac River, and the U.S. government purchased the property in 1808. The fort was named Fort Barberton. The first fort was completed in 1809 to protect Washington, but was destroyed by its own garrison during the War of 1812. Captain Sam Dyson commanded the fort. On August 27 as the British were leaving Washington, he had to abandon the fort with his small company of men. The British captured the fort and its supplies, and then sailed on to capture Alexandria. Capt. Dyson was court-martialed for this.

Major Pierre Charles L'Enfant, the architect for Washington, DC designed the next fort in 1815. After a quarrel with the War Department Lt. Col. Walker K. Armistead replaced him. The fort was completed in 1824, renamed Fort Washington and served until 1872.

**Fort Washington**

The fort is built of granite from Occoquan, Virginia. In 1939 the Department of the Interior took over the fort. During World War II the fort served as the Adjutant General's School, and then a prisoner of war camp. In 1946 the fort became part of the National Capital Park System.

Rosecroft Raceway. 6336 Rosecroft Drive. 301-567-4000. This is Maryland's oldest harness racing facility.

# Oxon Hill

The name probably came from the estate "Oxon Hill Manor", a home built in the 17th c by Col. John Addison, a privy counselor of Lord Baltimore.

## Attractions

Oxon Hill Manor. Oxon Hill Road. 301-839-7782. Tuesday-Friday. This property originally belonged to John Addison and was known as St. Elizabeth's in the late 1600s. His son, Thomas, built the original house, which burned in 1895. In 1767 Thomas' grandson later turned the land into an estate. John Hanson, President of the United States under the Articles of Confederation (1781-82) died here in 1783. Sumner Welles, Undersecretary of State for President Roosevelt also lived here and built the present house in the 1920's. The house is now listed on the National Register of Historic Places. The beautiful Georgian brick mansion overlooks the Potomac River and has lovely gardens.

Oxon Hill Farm. 6411 Oxon Hill Road. 301-839-1176. The 500 acre park has a farm, pastures, woods and ponds. The hands-on farm demonstrates the agricultural cycles of the year. The farm once belonged to St. Elizabeth's Hospital in Washington.

Fort Foote Park. Fort Foote Road. 301-763-4600. This Civil War fort was built in the 1860's and was used to guard Washington, Alexandria, and Georgetown.. William H. Seward, Jr., son of President Lincoln's Secretary of State supervised the building of the fort.

St. John's Episcopal Church. Rte. 210. The original church was built in the 1720s. The present structure was erected in 1766 and remodeled in 1820.

Harmony Hall. Livingston Road. Private. The estate was once known as Battersea and was thought to have been built by Enoch Magruder c1750. In 1792 Walter Dulaney Addison and his brother John brought their brides here, living in harmony for a year, and giving the house its name.

## Lodging

Best Western Potomac View-Oxon Hill. 6400 Oxon Hill Road. 301-749-9400
Red Roof Inn-Oxon Hill. 6170 Oxon Hill Road. 301-567-8030
Susse Chalet Inn- Oxon Hill. 6363 Oxon Hill Road. 301-839-0001

# A Side Trip to Washington

In 1790 Congress decided that the new capital would be located in the state of Maryland. In 1791 George Washington chose the site at the junction of the Eastern Branch (now Anacostia) and Potomac Rivers. Major Pierre Charles L'Enfant, who had served in the Continental Army during the Revolutionary War, came to the site to plan the city, based on the broad boulevards and circles in Paris. However he was dismissed in 1792 after he ordered the razing of Daniel Carroll's home on Capitol Hill which would block his plans for that area. Andrew Ellicott, a mathematician and Benjamin Banneker, an astronomer of Ellicott City began surveying the designated area, which was to be ten miles square.

Several special places related to the history of the Western Shore of Maryland are important to visit.

**Washington National Cathedral**

Washington National Cathedral. Mount St. Alban's. Charles Carroll Glover, a banker and civic leader held a meeting in his Washington home in 1891 to make

222

plans for a national cathedral. Two years later a charter was granted to the Protestant Episcopal Foundation. The Cathedral was part of Major L'Enfant's original plans for the capital.

Bishop Thomas John Claggett and his wife Mary Gantt were buried at Croom, and have since been moved to the Cathedral. Francis Scott Key wrote the inscriptions on their tombstones. Francis Scott Key was also a founder of Christ Church, Georgetown and Trinity Church, Washington.

The Maryland window is located on the right side of the Cathedral when you enter through the west entrance.

Dumbarton House. 2715 Q Street, NW. Dolley Madison fled to the home of Charles Carroll when the President's House (the White House) was burned during the War of 1812. The home was later owned by Joseph Nourse, first registrar of the Treasury. Today the house is the headquarters of the National Society of Colonial Dames of America, of which the author is a member.

Thomas Notley, a colonial governor of Maryland (1679-84), purchased most of Capitol Hill and southwest Washington in 1691 for 40,000 pounds of tobacco. His godson Notley Rozier inherited the land, and had a daughter Ann who married Daniel Carroll of Annapolis. He built five row houses in the 1800s that were called Carroll Row and torn down in 1887. During the Civil War the row houses became Carroll Prison for political prisoners. Her two sons Charles Carroll and Notley Young later inherited the estate part of which was to become the U.S. Capitol and the Navy Yard.

Duddlington Manor. 1st and 2nd Streets, SE. In 1791 Daniel Carroll who had inherited the land mentioned above, began to build his home on this site. Unfortunately the estate was situated in the plans laid out by Pierre L'Enfant, and he ordered the construction halted. George Washington and the local commissioners persuaded Mr. Carroll to move his house further east. Mr. Carroll was at that time a commissioner.

Suter's Tavern Site. 1000 block of Wisconsin Avenue, NW. In 1791 George Washington and the four commissioners, including Daniel Carroll met at the tavern with local landowners to persuade them to sell their property to develop the new capital. Pierre L'Enfant and Andrew Ellicott also met here to draw up plans for the city.

Christ Episcopal Church. 620 G Street, SE. The church was established in 1794 and first met in Daniel Carroll's tobacco barn.

Benjamin Ogle Tayloe House. The house, built in 1828, is situated at 21 Madison Place overlooking Lafayette Square, and is now part of the U.S. Court of Appeals for the Federal Circuit. Mr. Tayloe was a descendant of several Annapolis families. He is the author of "Our Neighbors on Lafayette Square", published in 1872 and containing many stories about the occupants of the White House, whom he knew. The house was occupied by Senator Mark Hanna during President McKinley's administration and was known as the "Little White House".

The Octagon House. 1799 New York Avenue, NW. Col. John Tayloe III built Octagon House in 1798. The architect was William Thornton, first architect of the U.S. Capitol building. Ann Ogle Tayloe was the daughter of Governor Benjamin Ogle of Maryland. President and Mrs. James Madison lived here after the British burned of the White House. President Madison signed the Treaty of Ghent, ending the War of 1812 at the house.

Corner of Madison Place and Pennsylvania Avenue, NW. In 1859 New York Congressman Daniel E. Sickles shot Philip Barton Key, son of Francis Scott Key, after Mr. Sickle's wife confessed to having an affair with Mr. Key. At his trial Mr. Sickle's was acquitted on grounds of temporary insanity. The site is now the Treasury Annex constructed in 1919.

Halcyon House. 3400 Prospect Street. This lovely home overlooking the Potomac River was built in the 1780's and was the home of the first Secretary of the Navy, Benjamin Stoddert, whose brother lived at West Hatton in Newburg.

722 Jackson Place, NW. In 1931 the Brookings Institution constructed a building on this site. The building was razed in 1963. The Brookings Institution is now located at 1773-75 Massachusetts Avenue, NW. The founder of the Institution, Mr. Brookings, is buried at St. Mary Anne's Church in North East.

Mary Surratt House. 604 H Street, NW. John Wilkes Booth and his co-conspirators plotted the death of President Abraham Lincoln, Vice President Andrew Johnson and Secretary of State William Seward here. Mary Surratt would eventually be tried and hanged for her role, the first woman hanged in Washington.

M Street, near Key Bridge. Francis Scott Key, while practicing law in Washington, lived here from 1805-30. The Whitehurst ramp is now located on the site.

308 C Street, NW. Francis Scott Key moved to this residence in 1833 to get away from the construction noise of the new Chesapeake and Ohio Canal near his Georgetown house. He lived here until his death in 1843. "The Star-Spangled

Banner was first sung in Washington at the McKeown Hotel, 615 Pennsylvania Avenue following a dinner for retiring Secretary of the Navy William Jones.

Wisconsin Avenue and R Street, NW. Governor Thomas Lee Sim of Maryland purchased this property and named it Lee's Hill. Later a reservoir was located here and is now the Georgetown Branch of the District of Columbia Library.

Mount Olivet Catholic Cemetery. 1300 Bladensburg Road, NE. Towards the back of the cemetery is inscribed a stone that only says "Mrs. Surratt". This marks the grave of the woman hanged for complicity in the Lincoln assassination who lived at Surratt House.

St. John's Catholic Cemetery. Forest Glen at Rosenteel Avenue. Silver Spring. The Rev. John Carroll built the first St. John's here in 1774. He was made Bishop of Baltimore in 1790 and Maryland's first archbishop in 1808. Rev. Carroll is buried in Baltimore, but his mother is buried here. The chapel is a replica of the original.


## Campgrounds

Woodlands Camping Resort. 265 Starkey Lane. Elkton. 410-398-4414
Riverside Ponderosa Pines Campground. 1435 Carpenter's Point Road. Perryville. 410-642-3431
Susquehanna State Park. Havre de Grace. 410-557-7994
Bar Harbor RV Park and Marina. 4228 Birch Avenue. Abington. 1-800-351-CAMP
Capital KOA Campground. 768 Cecil Avenue. Millersville. 410-923-2771
Duncan's Family Campground. 5381 Sands Road. Lothian. 410-741-9558
Breezy Point Beach & Campground. 530 Breezy Point Road. Chesapeake Beach. 410-855-9894
Point Lookout State Park. Rte 5, Scotland. 301-872-5688
Matoaka Beach Cabins. St. Leonard. 410-586-0269
Camp Merrylande. St. George's Island. 301-994-1722
Dennis Point Marina & Camp Ground. Drayden. 301-994-2288
Le Grande Estate Camping Resort. Leonardtown. 301-475-8550
St. Patrick's Creek. Colton's Point. 301-769-4099
Sea Side View Recreation Park. Ridge. 301-872-4141
Take-it-Easy Ranch Campsite. Callaway. 301-994-0494
Smallwood State Park. Rte. 1, Marbury. 1-800-784-5380
Aqua-Land Campground. Newburg. 301-259-2575
Goose Bay Marina and Campground. Welcome. 301-934-7613

# Chapter 4

# Yachting

*Lady Katie* and *Constellation* – Baltimore Harbor

## Yachts, Workboats and other Sailing Vessels

The earliest boats on the Bay and rivers were Indian dugout log canoes with a sail. Later, the coloonists used this same style boat. The bugeye is a two-master schooner descended from the canoe, and was used for oystering. The skipjack also was used for oystering and has a single raked mast and centerboard. Only about 30 skipjacks are left. A patent tonger is a vessel that uses rigs and cannot use power for dredging.

Early shipyards included the Stephen Steward Yard on the West River, Galesville which built scows, brigs, sloops, schooners, and brigantines. During the Revolution and later the War of 1812 and the Civil War, American cities were cut off from trade. Privateers or running blockades were necessary means of survival. John Paul Jones, Joshua Barney and others played important roles in the United States Navy. Most of Commodore Barney's flotilla was built at Fells Point in Baltimore, Washington and St. Michael's and included 13 barges.

John Henry Davis moved to Solomons Island in 1879 to build pungy schooners and bugeyes. His son founded the Davis Shipyard in 1885.Marcellus M Davis built boats into the 1920s. The company built steam-powered tugboats, bugeyes, and later racing yachts that included *High Tide* owned by Eugene Dupont and *Manitou* owned by John F. Kennedy. Pictures of these can be seen at the Calvert Marine Museum in Solomons. His son Clarence Davis also built yachts.

Many boatyards operated in Baltimore. In 1773 the Continental Congress commissioned the first ship for the Navy. George Wells built the *Virginia* on Fells Point. His house is still located at Bond and Thames Streets. The Baltimore Schooners helped win the War of 1812. The *Pride of Baltimore* is the only existing replica of an 1812 era Baltimore Clipper topsail schooner.

One of the most famous builder and designer of yachts, John Trumpy, purchased the Annapolis Yacht Yard which had constructed the Vosper patrol boats during World War II, and moved from New Jersey to Annapolis in 1947. The site had originally been the Chance Marine Construction Co. founded in 1913 by Charles Chance to build and repair boats for the watermen. During WWI six 110-foot submarine chasers were built for the Navy, and after that boats for pleasure. The Reconstruction Finance Corp. purchased it in 1937, after which it was again purchased, this time by Nelson-Reid, naval architects and boat builders, becoming the Annapolis Yacht Yard, Inc.

Small classic boats on the Bay are the Whirlwinds, built in Cockeysville by Molded Products from 1947-62. Their molded mahogany hulls were lightweight, low maintenance, low priced and easy to handle. About 12,000 Whirlwinds were built. They were known for their speed, often winning APBA championships. Unfortunately with the debut of fiberglass and the recession of 1960-61 the company was sold at auction in 1962. However, there are still quite a few around.

The Chesapeake 20s, Quadrants and various other boats were designed and built at the Hartge Yacht Yard in Galesville. Captain Ed Leatherbury of Shady Side also built a number of boats for the Bay.

### Ferries and Steamboats

Means of travel to the other side of the Chesapeake was limited until 1952 with the opening of the Bay Bridge to ferries, steamships or other types of vessels.

During the 1600's ferries crossed the South River at Londontowne. In the 1760's innkeeper Samuel Middleton of Annapolis operated a ferry across the Bay carrying people and horses.

During the 1830's the first steamboats were put into operation. The *Dreamland* could carry up to 3,000 passengers between Baltimore and Chesapeake Beach for 50 cents. The 185-foot *Emma Giles*, built in 1887, plied the Bay for 50 years carrying passengers, and beginning in 1932, freight until she was sold for scrap. Her captain's wheel is on display at the Galesville Community Hall and a model at the Salem Avery House in Shady Side. The boat was named for the owner's daughter, whose portrait had hung on the landing of the steamboat's grand stairway.

*The Victory Chimes*, now a National Historic Landmark, is the last American built three-masted schooner or larger sailing vessel still sailing. She was built as a Chesapeake Bay Ram in 1900 at Bethel, DE and christened *the Edwin and Maud*. There were 28 rams built c1870-1920. The Victory Chimes carried lumber along the East Coast and then was converted into a passenger ship. She sailed out of Annapolis until 1955, and then up in Maine, where she is part of the Windjammer fleet. She returned to the Bay the summer of 2000 to celebrate her 100th birthday.

The Chesapeake steamer, *President Warfield*, plied the Bay from 1913-1963. She took overnight passengers, and offered good dining and dancing. During World War II the *President Warfield* landed at Omaha Beach in Normandy and transported American troops up the Seine River. After the war she returned to Baltimore, but was sold to the Jewish underground army Haganah, Under the name *Exodus* she carried 4,500 Holocaust survivors from Europe to Palestine, and on July 18, 1947 tried to break the Royal Navy blockade of what is now Israel. In 1969 David Holly wrote the book *Exodus 1947* about the ship. In addition he has built models and studied steamboats of the Bay.

The *Starlight* steamed from the Patapsco River to Brown's Grove in Anne Arundel County with African American passengers. In 1919 the 201 foot side-wheeler *Governor Emerson C. Harrington* began the Annapolis-Claiborne run with cars and passengers in just a little over an hour.

The double-ended Governor *Albert C. Ritchie* was launched in 1926, an even larger vessel. The *John M. Dennis* was put into service in 1929 and the terminus was moved from Claiborne to Matapeake, making the crossing in about 45 minutes, and costing 50 cents round trip! The trip from Annapolis was from the King George Street dock. In 1943 this was moved to Sandy Point now taking only 25 minutes. The *Dennis* made the last crossing in 1952 when the Bay

Bridge opened. In June 1973 the second Chesapeake Bay Bridge span opened, one year late and cost $60 million more than the $65 million estimate.

## Lighthouses/Lightships

The Chesapeake Bay has many beautiful harbors, but also treacherous shoals. Lighthouses were built to warn the sailors of the shoals. The first lighthouse was built in Maryland in 1822, with 43 added after that.

Thomas Point Lighthouse, Annapolis was built in 1875 as a screwpile wooden hexagon, was the last manned lighthouse on the Chesapeake, and was automated until 1989.

Sandy Point Shoal, Annapolis was built 1882 as a caisson brick house.

Concord Point Lighthouse, Havre de Grace is on the site of a battery where the Susquehanna River meets the Chesapeake Bay. The lighthouse was built in 1827 by John Dunahoo and was the oldest lighthouse in continuous use in Maryland. The lighthouse was decommissioned in 1975.

Fishing Battery. Havre de Grace. The lighthouse was built in 1853 and located 2.5 miles from the shore.

Turkey Point. North East. The stone tower was built in 1833 and is located in Elk Neck State Park.

Pooles Island. Aberdeen Proving Grounds. The stone tower was built in 1825.

Fort Carroll. Baltimore. The wooden frame tower was built in 1898 and is located almost under the Key Bridge.

Bodkin Point Lighthouse erected in 1822 at the entrance to Baltimore Harbor was the first lighthouse in Maryland. The lighthouse remained in operation until 1856 and then was abandoned.

Drum Point. Solomons. The screwpile lighthouse was built in 1883 and is on display at the Calvert Marine Museum

Piney Point. St. Clement's Island. The stone tower was built in 1836.

Fort Washington. Fort Washington Park. The frame tower was built in the 1870s.

# Marine Information

U.S. Coast Guard. 1-800-418-7314
U.S. Coast Guard, Annapolis. 410-267-8108
U.S. Coast Guard, St. Inigoes. 301-872-4344
Natural Resources Police. 1-800-628-9944

## Special Yachting Events

June 2002 – Volvo Around the World Race will race into Baltimore and Annapolis

## Yacht Clubs/ Sailing Associations

Perryville Yacht Club. 31River Road. Perryville. 410642-6364
North East River Yacht Club. 410-287-6333
North East Yacht Club. 410-287-6660
Glenmar Sailing Association. Middle River
Middle River Yacht Club. 201 Nanticoke Rd. Essex. 410-687-1160
Annapolis Yacht Club. 2 Compromise Street. 410-263-9279
Eastport Yacht Club- 317 First Street, Eastport. 410-263-0415
Severn River Yacht Club. 519 Chester Avenue. 410-268-8282
Maryland Capital Yacht Club. 16 Chesapeake Landing. 410-269-5219
Severn Sailing Association. 311 Second Street. 410-269-6744
Podickory Point Yacht and Beach Club. 2116 Bay Front Terrace. 410-757-8000
West River Sailing Club. Tenthouse Creek.

## Towing/Recovery

Markley's Marina. Baltimore. 410-687-5575
Sea Tow. Annapolis. 410-267-1260
Sea Tow. Arnold. 410-267-7650
Sea Tow. Baltimore. 410-574-4188
TowBoat/US Annapolis. 410-263-1260
TowBoat/US Baltimore. 410-440-3319
TowBoat/US Upper Chesapeake. 410-885-5988
TowBoat/US Herring Bay. 301-261-5151
TowBoat/US Northeast. 410-885-5988
TowBoat/US Solomons. 410-326-6801

Vehicle Assist Solomons. 410-535-1554
Casa Rio Marina. Mayo. 301-261-7111

## Marinas/Docks

Cove Marina. 11 Main Sail Drive. Elkton. 410-620-5505
Triton Marina. Plum Point Road. Elkton. 410-398-7515
Anchor Marina, Inc. Iroquois Drive. North East. 410-287-6000
Bay Boat Works. Hances Point Road. North East. 410-287-8113
Jackson Marine Sales. North East. 410-287-9400
Tomes Landing Marina. 1000 Rowland Drive. Port Deposit. 410-378-3343
McDaniel Yacht Basin. 15 Grandview Avenue. North East. 410-287-8121
Penn's Beach Marina. Havre de Grace. 410-939-2060
Tidewater Marina. Bourbon Street. Havre de Grace. 410-939-0950
Havre de Grace Marina at Log Pond. 410-939-2161
Gunpowder Cove Marina. 510 Riviera Drive. Joppa. 410-679-5454
Maryland Marina. 3501 Red Rose Road. Essex. 410-335-8722
River Watch Marina. 207 Nanticoke Road. Essex. 410687-1422
Essex Marina and Boat Sales. 1755 Hilltop Avenue. Essex. 410-687-6149
Neris Marina. 400 Wagner Lane. Middle River. 410335-5533
Weaver's Marina. 730 Riverside Drive. Essex. 410-686-4944
Buedel's Marina. 1907 Old Eastern Avenue. Essex. 410-687-3577
Anchor Bay Marina & Ship's Store. Essex. 410-574-0777
Cutter Marine Yacht Basin. 1900 Old Eastern Avenue. Upper Middle River. 410-391-7245
Bowley's Marina. 400 Bowley's Quarters Road. Middle River. 410335-3553
Baltimore Public Docking. 410-396-3174
Inner Harbor Marina of Baltimore. 400 Key Highway. 410-837-5339
Inner Harbor East Marina. 801 Lancaster Street. Baltimore. 410-625-1700
HarborView Marina. Baltimore. 410-752-1122
Sunset Harbor Marina. Baltimore. 410-687-7290
Tidewater Yacht Service. Baltimore. 410-625-4992
Bay View Marina. Fells Point, Baltimore. 410-327-8600
Center Dock Marina. Fells Point, Baltimore. 410-685-0295
Old Bay Marina. Baltimore. 410-477-1488
Porter's Seneca Marina. 918 Seneca Park Road. Baltimore. 410-335-6563
Hendersons's Wharf Marina & Inn. 10001 Fells Street. Baltimore. 410-732-1049
Anchorage Marina. Canton, Baltimore. 410-522-7200
Baltimore Marine Center. 2600 Lighthouse Point West. Canton. 410-675-8888
Canton Cove Marina. Canton. 410-675-1148
Pleasure Cove Marina. Bodkin Creek. Pasadena. 410-437-6600
Ventnor Marina. 8070 Ventnor Road. Pasadena. 410-255-4100
Oak Harbor Marina. 1343 Old Water Oak Road. Pasadena. 410-255-4070

White Rocks Marina. 1402 Colony Road. Pasadena. 410-255-3800
Magothy Marina. 360 Magothy Road. Severna Park. 410-647-2356
Ferry Point Marina and Yachtyard. 700 Mill Creek Road. Arnold. 410-647-8722
Smith's Marina. 529 Ridgely Road. Crownsville. 410-923-3444
Podickory Yacht and Beach Club. 2116 Bayfront Terrace. Annapolis. 410-757-8000
Annapolis City Marina. 410 Severn Avenue. 410-268-0660
Annapolis Landing Marina. 980 Awald Drive. Annapolis. 410-263-0900
Mears Marina. 519 Chester Avenue. Annapolis. 410-268-8282
Port Annapolis Marina. 7078 Bembe Beach Road. Annapolis. 410-269-0939
McCleary's Pier 4 Marina. 301 Fourth Street. Annapolis. 410-990-9515
Liberty Yacht Club & Marina. 64 Old South River Road. Edgewater. 410-266-5633
Selby Bay Yacht Basin, Inc. Edgewater. 410-798-0232
Rhode River Marina. Edgewater. 410-269-0699
South River Marina. 1061 Turkey Point Road. Edgewater. 800-262-8351
Warehouse Creek Marina. 58 Leland Road. Edgewater. 410-956-1880
Holiday Point Marina. 3774 Beach Drive Blvd, Edgewater. 410-956-2208
Turkey Point Marina. 1107 Turkey Point Road, Edgewater. 410-798-1369
Holiday Hill Marina. Mayo. 410-626-1345
Hartge Yacht Yard. 4480 Church Lane. Galesville. 410-867-2188
Bluewater Marina. Rhode River. 410-798-6733
Leatherbury Point Marina. Shady Side. 410-261-5599
Shipwright Harbor. 6047 Herring Bay Road. Deale. 410-867-7686
Herrington Harbour. Deale. 410867-4343
Herrington Harbour South Resort. Rose Haven. 410-213-9438
Rod-N-Reel Dock. Rte. 261 and Mears Avenue. Chesapeake Beach. 301-855-8450
Halle Marina, Inc. Halle Marina. 410-257-2561
Kellam's Marina & Boatyard. 8020 Bayside Avenue. 301-855-8968
Fishing Creek Landings Marina. 4055 Gordon Stinnett Avenue. Chesapeake Beach. 301-855-3572
Abner's Marina. 3725 Harbor Road. Chesapeake Beach. 301-855-8985
Breezy Point Marina. 530 Breezy Point Road. Chesapeake Beach. 410-855-9894
Hallowing Point Marina. Barstow. 410-535-4802
Flag Harbor Yacht Haven. St. Leonard. 410-586-0070
Len's Marina. 8995 Broomes Island Road. Broomes Island. 410-586-0077
Broomes Island Marina. 3939 Oyster House Road. Broomes Island. 410-586-2941
Mill Creek Boating Center. 12565 Rousby Hall Road. Lusby. 410-326-7089
Vera's White Sands Marina. 1200 White Sands Drive. Lusby. 410-586-1182
Calvert Marina. Dowell Road. Solomons. 410-326-4251
Comfort Inn Beacon Marina. Solomons. 410-326-6303
Harbor Island Marina. Solomons. 410-326-3441

Hospitality Harbor Marina. Solomons. 410-326-1052
Quantum. Solomons Island. 410326-2600
Spring Cove Marina. Back Creek and Lore Street. Solomons. 410-326-2161
Town Center Marina. 255 A Street. Solomons. 410-326-2401
Zahniser's Yachting Center. 245 C Street. Solomons. 410-326-2166
Solomons Point Marina. Charles & William Streets. Solomons. 410-394-0585
Beacon Marina. Lore Road. Solomons. 410-326-6303
Dennis Point Marina. Carthegena Creek. Drayden. 301-994-2288
Blackstone Marina. Hollywood. 301-373-2015
Boatel California. N. Patuxent Road. California. 301-737-1401
Buzz's Marina. Ridge. 301-872-5887
Cape St. Mary's Marina. Sandgates. 301-373-2001
Cather Marine, Inc. Colton's Point. 302-994-1155
Drury's Marina. Ridge. 301-862-4480
Feldman's Marina. Drayden. 301-994-2629
Combs Creek. Compton. 302-475-2017
Fitzies Marina. Compton. 301-475-1919
Haskell's Marina. Piney Point. 301-994-1008
Kopel's Marina. St. Patrick's Creek. Colton's Point. 301-769-3121
Phil's Marina. Ridge. 301-872-5838
Point Lookout Marina. Smith's Creek. Ridge. 302-872-5000
Tall Timbers Club & Marina. Tall Timbers. 301-994-1508
Weeks Marina. Hollywood. 301-373-5124
Sweden Point Marina. Smallwood State Park. Rte. 1, Marbury. 301-743-7613
Cobb Island Marina. Cobb Island. 301-259-2879
Saunders Marina. Cobb Island. 301-934-9266
Shymansky's Marina. Cobb Island. 301-259-2221
Port Tobacco Marina. Port Tobacco. 301-932-0063


**Boat Builders**

Belkov Yacht Company. 311 Third Street. Annapolis. 410-269-1777. Builds classic wooden "picnic boats"
Mast & Mallet. Galesville. 1014 B E. Benning Road. 410-867-1587. Mike Kaufman designed the Thomas Point series. The yard's 38-foot Sanctuary combines the lines of the traditional Maine lobster boat and the Chesapeake dead rise. Mast & Mallet also builds skiffs and Chesapeake 20s.
Eastport Electric Boat Co. Annapolis. 410-263-6060
Markley's. Middle River. The yard still produces workboats such as deadrisers that are native to the Chesapeake Bay region.

# Sailmakers and Canvas Works

Concord Point Sails and Rigging. 311 St. John Street, Havre de Grace. 410-939-2196
Skelley Sails. 750 N. Adams Street, Havre de Grace. 410-575-7867
Banks Sails. 910 Commerce Road. 410-356-1060
Canvas Creations. 919 Bay Ridge Road. Annapolis. 410-267-0333
The Cover Loft. 412 Fourth Street. Annapolis. 410-268-0010
Christopher Ford Yacht Canvas. 7416 Edgewood Road. Annapolis. 410-268-7180
Housley, Inc. Sailmakers. 1810 Virginia Street. Annapolis. 410-263-4913
North Sails Chesapeake. 317 Chester Avenue. Annapolis. 410-269-5662
Quantum Sail Design Group. 951 Bay Ridge Road. Annapolis. 410-268-1161
Scott Allan-UK Sailmakers. 108 Severn Avenue. Annapolis. 410-268-1175
Scott Sailmakers, Inc. 7416 Edgewood Road. Annapolis. 410-268-2268
Hood Sailmakers. 616 Third Street. Annapolis. 410-268-4663
The Tailored Yacht. 7310 Edgewood Road. Annapolis. 410263-4913
Neil Pryde Sails Annapolis. 2013 Admiral Melville Circle. Annapolis. 410-626-1234
Sail Menders. 1414 Snug Harbor Road. Shady Side. 410-867-4071

## Rigging

Fawcett Boat Supplies. 110 Compromise Street. Annapolis. 410-280-5272
Atlantic Spars & Rigging, Inc. 317 Chester Avenue. Annapolis. 410-269-6042
Northern Bay Yacht Rigging. 1755 Hilltop Avenue. Baltimore. 410-780-9500
Eastport Spar & Rigging. 919C Bay Ridge Road. Annapolis. 410-267-9464
Chesapeake Rigging. Jabin's Yacht Yard. Annapolis. 410-268-0956
Chesapeake Rigging. Herrington Harbor North. Deale. 301-261-2005
West River Rigging. 831 Shady Oaks Road. West River. 410-867-1012

## Sailing Schools/Training

Havre de Grace Sailing School. Havre de Grace. 410-939-2869
Downtown Sailing Center. 1425 Key Highway, Baltimore. 410-727-2884
Getaway Sailing School. 2701 Boston Street, Baltimore. 410-342-3110
Virginia Marine Institute. 905 Bay Ridge Avenue. Annapolis. 410-280-5544
Annapolis Sailing School. 601 Sixth Street, Eastport. 410-267-7205
Chesapeake Sailing School. 7074 Bembe Beach Road. Annapolis. 410-269-1594
J World Annapolis. 213 Eastern Avenue. Annapolis. 410-280-2040
Womanship Inc. 410 Severn Avenue. Annapolis. 410-267-6661
Solomons Sailing School. Solomons. 410-326-1444

United States Power Squadron. 1-888-367-8777

## Yacht Sales

Brigadoon Marine Facility. 3644 Bowley's Quarters Road. Middle River. 410-335-7190
McDaniel Yacht Basin. North East. 410-287-8121
Giordano and Dour Yacht Sales. Hances Point Road. North East. 410-287-5030
Havre de Grace Yacht Sales. 326 First Street. Annapolis. 410-263-5580
Shady Oaks Marina. West River. 410-867-7700
Zahniser's Yachting Center. 245 C Street, Solomons. 410-326-2166
Interyacht. 7076 Bembe Beach Road. Annapolis. 410-269-5200
Bristol Yacht Sales. 623 Sixth Street. Annapolis. 410-280-6611
Farr International, Inc. 613 Third Street. Annapolis. 410-268-1001
Wagner-Stevens Yachts. Annapolis. 410-263-0008
Annapolis Yacht Sales. 7416 Edgewood Road. Annapolis. 410-267-8181
Sail Yard Inc. 326 First Street. Annapolis. 410-268-4100
Brittania Boats Ltd. P.O. Box 5033. Annapolis. 410-267-5922
Free State Yachts Inc. 64 Old South River Road, Edgewater. 410-266-9060
Hartge Yacht Sales. 4880 Church Lane, Galesville. 410-867-7240
Allied Yachts. 326 1st Street. Annapolis. 410-280-1522

## Boat Charters/ Rentals

South River Boat Rentals. Pier 7 Marina. Edgewater. 410-956-9729
Catherine M. Pasadena. 410-437-2715. Fishing charter
Admiral of the Bay. Annapolis. 410-437-4068
AYS Charters & Sailing School. Annapolis. 7416 Edgewood Road. 410-267-8181
Annapolis Bay Charters, Inc. Annapolis. 7310 Edgewood Road. 410-269-1776
Careless Yacht Charters. Annapolis. 410 Severn Avenue. 410-263-8064
Conklin Marine Center. 7040A Bembe Beach Road. Annapolis. 410-263-0706
Chesapeake Marine Tours and Charters. Annapolis. 410-268-7601
Chesapeake Yacht Charters. PO Box 6529. Annapolis. 410-266-9751
Solomons Boat Rentals. Solomons Island. 410-326-4060
Breezy Point Charter Boat Association. 5230 Breezy Point Road. Chesapeake Beach. 410-760-8242
Bunky's Charter Boats, Inc. 14448 Solomons Island Road South. Solomons. 410-326-3241
Calvert Marine Charter Dock. Dowell Road. Solomons. 410-326-4251
Chesapeake Beach Fishing Charters. Harbor Road. Chesapeake Beach. 301-855-4665

Rod-N-Reel Charter Captains. Chesapeake Beach. 301-885-8450
Solomons Charter Captains Association. Solomons. 410-326-2670

## Harbor Cruises

Skipjack Applegarth. Havre de Grace. 410-879-6941
Martha Lewis, Havre de Grace. 800-406-0766
The Lantern Queen. Havre de Grace. 410-287-7217
Clipper City. Baltimore Inner Harbor. 410-539-6277
Bay Lady and Lady Baltimore. 301 Light Street. 410-727-3113
Water Taxi. Baltimore. 410-563-3901
Baltimore Harbor Tours. 301 Light Street. 410-783-4660
Chesapeake Marine Tours and Charters. Annapolis. 410-268-7601
Patuxent River Cruises on the Wm. B. Tennison. Calvert Marine Museum.
Solomons. 410-326-2042
St. Clement's Island Boat Tours. St. Clement's Island-Potomac River Museum.
St. Clement's Island. 301-769-2222

## Sailing Publications

Spin Sheet. 301 Fourth Street. Annapolis. 410-216-9330
Chesapeake Bay Magazine. 1819 Bay Ridge Avenue. Annapolis. 410-263-2662
Cruising World Magazine. 105 Eastern Avenue. Annapolis. 410-263-2484
Soundings Publication. 326 First Street. Annapolis. 410-263-2386
U.S. Naval Institute. U.S. Naval Academy. Annapolis. 410-224-3378
Cruising World Magazine. 105 Eastern Avenue. Annapolis. 410-263-2484
PassageMaker, The Trawler and Ocean Motorboat Magazine. Horn Point
Marina. Annapolis. 888-487-2952
The Mariner. 500 S. Main Street, North East. 410-287-9430
Nor'easter Magazine. 22 N. Main Street, North East. 410-287-8840

## Associations

American Boat & Yacht Council. 3069 Solomons Island Road. Edgewater. 410-956-1050
The Maryland Watermen's Association, Inc. 1805-A Virginia Street. Annapolis.
410-268-7722

# Museums

Capt. Salem Avery House Museum. Shady Side. 1418 East-West Shady Side Road. Shady Side. 410-867-4486. The museum has exhibits of local interest – oystering, boating, maps and photos of a bygone era.

Hartge Maritime Museum. Galesville

Black Watermen of the Chesapeake Living History Museum. Shady Side. 410-867-2100

The Steward Colonial Shipyard Foundation. Galesville. 410-867-7995

Calvert Marine Museum. Solomons. 410-326-2042.

St. Clements Island- Potomac River Museum. Colton's Point. 301-769-2222

# Famous Yachtsmen

Laurence Hartge, Galesville developed the "Quadrant" class boat. Eighteen boats were built between 1953-62. He is a member of the Hartge family that owns the boatyard on the West River.

Gary Jobson, Annapolis won his status through America's Cup fame, and is now a CNN telecaster. He was instrumental in getting the Whitbread around the World Race to the Chesapeake, and is a major supporter of yachting events worldwide.

Bruce Farr, Annapolis is a New Zealander who built two America's Cup boats, including the 1987 *Kiwi* and more recently designed *Chessie Racing*, and seven other boats for the Whitbread. He is president of Bruce Farr & Associates. Mr. Farr has designed 16 of the 21 boats in the Admiral's Cup race, mainly Mumm 36's.

Jim Muldoon, Annapolis owner of the new Donnybrook, once had Starlight Express (also Donnybrook) which set the record for the Annapolis-Newport Race in 1987 with a time of 53 hours and 31 minutes.

George Collins, Gibson Island is the owner of *Moxie* and sponsor of *Chessie Racing*, the Chesapeake entrant in the 1997-98 Whitbread Around the World Race. He has continued to race in Key West and in January 2000 won the PHRF-A.

Some Annapolis members of the 1997-98 Whitbread crews included on *Chessie Racing* were "Fuzz" Snapback, Dave Scott, Rick Deppe, Jonathan Swain, Greg Gendell, and Gavin Brady. North Sails provided sails for all nine boats in the 1997-98 Whitbread around the World Race.

Chris Larson, Annapolis of North Sails-Chesapeake (won 1996 J/24 World Championship and was 1997 Rolex Yachtsman of the Year), Gavin Brady, Geoff Stagg of Farr International, Grant Spanhake, and Terry Hutchinson of Quantum Sail design sailed in Admiral's Cup in England 1997.

The Nautica 2000 Star World Championship Regatta was held in Annapolis in May 2000. A number of local sailors participated in the event – John Sherwood, Annapolis; Steve Kling, Annapolis; Larry Parrotta, Aberdeen; Elliott Oldak, Annapolis; Kevin McNeil, Annapolis; John Vanderhoff, Havre de Grace; Jonathan Bartlett, Annapolis; Tom Price, Pasadena; Jim Allsop, Annapolis; and Gavin Brady, Annapolis. Other top Star skippers are Rob Emmet and Jim Key of Annapolis.

Charlie Scott, Annapolis won J24 Worlds and has raced in many other events.

Walter Cronkite has owned a number of boats named Wyntje, the most recent one a 60 foot Camper Nicholson.

There are many Naval Academy graduates who have contributed to Naval history and sailing. The Academy maintains many lovely boats of all sizes open to the Midshipmen for racing, cruising or day sailing. Graduates include Rear Adm. Robert McNitt author of "Sailing at the Naval Academy"; Nicholas Brown, former director of the National Aquarium in Baltimore; Adm. Holloway, and more recently the twice superintendent Adm. Larson. The Naval Academy is home of the College Sailing Hall of Fame. Adm. McNitt was a recent inductee.

Thomas Gillmer is a 1935 graduate of the U.S. Naval Academy and retired as a professor of naval architecture from the Academy. He designed the model towing basin at the academy. He also designed the first fiberglass boat, the *Apogee,* to circumnavigate the globe. He also drew the construction plans of the *Peggy Stewart*, the brig made famous by its tea party in Annapolis, prior to the American Revolution. In 1975 he drew plans for the *Pride of Baltimore* and the *J.T. Leonard*, the last indigenous oyster sloop of the Chesapeake Bay. He also writes on maritime subjects.

Gavin Brady, Annapolis won the 1997 Mumm 36 World Championship on board "Thomas I Punkt".

Tony Smith, owner of Performance Cruising in Mayo, came here in 1973 from England.

# Did You Know?

The schooner *America* was used as a training ship for the Naval Academy. In 1851 she won the first America's Cup race "the Hundred Guinea Cup". She was designed by George Steers 95 feet long with 180-ton displacement and carried 5,263 square feet of sail. She was sold in England, and became a Confederate blockade-runner. At the end of the war she served as a training ship at the Naval Academy and then was sold to Gen. Benjamin Butler of Massachusetts. She was given back to the Academy in 1921. During the blizzard of March 29, 1942 she was destroyed at the Annapolis Boatyard when the boathouse roof collapsed.

*Vamarie,* a Cox & Stevens wishbone ketch sailed in the 1947 inaugural Newport-Annapolis, now Annapolis-Newport Race, taking 8th in her class. Hurricane Hazel destroyed her in 1954 when she was blown against the Naval Academy seawall.

Phil Rhodes designed the Penguin, a 12-foot boat, in the 1930's for frostbiting. Bill Heinz of the West River Sailing Club built Hull No. 1. Today they are still seen on the Bay, often as a family boat. Bill Heintz founded the West River Sailing Club in 1930.

The Chesapeake 20 was designed and built by Dick Hartge of Galesville in 1938. A number of these original boats are still around, including several at the Chesapeake Bay Maritime Museum in St. Michael's and the Steward Colonial Shipyard Foundation. The Hartge boatyard still produces memorable boats of all sizes and sizes.

Waterman is probably an English term for the hard working fishermen of the Chesapeake.

Oystermen are tongers or dredgers "drudgers". Tongs have been around since c 1700. They look like a double rake with a basket.

Charles L. Marsh, a blacksmith on the Patuxent River invented patent tongs, in 1887. These operated remotely with a winch, and could get into deeper places with less effort.

William Barrett and T. Rayner Wilson patented a hydraulic tong in 1958.

The Severn River Association, founded in 1911, is the oldest organization in America to preserve a river.

# Chapter 5

# Waterfowl

**Havre de Grace Decoy Museum**
Courtesy of Havre de Grace Decoy Museum – Katie Moose photo)

A guidebook to the Western Shore would not be complete if waterfowl were not mentioned. This Bay region has been on migration paths for thousands of years, with numerous rivers, creeks, brackish wetlands and marshland to attract many species of wildlife.

The Upper Bay around the Susquehanna Flats has been famous for its waterfowl since about 1880, though Native Americans certainly hunted in the region. The Flats are a shallow area about 36 square miles where the Susquehanna River and Chesapeake Bay meet. Wild celery and wild grasses provided food for the waterfowl. According to reports the skies were blackened with ducks or geese, and some hunters were known to bag over 500 ducks in a sitting. Hunting took place mainly from sinkboxes, low lying floating blinds. Decoys and dogs aided the hunters in catching their game.

The "Upper Chesapeake Bay's Legacy" offers much insight into the history, hunters and decoys makers of this region. Bagging large numbers of ducks would be limited by federal law in 1930 to 25 a day, then reduced to twelve and then two. Today there is a point system for bagging, and until recently canvasback ducks were banned until their comeback. Sinkboxes were banned in 1934.

One of the most famous clubs was the Spesutie Island Rod and Gun Club. The 700-acre Spesutie Island was bought in 1899 by a group of New Yorkers from Robert F. MaGaw. People came from all over the United States to hunt here and enjoy the clubhouse. After World War I the island was acquired by Aberdeen Proving Grounds.

The area offers wood carvers, bird watchers, animal lovers and hunters a chance to see wildlife in beautiful natural settings along the Bay, its rivers and creeks. A number of different birds can be spotted including the canvasback duck, Canada geese, loon, swans, eagles, duck, cormorants, hawks, osprey, bald eagles, great blue heron, pelican, terns and cattle egret. Trumpeter swans had been very common in the region until recently. Several years ago the Migratory Bird Program introduced ultra-light aircraft to teach the trumpeter swans to be led back to the Chesapeake Bay.

## Decoys

Maryland is renowned for its decoys and bird carvings. William I. Tawes in his book *Creative Bird Carving* traces the history of this craft back to early Egyptian history when wooden carvings were found in the tombs of the pharaohs and others, including Hammarubi. In this country the Indians also carved wood for utensils, totem poles, and included birds and other animals. Gods were often represented as birds.

Decoys were used by Native Americans and later European colonists. Unlike in Europe where game belonged to the Crown and only royalty could hunt, everyone could hunt in America. The Indians hunted in log canoes using reed decoys and arrowheads. The early settlers began to use large guns. These and lights were eventually outlawed for hunting. During the 1800s rail and ship transportation permitted rapid transport to growing markets for wildfowl and seafood.

Carving is a beautiful and unique art. Each feather, each marking is so delicately carved and painted. A true master carver does not come about his work in a brief time, but learns to observe every detail of the model to be carved. Decoys have regional characteristics. They were once used for luring fowl to hunters. Today prize decoys can sell for thousands of dollars.

## Famous Decoy Carvers

R. Madison Mitchell was the most noted Havre de Grace decoy maker, working full time as an undertaker, and then enjoying the sport of hunting. His Uncle E. Madison Mitchell owned hundreds of decoys and did most of his hunting off Plumb Point.

Robert McGaw was also from Havre de Grace. His carving of a canvasback duck has appeared on the U.S. postage stamp. Until 1929 he carved all of his decoys by hand and then acquired a duplicating lathe which he passed on to R. Madison Mitchell.

The Holly family produced decoys beginning around the time of the Civil War. John Holly, Sr. (Daddy) was born in Havre de Grace in 1818. His four sons were also skilled carvers and influenced the "Havre de Grace" style decoy, which was to influence Madison Mitchell and other decoy makers. His son James was a noted painter, and especially for his oil of a sinkboat shooting on the Susquehanna Flats. He also designed and built bushwhack boats and sinkboats.

Other noted Havre de Grace decoy carvers are Paul Gibson, Harry Jobes, Jim Pierce, and Charlie Joiner. Charlie Joiner began carving in the 1940s and studied under R. Madison Mitchell.

## Museums

Havre de Grace Decoy Museum. 215 Giles Street. 410-939-373. The museum was built in 1986 on the site where Jim Currier carved his duck decoys, many of which are now displayed in the museum.

## Special Events

Decoy, Wildlife Art and Sportsmen Festival. Havre de Grace Decoy Museum. First week-end in May
Duck Fair. Havre de Grace Decoy Museum. Second week-end in September
Carver's Celebration. Havre de Grace. Second Sunday in December

# Decoy Makers

Charles Jobes. 855 Otsego Street, Havre de Grace. 410-939-3005

## Shops

Susquehanna Trading Company. 324 N. Union Avenue, Havre de Grace. 410-939-4252
Vincenti Decoys. 353 Pennington Avenue, Havre de Grace. 410-734-7709
Captain Bob's Decoys. 721 Otsego Street, Havre de Grace. 410-939-1843
Pierce's Decoys. 319 Lapidum Road. Havre de Grace. 410-939-2272
Walker Decoys. 221 N. Lapidum Road. Havre de Grace. 410-939-3743
The Duck Boat. 1734 Jerry's Road. Street. 410-692-6434
Vernon Bryant. 90 Greenbank Road. Perryville. 410-287-8548

## About the Author

Katie Barney Moose, born in Baltimore, is a descendant of the Claggett (Clagett) family of Maryland, and many old New England whaling families. She has lived in many of the U.S.' great architectural, historical and waterside gems besides Annapolis - New Castle, DE; Newport and Providence, RI; Cold Spring Harbor, NY; San Francisco; Philadelphia; Greenwich, CT; Alexandria, VA; Washington, DC; and New York City. She and her family also maintain homes on historic Nantucket Island.

Mrs. Moose is the author of "Annapolis: The Guidebook", "Eastern Shore of Maryland: The Guidebook", "Chesapeake's Bounty", and Nantucket's Bounty". She is also a consultant on international business and protocol. Her hobbies include gourmet cooking, fine wines, history, sailing, genealogy, theology and travel.

# *Order Form for Conduit Press Books*

Please send me_____ copies of Nantucket's Bounty @ $17.95

Please send me _____ copies of Chesapeake's Bounty @ $16.95

Please send me_____ copies of Annapolis: The Guidebook @ $13.95

Please send me_____ copies of Eastern Shore of Maryland: The Guidebook @ $15.95

Please send me_____ copies of Maryland's Western Shore: The Guidebook @ $15.95

Add postage first book @ $3.00_____
Postage for each additional book to same address @ $1.00_____
Gift wrap per book @$2.00_____
Total Order_____

❑   Check or money order enclosed
❑   Make check payable to Conduit Press
❑   Credit Card_____ex._____
❑   Please personalize to:

Mail to:

Conduit Press
111 Conduit Street
Annapolis, MD 21401

Ship the books to:

Name_____

Address_____

_____

Telephone_____

For further information please
● Call 410-280-5272
● Fax 410-263-5380

●   E-mail   kamoose@erols.com

245

# Notes